THE SITUATION ROOM

√THE SITUATION ROOM

———◆———

*The Inside Story of
Presidents in Crisis*

GEORGE STEPHANOPOULOS
WITH LISA DICKEY

GRAND
CENTRAL

New York   Boston

Grand Central Publishing
Hachette Book Group
1290 Avenue of the Americas, New York, NY 10104
grandcentralpublishing.com
@grandcentralpub

First Edition: May 2024

Grand Central Publishing is a division of Hachette Book Group, Inc.
The Grand Central Publishing name and logo is a registered trademark of Hachette Book Group, Inc.

The publisher is not responsible for websites (or their content) that are not owned by the publisher.

The Hachette Speakers Bureau provides a wide range of authors for speaking events. To find out more, go to hachettespeakersbureau.com or email HachetteSpeakers@hbgusa.com.

Grand Central Publishing books may be purchased in bulk for business, educational, or promotional use. For information, please contact your local bookseller or the Hachette Book Group Special Markets Department at special.markets@hbgusa.com.

Print book interior design by Taylor Navis

Library of Congress Cataloging-in-Publication Data

Names: Stephanopoulos, George, 1961- author. | Dickey, Lisa, author.

Title: The situation room : the inside story of presidents in crisis / George Stephanopoulos with Lisa Dickey.

Other titles: Inside story of presidents in crisis

Description: First edition. | New York : Grand Central Publishing, 2024. | Includes bibliographical references and index.

Identifiers: LCCN 2023041729 | ISBN 9781538740767 (hardcover) | ISBN 9781538767351 | ISBN 9781538740781 (ebook)

Subjects: LCSH: Presidents--United States--Decision making. | United States--Foreign relations--1945-1989. | United States--Foreign relations--1989- | United States. White House Situation Room. | Presidents--United States--Staff. | Executive power--United States. | Political leadership--United States.

Classification: LCC E840 .S74 2024 | DDC 973.09/9 [B]--dc23/eng/20231002

LC record available at https://lccn.loc.gov/2023041729

ISBNs: 9781538740767 (hardcover), 9781538740781 (ebook), 9781538769416 (large print), 9781538767351 (signed edition), 9781538770184 (intl. trade pbk.)

Printed in the United States of America

LSC-C

Printing 1, 2024

For Ali, Elliott and Harper

CONTENTS

Prologue: Center of the Storm 1

Chapter 1: At the Creation 8

Chapter 2: All Through the Night 30

Chapter 3: "All hell has broken loose" 51

Chapter 4: S.O.S. 69

Chapter 5: Close Encounters 88

Chapter 6: The Helm Is Right Here 116

Chapter 7: Right Side of History 148

Chapter 8: Please Hold for the President 174

Chapter 9: "This is where we fight from" 203

Chapter 10: The Pacer 235

Chapter 11: Postcards from the Edge 271

Chapter 12: Tiger Team 299

Epilogue: WHSR 319

Acknowledgments 327
Notes 330
Index 338

THE
SITUATION
ROOM

Prologue

CENTER OF THE STORM

————◆————

DAWN HAD NOT yet broken when Mike Stiegler steered his blue Toyota Camry toward the White House on January 6, 2021. It was 4:20 a.m., and Stiegler was arriving early for his twelve-hour shift as a desk officer in the White House Situation Room.

Normally at this hour, downtown Washington, D.C., was deserted, its monuments and office buildings silent under the black night sky. But when Stiegler stepped out of his car, he sensed something strange. "All these people on the street that you don't normally see, and a bunch of cars parked," he told me. "I've tried to describe this many times to many people, but it just felt different."

That afternoon, Congress was scheduled to certify the election of Joe Biden as the forty-sixth president of the United States. But the incumbent he defeated was doing everything he could to block the transfer of power. Thousands of his followers had come to Washington at his request to stop the certification, and no one knew for sure how the day would play out. The Situation Room staff was on alert, monitoring events, synthesizing public information and private intelligence, and preparing to report to the president—as they did with all crises, domestic or foreign, that might require his attention. But on this day, they never called him. He didn't call them. The president himself was the cause of the crisis.

This doesn't feel right, Stiegler thought as he began his shift. An intelligence analyst in his thirties, he had been thrilled in the summer of 2019 to get the call to serve in the Situation Room—a plum assignment for any intelligence professional. In the eighteen months since then, "I witnessed two impeachments. I went through Covid. I went through the Black Lives Matter protests and the riots," he told me. "It was just one thing after another." Now, as the sun rose, he steeled himself for what might come.

All morning, protestors flocked to the Ellipse, the grassy oval expanse just south of the White House. At noon, President Donald Trump stood in front of his edgy and excited supporters and called on Vice President Mike Pence to send the vote back to the states. He claimed that "radical-left Democrats" had stolen the election. He urged the crowd to "fight like hell. And if you don't fight like hell, you're not going to have a country anymore." And then he told them to march down Pennsylvania Avenue to the Capitol.

Trump wanted to join them, but his Secret Service detail refused to take him, because pandemonium had erupted on the Capitol grounds. Protestors stormed police barriers, attacking multiple officers. "We have been flanked, and we've lost the line!" shouted D.C. police commander Robert Glover as the mob surged forward, smashing windows and flooding into the building. Secret Service agents hustled Vice President Pence to a secure location, and lawmakers huddled in terror as mobs charged the hallways, breaching the U.S. Senate chamber. Rioters emptied cabinets and upended furniture. Gunshots echoed through the hallowed corridors in the 228-year-old seat of our nation's legislature.

Back in the Oval Office, President Trump sipped Diet Coke as he watched the spectacle on television. Aides and allies implored him to condemn the riot and call off the mob. Instead, at 2:24, with the violence raging, he sent out a tweet calling out Mike Pence for lacking "the courage to do what should have been done."

With reports coming in from the Secret Service and other officials on Capitol Hill, the Situation Room scrambled into action. "Things got very chaotic," Stiegler told me. "We went into a continuity-of-government situation."

Stop there. Take that phrase in: "continuity-of-government situation." That bland bit of bureaucratic jargon masks a deadly serious set of policies and actions first ordered by President Eisenhower at the height of the Cold War. "COG" was designed to ensure the government would still function after a disaster such as nuclear war. It involves secret command centers—the Sit Room being a critical one—elaborate chains of command, the relocation of Congress and the replacement of executive branch officials killed in attacks. It had been activated only once before, in the immediate aftermath of the September 11, 2001, terror attacks.

The situation was "surreal," said Stiegler. But he was wary of disclosing more. "I have to be careful," he told me. "I have been giving a lot of testimony, and I don't know where the lines quite are." I ventured that one of his points of contact must have been the Secret Service. He paused, then said, "That's fair." Which meant that he was getting real-time updates directly from the chaos in the Capitol building, as the mobs surged through the halls.

The most harrowing part?

"How close we came to losing the vice president," he told me. He paused, then looked up at the ceiling, struggling to compose himself. "The screams, the yelling. The different things that we heard that day." Stiegler is a young man with a cheerful disposition, but when he talked about January 6 he seemed to age before my eyes.

"It was horrific," he said quietly. "There's a group of us that were on duty that day, and we don't know how to process it still… We don't know how to talk about it. And we don't know who to talk about it with. There are a lot of things we witnessed that day that we can't talk about. And how do you deal with that?"

In the six decades since the creation of the Situation Room, it has been the crisis center during America's catastrophes. The men and women of the Sit Room have dealt with nuclear scares, the assassination of a president and attempts on two others. They stayed at their posts on 9/11, when the White House itself was the target of terrorists. And they tracked and analyzed American wars that cost hundreds of thousands of lives and billions upon billions of dollars. But never before had they dealt with an insurrection against our own government, inspired by the president of the United States.

If the election certification hadn't gone through, Stiegler told me, "I think we would have possibly seen an institution just crack, crumble. I think a lot of us would have walked out." These staffers serve the person who lives in the White House, but they work for the *presidency*, not the president. "Your allegiance to your country supersedes your allegiance to your role," said Stiegler. Those dueling loyalties had never been tested like this.

VOLUMES HAVE BEEN written about the twelve U.S. presidents who've served since the Situation Room was created in 1961—but few accounts have chronicled the history and inner workings of the site itself, despite its vital place in America's story.

It's located in the White House basement, just off the mess where staffers go for coffee and meals. For most of its history the Sit Room wasn't much to look at—nothing like the vast war room in the movie *Dr. Strangelove* or the comfortable and coolly lit spaces of *The West Wing* and *24*.

Hollywood's idea of a Situation Room: the ridiculously vast War Room in *Dr. Strangelove*. | *Michael Ochs Archives / Getty Images*

The reality for decades was much more modest: a cramped conference room, three smaller ones off to the side, and a watchstanders' office where Sit Room staff collect and analyze information for the president and his aides. Even for those like me who've worked in the White House, it's hard to reconcile the flow of sensitive and sometimes scary information, the mysteries being uncovered and the earth-shaking matters being discussed and debated, with such a mundane place.

In the course of researching this book, I interviewed more than a hundred people, most of whom worked in the Situation Room—from cabinet secretaries and top White House aides to desk officers and Sit Room directors. Their most common reaction to seeing the space for the first time is…"This is *it?*" The word I heard most often echoes my own reaction when I first walked in: "underwhelming."

Henry Kissinger called it "a tiny, uncomfortable, low-ceilinged, windowless room" that was "unaesthetic and essentially oppressive." And diplomat Richard Holbrooke memorably described it as "a room that, to me, symbolizes the problem; a windowless below-ground room in which the distance from real knowledge to people is at its very greatest."

Yet while the physical space was unimpressive, the work performed by the professionals who staff the Sit Room is unparalleled. "It's the communications nerve center of the United States government," President Obama's national security adviser Tom Donilon told me. "If there's one geographic spot in the world that could fairly be called the nerve center operationally, in terms of intelligence and information, it's the five thousand square feet right in the basement of the White House." As former NATO ambassador Doug Lute adds, "It's a place, but it's also a set of people and a process"—the three Ps. "They've got to come together." When they do come together, wars are won, terrorists taken down and disasters forestalled. When they don't, the crises cripple presidencies.

In the chapters that follow, you'll learn about the place, and how it's transformed over time. You'll learn about the people who have served there, and how they performed under enormous pressure. You'll learn about secret meetings, presidential foibles, shocking security breaches and MacGyver-style technological improvisation. But most important, you'll see presidents and their teams managing the crises that have defined the modern presidency, wrestling with the tough calls that can make or break their legacies. This is the room where their character and resolve were tested. Some rose to the test, others failed.

The history of the Situation Room is a largely hidden history of our country over the past six decades. Many of the stories you're about to read have never been told before. Some were under wraps for decades, known only by people with the highest security clearances. I've studied all the presidents and spent many hours in the Sit Room—but even I was surprised to learn so many never-revealed details of what has happened within those walls. In this book, you'll hear them from the people who lived them.

It all began with JFK.

Chapter 1

AT THE CREATION

---•---

THEY CALLED HIM God.

He was a man of contradictions: A deeply patriotic American who spoke English with a pronounced French accent, thanks to a childhood spent in Paris. A debonair, water-skiing Air Force brigadier general whom Jacqueline Kennedy once described as "gay and impetuous." And a close friend and confidant of both President and Mrs. Kennedy, despite the fact that years earlier, he and Jackie had dated.

Godfrey McHugh—"God" for short—served as John F. Kennedy's Air Force aide in the White House. McHugh came to the administration with a wealth of worldly experience. As a younger man, he dined with Franklin D. Roosevelt and Winston Churchill at the White House. He sailed with Harry S. Truman on his yacht, the *Williamsburg*. He threw parties that the cream of Washington society clamored to attend. He was a handsome and dashing man about town, like JFK himself.

But to the Kennedys, McHugh was much more than that. He was JFK's go-to guy for all things at the intersection of politics, family and diplomacy. He vetted letters that the president wrote, sometimes sign-ing his name to them. When the Kennedys' infant son Patrick fell ill, he arranged for the doctor of their choice to be flown to the child's bed-side. At JFK's request, he personally escorted Emperor Haile Selassie from Addis Ababa to Washington, D.C. He even persuaded Kennedy to let him use Air Force One to take a group of U.S. nuclear physicists to the Soviet Union.

McHugh was larger than life, like a character out of a Fitzgerald novel. He was also the person who introduced JFK to the term "Situa-tion Room," setting in motion the events that would lead to its creation.

McHugh didn't coin the phrase himself. But in the spring of 1961, he forwarded a study to Kennedy that contained what appears to be the first use of the term. The "Concept for National Cold War Operations" paper had been prepared by unnamed military researchers in the Air Force's Long Range Objectives division. In his cover memo, typed on White House stationery, McHugh wrote that "this essay is forwarded to you, Sir, in view of your deep interest in this subject."

In thirteen tightly argued pages, the authors focused on how best to combat the threat of Communism. "The need for more effective prosecution of the cold war is evident in the face of greatly expanded Sino-Soviet efforts and the revolutionary changes occurring in many parts of the world today," they wrote in the summary. Then came this recommendation: "Establish a National Daily Situation Room within the structure of the Executive staff to assist in the continuing review and direction of cold war matters."

The paper detailed the proposed room's functions, personnel and communications setup:

> The National Daily Situation Room would be a perma-nent organization . . . It would serve as a management tool by

providing intelligence, communications, briefing, display and monitor facilities...

Personnel of the highest caliber should be assigned to the facility from the various departments and agencies. They should have a comprehensive background in both international affairs and the interrelationship of governmental departments and agencies. It is estimated that approximately eighty specialists will be required to operate the situation room.

The National Daily Situation Room should be equipped with the most up-to-date communications, display and briefing equipment. The communications system should provide maximum speed and security for both world-wide and internal service.

McHugh forwarded the study to President Kennedy on April 7, 1961. Remarkably, this was ten days before the disastrous Bay of Pigs invasion—the event that provoked Kennedy into creating the White House Situation Room. While the communications failures of that crisis hastened the process, God McHugh is the one who began it.

KENNEDY HAD BEEN president for just eighty-seven days when he launched the Bay of Pigs invasion. A CIA-backed attempt to overthrow Fidel Castro's Communist government in Cuba, the operation was a fiasco from start to finish. The CIA had recruited 1,400 Cuban exiles to storm the island, but Castro's forces outnumbered and crushed them. More than a hundred were killed and hundreds more were captured, a debacle that became a huge embarrassment for the fledgling Kennedy administration.

The president was angry and dismayed, not only at the outcome, but at the process that led to it. Originally, the invasion was to take place at Trinidad, on the central southern coast of Cuba. Kennedy felt that plan was "too spectacular...too much like a World War II invasion," so he directed the CIA to plan a stealthier attack in a less populated place.

The CIA recommended the Bay of Pigs, about a hundred miles up the coast, without informing the president that it was surrounded by swamps that would bog down the invading forces. As national security adviser Walt Rostow would later observe, "When the CIA changed the site, the impact of the shift didn't filter up to the president...Had Kennedy known the details of the landing site change, he might have made different decisions."

Communications on the day of the attack were also shockingly poor. "Decisions affecting the movement of U.S. Navy ships and U.S. Air Force planes [were] relayed...from the Cabinet Room to the Pentagon over unclassified telephone lines," recalled National Security Council aide Bromley Smith. In fact, it was even worse than that. Naval aide Tazewell Shepard described a process that resembled a game of telephone: "I sat outside during the meetings. If the president decided to reposition U.S. forces, Admiral Burke stuck his head out the door and passed the orders on to me. I then called the Joint Chiefs of Staff and relayed the president's instructions."

Publicly, Kennedy took full responsibility for the disaster. Privately, he was fuming. Why didn't he have the information he needed? And why should he have to rely on secondhand summaries of data that he could have received directly? The president felt irritated that he'd allowed "experts" to lead him by the nose, rather than taking charge of the process himself. "The first advice I'm going to give my successor," he told his friend *Washington Post* editor Ben Bradlee, "is to watch the generals and to avoid feeling that just because they were military men their opinions on military matters were worth a damn."

President Kennedy didn't want some CIA officer's description of a situation; he wanted the same raw intel the officer had, so he could make up his own mind. Kennedy had taken a speed-reading course with his brother Bobby in 1954 and claimed he could read 1,200 words per minute. While some people prefer oral presentations, he vastly preferred the written word. He read fast, and he retained what he read.

What the president wanted was an information clearinghouse with secure communications. Rather than having aides run all over the White House to deliver reports and make calls, a central location would coordinate smoother—and faster—information flow. As the State Department's Lucius Battle recalled, "In those days we had none of the mechanical devices that have since sped things up enormously. We were still working by dog sled."

Shortly after the Bay of Pigs, Taz Shepard advised Kennedy to create a "watch center" in the White House. A March 10, 1961, memo written by Colonel E. F. Black had proposed a "Nerve Center" that would serve as a "war room for the cold war." Other memos had dubbed it the "Executive Coordination Center." And a Cuba Study Group report had called for a new "headquarters for the cold war." But the name in the study that Godfrey McHugh forwarded to JFK on April 7 is the one that stuck in the president's mind.

On April 30—less than two weeks after the Bay of Pigs—Kennedy decided to act. Naval aide Gerry McCabe described the scene:

> It was a Sunday afternoon…The president and [national security adviser McGeorge] Bundy and Shepard and I walked from the South Lawn through the door into [secretary Evelyn]

Lincoln's office. And Bundy and the president went into the president's office and chatted for about fifteen or twenty minutes while Shepard and I stood outside...

As a result of that discussion apparently, Bundy came out and he turned to Shepard and me and he said, "We really need a situation room in the White House. How long would it take you to get one started?"

And off the top of my head I estimated two weeks, for a very crude one, and he said, "Okay, do it."

And that was really the only marching orders we had.

Two weeks to build, furnish, equip and staff a crisis management center in the White House—arguably the most important crisis management center in the entire world. One hundred and seventy-two years to the day since George Washington first took the oath of office, President Kennedy finally ordered what seemed like a blazingly obvious intelligence tool.

So, how was it that thirty-four presidents had served this country before anyone thought to create one?

A FEW EARLIER presidents actually did have something resembling a situation room.

During the Civil War, Abraham Lincoln spent hours in the telegraph office at the War Department, where the Eisenhower Executive Office Building (EEOB, formerly known as the Old Executive Office Building or OEOB) now stands. "He came over from the White House several times a day, and, thrusting his long arm down among the messages, fished them out one by one and read them," according to an account by Army major A. E. H. Johnson. Lincoln was amazed by telegraphs, which he called "lightning messages." He was so eager for instant news, he sometimes slept over in that office, folding his six-foot-four frame into a cot so he wouldn't miss an update from the battlefield.

By the time William McKinley became president in 1897, telephones were added to the wonders of available technology. During the Spanish-American War, McKinley set up a "War Room" in the White House, equipping it with telegraphs, telephones, maps and a brigade of mustachioed young men who tracked battles and relayed orders to the field. Located in what's now called the Lincoln Sitting Room, this could have been a precursor to a dedicated Situation Room. But once the Spanish-American War ended, so did McKinley's use of it.

In the first half of the twentieth century, presidents most often used the Oval Office for high-level meetings. In 1934, when the ornate, high-ceilinged Cabinet Room was completed, it also became a hive of activity. It wasn't until 1942 that President Franklin D. Roosevelt again established a nerve center for managing U.S. involvement in a war.

FDR chose a former billiard room for his war headquarters. Located on the ground floor of the White House, the area sat unfinished and unused until the early 1880s, when President Chester Arthur installed a pool table. The Wilson and Coolidge families spent hours playing there, but President Hoover removed the table in the 1930s, turning the space into a meeting room. Following the Japanese attack on Pearl Harbor, with the country now at war, FDR directed staff to hang maps on the walls, creating a central location where he could track the fighting. It would forever after be known as the Map Room.

This was a true Situation Room–style setup. A staff of watch officers was on duty around the clock, monitoring information and updating the president and his advisers on the war's progress. Communications, both classified and unclassified, flowed through the room. As described by one watch officer, Navy ensign George Elsey, FDR visited at least twice a day—once on his way to the Oval Office and once on his way back to the residence.

"We pushed the wheelchair first to the main desk, where the latest war news—or possibly the latest message from Churchill—awaited in a black leather folder with 'The President' stamped in gold leaf on the front," Elsey related in a 1964 oral history. "Then we made a slow tour of the room…Furniture was clustered in the center, leaving aisles on the four sides so FDR could study the maps at close range."

When Roosevelt died, incoming president Harry S. Truman continued using the Map Room to monitor the fighting. But presidents only seemed to want these Sit Room–style setups during wartime, so after the Japanese surrendered in 1945, Truman shut down the nerve center.

More than a decade later, Dwight Eisenhower—a five-star Army general who led the Allied forces in World War II—became the first president to express a desire for a permanent White House crisis center. James W. Lucas of the Defense Intelligence College describes a moment in which Eisenhower asked his chief of staff, General Andrew Goodpaster, for an update on how a battalion of U.S. Marines was faring in Lebanon. "Sir," the general said, "if I call the Joint Chiefs of Staff, or if we go over there, maybe they'll tell us."

Dissatisfied with that answer, Ike replied, "You know, Andy, I think I might need a little watch office." This might have remained a minor apocryphal moment, if it weren't for what happened next. As described by Lucas:

So, a study was undertaken, typical of the way that we do things in the American government: A committee was formed and a commission was chartered and 18 months later a recommendation was made. The recommendation to President Eisenhower was, if you will give up either the bowling alley or the swimming pool...you could probably put in a little watch office, operations center, or command and control center, if you want to call it that, at the White House.

Eisenhower never acted on the report. But following the Bay of Pigs, it was revived and circulated among Kennedy's aides. The Cold War with the Soviet Union was a different kind of struggle from World Wars I and II. But Kennedy understood that it would require just as much attention, planning, monitoring and strategizing as the hot wars of years gone by.

Already primed by the concept paper Godfrey McHugh had sent him earlier that month, President Kennedy ordered a Situation Room to be built. And he wanted it located in a spot recommended in the Eisenhower report: an old bowling alley in the basement of the West Wing.

Gerry McCabe had estimated it would take two weeks to build a rudimentary Situation Room. Taz Shepard recalled that it was finished even faster than that. "I got the Seabees from Camp David, which is under my charge, and had them come down and work at night. In a week, they put in a Situation Room." The cost, which came out of the president's emergency funds, was $35,000.

"Situation Room" was a misnomer from the beginning, as it's

actually several rooms. Shepard's Seabees—the U.S. Navy's Construction Battalion, or "CBs" for short—transformed the bowling alley into a four-room complex. The conference room was the centerpiece, an 18-by-18-foot space with all the charm of a cardboard box. Photos from the time show cherrywood-paneled walls, dark gray carpet and a low white acoustical-tile ceiling. A long brown conference table was surrounded by eight low-slung off-white leather chairs, and at each seat was a pad of paper and a freshly sharpened pencil. In the middle of the table sat a crucial item for any 1960s conference room: a large glass ashtray.

The other three rooms in the complex were a file storage area, a watchstanders' station and an office. All three were small and plain, with the file room being particularly cramped, as it was lined with gray metal racks stuffed to bursting with tabbed folders. It also served as the projection room, with a bulky green metal projector aimed through a window at a screen in the conference area.

McCabe recalled that the original complex was "very crude" and "not very secure," but Mac Bundy quickly began holding staff meetings there every morning. Sensing an opportunity, he also moved his office from the OEOB to the West Wing, to be closer to the action. Bundy, whom author Patrick Anderson memorably described as "witty, acidulous, aristocratic, ambitious, overbearing, self-satisfied [and] self-serving," was proud of his role in creating the Sit Room. And he wasn't shy about insisting that Kennedy use it.

On May 16, 1961, Bundy sent a memo chastising JFK. "You should set aside a real and regular time each day for national security discussion and action," he wrote, noting that although the president had asked him to set up a morning meeting, "I have succeeded in catching you on three mornings, for a total of about 8 minutes, and I conclude that this is not really how you like to begin the day . . . You have to mean it, and it really has to be every day," he finger-wagged, before imploring Kennedy to use his new complex. "Perhaps the best place for it would be the new Situation Room, which we have just set up in the basement of the West Wing."

To Bundy's dismay, Kennedy never did use the Sit Room for regular meetings. In fact, he rarely set foot in it—and when he did, he was deeply unimpressed. In January 1962, Bundy sent a memo to JFK's appointments secretary, Kenneth O'Donnell, already begging for more space for the complex. "We are currently extremely crowded. So is nearly everyone in the building, but our position is extreme. Come and see. (The president called it a pigpen, and my pride is hurt.)"

The room is, as Kennedy wanted, an information clearinghouse and a communications hub. But it is not meant to be a command post—a fact clearly laid out by its architects, including Bromley Smith:

> The new unit was called the Situation Room rather than the operations center, to make clear that it was a facility—not a command post except in most unusual circumstances. Its purpose was to serve as a funnel for all classified information coming from all national security agencies and present it to the president and his national security staff in an orderly fashion. It aimed at coordinating the many information channels to the White House...including those of the Central Intelligence Agency, the State and Defense Departments and the Chiefs of Staff through their aides in the White House.

Even in the original study that Godfrey McHugh sent JFK in April 1961, the authors made clear that the Situation Room "would not usurp the operating responsibilities of any department or agency."

Rather, it would "serve as a management tool by providing intelligence, communications, briefing, display and monitoring functions." It would draw on the resources of cabinet agencies, supplement that intelligence with public and press reports, and funnel it all to the president and his top aides.

And it would, incredibly, do this with a single duty officer working a twenty-four-hour shift.

———◄o►———

"My workday, beginning at 9:30 a.m., was twenty-four hours long, followed by forty-eight hours off," recalled Charles D. "Chuck" Enright, the Situation Room's first duty officer. A CIA analyst who found himself detailed to the new nerve center in the White House basement, Enright described his typical day:

9:30 a.m.   Arrive at Sit Room, review night's activity.
10 a.m.   Go to [National Security Council] staff office, 3rd floor of Executive Office Building. Spend the next seven hours screening material for the NSC staff.
5 p.m.   Return to Sit Room, continue screening anything "hot."
5:30 p.m.   White House Staff Mess brings supper (for which I paid cash).
9:30 a.m.   (Next day) Duty ends.

What Enright didn't note is that a cot had been rolled into the complex, so the duty officer could sleep at night—a rather absurd scenario for what was meant to be a 24/7 watch operation. The duty officers would soon be supported by a small staff, including technicians from the White House Communications Agency (WHCA), but the one-day-on/two-days-off schedule continued throughout the Kennedy administration and beyond.

CIA director Allen Dulles wanted to make sure that it would be his employees who served as Sit Room duty officers. On May 18, 1961, he sent a memo to President Kennedy stating: "There is some question in my mind...whether the present arrangements, under which CIA supplies one of several watch officers, will completely meet your needs. I would be more satisfied...if CIA were represented in this watch full time."

JFK agreed, so in the beginning, Sit Room duty officers were drawn almost exclusively from the CIA. It wasn't until the Reagan administration that the ranks would expand to include duty officers from the State Department, NSA and Defense Intelligence Agency, all of whom come to the White House for a two-year term, on temporary loan from their respective departments.

As evidenced by Chuck Enright's seven-hour daily stints at the National Security Council office, the Situation Room and NSC were (and still are) inextricably linked. Established by Harry Truman in 1947, the NSC is a group of aides and cabinet officials who advise the president on defense, foreign policy and national security. Its members are a Who's Who of high-level Washington officials, including the vice president; the secretaries of defense, state, energy and treasury; the Joint Chiefs of Staff (JCS); and the intelligence directors. Even when presidents choose not to take meetings in the Sit Room—Nixon and Ford come to mind—the NSC often meets there to discuss matters before bringing recommendations to the president.

Yet the beating heart of the Situation Room is not these marquee names. It's the people who staff it. In the many interviews I did for this book, every time I asked about the quality of staff, I got variations of the same response. Secretary of state Condoleezza Rice: "The best of the best." Deputy national security adviser Jim Steinberg: "The most wonderful, terrific, dedicated, on-top-of-it group of people." White House coronavirus response coordinator Deb Birx: "They were amazing…and incredibly kind." Obama adviser Valerie Jarrett: "The conscientiousness with which they do their jobs is pretty extraordinary."

A good Sit Room officer must be focused, organized, intelligent, judicious, apolitical, a fast reader, a critical thinker and cool under pressure. These skills are as disparate as they are valuable, and it's the rare person who possesses them all. As former Reagan aide Richard S. Beal once put it, he could "go through the length and breadth of this land and not find twenty people who have that capacity by virtue of training."

That said, with all of their sharply honed skills, duty officers often find themselves answering some amusingly basic requests. Chuck Enright described one such episode from 1962:

> The naval aide called from Hyannis Port one Sunday evening at 10 and said the President wanted a copy of every *Time* and *Newsweek* magazine for the past year at his bedside in Hyannis Port when he got up in the morning. I groaned, phoned the librarian for the NSC, and she told me that she had only a few issues in her office but could get others from D.C. public libraries, to which she had access at any time. I arranged for the copies to be put aboard the courier plane that left at 4 a.m., and the deadline was met.

It's funny now to imagine an NSC researcher hustling down darkened D.C. streets to the public library to fulfill a presidential request. The biggest change in the Sit Room's six decades of existence has, of course, been the rise of computers and the Internet, which made such tasks obsolete. But what was the technology like in that first Sit Room complex? It would presumably have been state-of-the-art for its time—but what did that mean in the early 1960s?

The first communications system was, as described by Reagan-era Sit Room director Michael K. Bohn in his 2003 book *Nerve Center*, a "rudimentary affair":

> At first, military communications technicians pulled incoming cables off the teletype printers and hand-carried them to the Situation Room in the West Wing. A few years later, engineers built pneumatic tubes to carry cables to the Situation Room.

Yes, pneumatic tubes—just like the ones they used to have at banks so you could drive through and deposit your paycheck from your car, getting a lollipop for your kid in return. Until personal computers came along in the 1970s, enabling staff to send documents electronically, these tubes were the fastest, most efficient way to transmit cables from the East Wing to the West Wing.

The complex did have an early version of a fax machine, a secure device that was used to transmit top secret information between the CIA, the State Department and the National Military Command Center (NMCC). It also had multiple telephones, with both classified and unclassified lines. Communications techs set up direct phone connections with world leaders, including French president Charles de Gaulle and German chancellor Konrad Adenauer. And then there was the dedicated telephone linking British prime minister Harold Macmillan with the Kennedy White House—better known as the "Mac-Jack line."

Dusty, cramped, airless, with the occasional rat and cockroach skittering through, the complex was far from glamorous. But once it began humming with activity in the spring of 1961, the Sit Room quickly became a focal point in the White House. And just as its creators envisioned, it would prove its true worth in a frightening and fast-moving Cold War clash: the Cuban Missile Crisis.

In October 1962, a U.S. Air Force pilot flying reconnaissance in the Caribbean photographed ballistic missile launch sites in the Cuban countryside. Located less than three hundred miles from Miami, the missiles, which had been placed in Cuba by the Soviet Union, were capable of striking American soil within minutes of launch. The Situation Room passed the photos to the president, who immediately met with his top advisers to game out a response. Over the next thirteen days, the showdown between the United States and the Soviet Union came terrifyingly close to nuclear war.

While Kennedy didn't convene his meetings in the Situation Room, he did make other vital use of it. As recounted by Paul Brandus, the author of *Under This Roof: The White House and the Presidency*:

> Throughout the tense fortnight—as the threat of nuclear war hung over the world like the sword of Damocles—the Situation Room worked as the president had intended. Kennedy got the information he needed and he got it faster, allowing him and the so-called EXCOMM—the Executive Committee of the National Security Council—to work through the crisis more efficiently.
>
> The president himself often went downstairs to the command center itself…to read newswire reports. There were meetings held there as well, usually chaired by the president's

national security adviser, McGeorge Bundy. In addition to embassy cables and military reports, the Situation Room was also plugged into the CIA's Foreign Broadcast Information Service (FBIS), which allowed it to monitor news broadcasts from around the world.

In fact, the Sit Room's monitoring of FBIS would lead to the biggest breakthrough of the crisis. Because there was no direct line between the Kremlin and the White House, communications went through slow-moving diplomatic channels. When Soviet leader Nikita Khrushchev decided to remove the missiles, he wanted to get the news to Kennedy as quickly as possible—so he announced his decision on Radio Moscow. The Sit Room staff received the information via FBIS and rushed it to the president.

Both sides were looking for a way out, and Kennedy had now found his. If the Sit Room had not yet existed, Khrushchev's overture would have taken longer to arrive, and the Cuban Missile Crisis might have taken a much darker turn. As Brandus wrote: "Never had the White House had a room so inconspicuous, and yet so critically important to the nation's security and future."

———————◀O▶———————

Press secretary Pierre Salinger: Situation Room, this is WAYSIDE. Do you read me? Over.
Duty officer Oliver Hallett: This is the Situation Room. I read you. Go ahead.

Transcripts of tapes from the White House Situation Room are exceedingly rare. While staffers create detailed, nearly verbatim memos of phone calls between the president and other heads of state, they're produced in real time using several transcribers, rather than being recorded. A few tapes do exist, most notably those made during Lyndon Johnson's presidency, when he secretly recorded some of his many phone calls to duty officers, and an extraordinary recording from the day John Hinckley shot Ronald Reagan—both of which we'll detail in later chapters. For most administrations, though, whatever happens in the Sit Room is supposed to stay in the Sit Room. At least for a while.

Yet five remarkable transcripts exist from the Kennedy presidency, providing a record of calls between press secretary Pierre Salinger and the Sit Room on November 22, 1963—a stark reminder of the chaos and confusion of the day Kennedy was assassinated.

At the moment shots rang out on Dealey Plaza in Dallas, Salinger was high above the Pacific Ocean in a government plane, flying with secretary of state Dean Rusk and five other cabinet members to Japan for meetings. The shocking news came in through a UPI ticker in the aircraft's forward cabin, and at 12:45 p.m. Central Time, just fifteen minutes after Kennedy was shot, Salinger called the White House from the air to get more details. The White House operator connected Salinger, who identified himself using the code name WAYSIDE, with the Sit Room.

Duty officer Oliver Hallett picked up the call. Though Sit Room staffers were normally stoic, Hallett's voice betrayed his shock at the unfolding events.

> **Salinger:** Give me all available information on president. Over.
> **Hallett:** All available information on president follows:
> Connally—John—he and [Hallett takes a deep breath]
> Governor Connally of Texas have been hit in the car in which
> they were riding. We do not know how serious the situation is.

We have no information. Mr. Bromley Smith is back here in the Situation Room now. We are getting our information over the tickers. Over.

Salinger: That is affirmative, affirmative. Please keep us advised out here. This plane, on which secretary of state, other Cabinet ministers headed for Japan, turning around, returning to Honolulu. Will arrive there [in] approximately two hours.

The two men discussed logistics, including whether Salinger and the cabinet members should travel directly to Dallas. Then:

Hallett: The Associated Press is coming out now with a bulletin to the effect that they believe the president was hit in the head. That just came in. Over.

Salinger: The president was hit in the head. Over.

Salinger left the call to inform the cabinet members of this latest update. When Hallett spoke again, he struggled to control his voice.

Hallett: Ah, this is … Oh. Hold on the line there, WAYSIDE. We have some more information coming up … WAYSIDE, WAYSIDE, this is the Situation Room. I read [to you] from the AP bulletin: "Kennedy apparently shot in head. He fell face down in back seat of his car. Blood was on his head. Mrs. Kennedy cried, 'Oh no,' and tried to hold up his head. Connally remained half-seated, slumped to the left. There was blood on his face and forehead. The president and the governor were rushed to Parkland Hospital near the Dallas Trade Mart where Kennedy was to have made a speech." Over.

Twenty minutes later, at 1:10 p.m. CT, the White House operator patched through another call. Once again, Hallett and Salinger spoke.

> **Hallett:** WAYSIDE, this is Situation Room. I read [to] you latest bulletin: "President Kennedy has been given blood transfusions today at Parkland Hospital in an effort to save his life after he and Governor John Connally of Texas were shot in an assassination attempt." Over the TV we have the information that the Governor has been moved to the operating room. The President is still in the emergency room at Parkland Hospital. Do you read me so far? Over.
>
> **Salinger:** I read that loud and clear. Go ahead.
>
> **Hallett:** WAYSIDE, this is Situation Room. Are you getting the press coverage, or do you want us to continue to relay it to you? Over.
>
> **Salinger:** Situation Room, this is WAYSIDE. We are getting very garbled, very garbled transmissions. We'd appreciate [being] kept informed. Over.

At 1:40 p.m. Central Time, an operator at Andrews Air Force Base called the Sit Room to connect Salinger. Heartbreakingly, as the recording starts, an announcer from NBC Television News is audible in the background, saying, "The last rites have been given…"

> **Hallett:** This is Situation Room. Relay following to WAYSIDE: We have report quoting Mr. Kilduff in Dallas that the [speaks slowly and deliberately] president is dead, that he died about 35 minutes ago. [Pause.] Do you have that? Over.
>
> **Salinger:** The president is dead. Is that correct?

Hallett: That is correct. That is correct. New subject. Front office desires plane return Washington, with no stop Dallas. Over.

But Salinger had left the line once again, to relay the most horrific news any of the men on the plane would ever hear.

———◄○►———

ON ANOTHER PLANE, idling on the tarmac at Dallas's Love Field, Jacqueline Kennedy sat next to the casket containing the body of her murdered husband. Still dressed in her pink Chanel suit, now spattered with the president's blood and brain tissue, she didn't want to leave his side. But the new president, Lyndon Johnson, was about to be officially sworn in by Judge Sarah T. Hughes in the front of the cabin. He needed Jackie there to give legitimacy to his ascension to the presidency.

Political aide Ken O'Donnell came to the back of the plane. "Do you want to go out there?" he asked Jackie. "Yes, I think I ought to," she said. "At least I owe that much to the country." She then turned to the Air Force general who had been sitting with her by the casket. "Don't leave him," she said. "Stay with him." She couldn't bear the thought of her husband's body lying there alone—and this general was a man she trusted.

The general had no intention of leaving. He knew that military tradition calls for a high-ranking officer to remain with the body of a slain commander in chief. But more important, he was not only the Air Force aide, but a longtime close friend of President Kennedy. He stayed with the president's body for the flight back to Washington, and at Jackie's request, he helped carry the casket off the plane. He was present for the autopsy, and he arranged for Air Force fighter jets to fly over Kennedy's funeral service. And then, when Jackie couldn't bear to do it, he stepped in to host a party for little John-John, whose third birthday was the same day as his father's funeral.

Years later, the general told an interviewer that "I was in total adoration of a great human being. I respect the presidency. Whoever was president, I respected. But I think he added extraordinarily to the presidency, and it was way too short for him to make a strong mark on it." He later told his daughter that when Kennedy died, he lost his best friend.

His name was Godfrey McHugh.

Chapter 2

ALL THROUGH THE NIGHT

—◆—

THURSDAY, MAY 20, 1965. It's two o'clock in the morning, and downtown Washington, D.C., is dark. The National Mall is deserted save for the occasional car crawling past. The White House is empty except for overnight staff. But in the Situation Room, the lights—as always—are on.

The phone rings, and a duty officer picks up. It's an operator with the White House switchboard, connecting a call from President Johnson, who's up in the residence. The duty officer presses a button to begin capturing the call on a Dictabelt, a box-shaped device that uses a clear vinyl ribbon rotating on metal cylinders to record conversations. LBJ inherited President Kennedy's Dictabelt when he moved into the Oval Office following the assassination, and over time, he directed the White House Communications Agency to install more such recorders—not only all over the White House, but also at the LBJ Ranch in Texas and at Camp David.

Presidential phone calls haven't been recorded since the Nixon tapes sunk his presidency. But during Johnson's administration, these analog machines captured LBJ's questions and ruminations—the agony of a commander in chief trapped by a war he didn't start but couldn't quit. Vietnam was the subject of that two a.m. call:

> **Sit Room:** Good morning, Mr. President.
>
> **LBJ:** What's this story on this colonel [who] got killed?
>
> **Sit Room:** He did indeed get killed. Now, we have several reports, one that—an FBI report that says that he was shot by Americans, accidentally shot in the back. We have nothing to back this up other than this FBI report[. . .]
>
> **LBJ:** What about our planes? Are any of them back [from] Vietnam?
>
> **Sit Room:** None back yet, sir, that—no word.
>
> **LBJ:** I'm sure anxious on those that are going up there close to Hanoi there.
>
> **Sit Room:** Yeah, we're watching that very carefully tonight, sir.
>
> **LBJ:** You let me know if we lose any.
>
> **Sit Room:** Yes, sir, I will.
>
> **LBJ:** Whatever time of night it is.
>
> **Sit Room:** Yes sir. I will do that.

LBJ was desperate for any piece of information from Vietnam, day or night, no matter how minor. "Johnson was so involved in the details I don't know how he survived," recalled his national security adviser Walt Rostow in an October 1999 roundtable discussion. "He had three days: He'd wake up in the morning and be very active; then he'd nap and have a second life with a party or something in the White

House; and then he had a third life reading until three in the morning." Yet reading wasn't LBJ's only activity during those early morning hours. He was also calling—and often visiting—the Situation Room.

Judging from the recordings from 1965, LBJ rarely got a full night's sleep. Conversations were recorded on various dates at 1:25 a.m., 2:00 a.m., 2:43 a.m., 3:27 a.m., 4:45 a.m. and 5:52 a.m. "He called almost always before going to sleep, or upon awakening, to the Situation Room," former LBJ aide Tom Johnson told me. "He particularly wanted to know the number of aircraft that had returned to their carriers from their missions over North Vietnam. And he wanted to know the most recent body count." The toll of the war was always on the president's mind, Tom Johnson recalled. "His sleeps often were anguished sleeps after difficult, difficult days."

The president's calls to the Sit Room generally started the same way, with little or no pleasantries, just a direct question about what was happening in Vietnam. LBJ's voice was low and gruff, roughened by years of Cutty Sark and cigarettes. It had an intimate quality, as if he were leaning over to talk into your ear, rather than through a telephone. George Reedy, his press secretary from 1964 to 1965, once said that it felt like LBJ could "crawl through that wire" to talk to you.

A March 30, 1965, call at 8:10 a.m. demonstrates the granular level of detail the president sought:

> **LBJ:** What have you got on our Saigon development?
> **Sit Room:** Well, we have a total—we have some more casualty
>   figures in now. The total of two U.S. killed. And—
> **LBJ:** Do you know who they are? Soldiers, women, or what?
> **Sit Room:** We have women listed so far: two women.
> **LBJ:** Know who they are?
> **Sit Room:** Yes, sir, we do have the names...

LBJ: Both American?

Sit Room: Both American, yes, sir.

More than 58,000 Americans would ultimately die in the Vietnam conflict. President Johnson's insistent questions about these two show just how immersed he became in every aspect of the war.

Later in that same call, he probed for details about an air strike:

LBJ: Any other news of pertinence?

Sit Room: The only other news, sir, is the South Vietnamese air force conducted a strike on an airfield.

LBJ: What—

Sit Room: All the planes have returned safely, and the pilots estimate 90 percent damage.

LBJ: What kind of airfield? Jet airfield?

Sit Room: Yes, sir. It was a jet airfield in North Vietnam just over the 17th Parallel.

LBJ: It must have been right on the demarcation line?

Sit Room: Just north of it, sir.

I asked President Johnson's younger daughter, Luci Baines Johnson, why she thought her father was so fixated on such details. She told me that he wanted to get to "the pulse of the decision-making."

"He used to often say, 'Luci Baines, your decisions are only as good as your information. And my problem is, I'm trying to get the best information, but I have to act in certain time frames, and I'm afraid too often I will find later on that there was more information that I needed,'" she recalled. In other words, he was terrified of missing any detail that might have helped save lives. What he didn't understand was that the details he was looking for didn't really matter.

Body counts couldn't tell him the war was being won. And many of the reports he was getting were based more in hope than in reality. Beyond all this, the toll of the war was personal to him. Both of his sons-in-law would end up fighting in Vietnam, making LBJ the last U.S. president to have immediate family members serving in combat while in office. The Situation Room gave Johnson regular updates on how they were doing.

And so he wanted to know everything possible about what was going on over there. Lady Bird Johnson recalled a night in February 1965 when the president nervously awaited updates about a planned attack. "It came at one o'clock, and two o'clock, and three, and again at five—the ring of the phone, the quick reach for it, and tense, quiet talk." As she recorded in her diary, "Lyndon [asked] to be waked up whenever there was an operation going out. He won't leave it alone. He said, 'I want to be called every time somebody dies.' He can't separate himself from it."

LBJ was the undisputed master of domestic politics. In 1965, the same year these transcripts were recorded, he pushed through an astonishing amount of landmark legislation: the Voting Rights Act, the Immigration and Nationality Act, the Water Quality Act and the Motor Vehicle Pollution Control Act, the creation of the National Endowment for the Arts and the Department of Housing and Urban Development. Head Start, Medicare, Medicaid, the Highway Beautification Act—the list goes on and on. LBJ's domestic achievements were legion, and his skills legendary.

But his mastery of the home front was matched by his muddling in Vietnam. Johnson confessed to being "no military man at all." The confidence he displays in hustling up support for legislation vanishes when he discusses Vietnam. Even when talking with Sit Room staffers, he is tentative.

On Tuesday, March 2, 1965, Johnson pressed the Situation Room for information about the opening bombing raid of Operation Rolling Thunder, a long-planned aerial assault campaign against North Vietnam. Desperate for news, the president jumped the gun:

> **Sit Room:** Their time over target was to be about seven minutes ago, sir. So we don't even have—of course, it's too early to have even a preliminary report on just how they're making out, but they are now over the target.
>
> **LBJ:** How many of them are there?
>
> **Sit Room:** Well—
>
> **LBJ:** Forty?
>
> **Sit Room:** Well, of our own, sir, there are roughly about 40, sir. Roughly about 40 of ours; there's about 19 of the Vietnamese planes.
>
> **LBJ:** Any other news?
>
> **Sit Room:** No, sir, no other news. It's all quiet, sir.
>
> **LBJ:** How long before you should hear something?
>
> **Sit Room:** Well, let's see, we should know . . . let's see, it would probably be about 5:00 or 5:30, I would imagine, before we know how many got back safely, sir.
>
> **LBJ:** Call me.

Here Johnson is three months into what historian Michael Beschloss called the "pivotal" year of the war and his presidency. Despite telling defense secretary Robert McNamara early in 1965, "I don't see any way of winning in Vietnam," LBJ creeps toward catastrophe. Concern about the credibility of U.S. commitments kept him in the war; fear of losing dug him in deeper. But there was no strategy for subduing a country that would fight to the death. The tapes from that time reveal an uncertain man, angry, often depressed, lashing out at enemies both real and perceived. Aides like Richard Goodwin and Bill Moyers were so concerned about his paranoia, they consulted psychiatrists to try to get a handle on his mental state.

If you're a Situation Room duty officer, how do you deal with a president in this condition? Nearly all the tapes reveal a calm, cool demeanor among the Sit Room staff. Yet occasionally, a younger or newer duty officer displays a nervous wobble in his voice.

On Tuesday, April 6, 1965, Johnson called down to the Sit Room at 4:45 a.m. to ask if there was any news.

> **Sit Room:** Nothing, Mr. President. Very, very quiet night. No problems whatsoever.
> **LBJ:** Mm-hmm.
> **Sit Room:** No action last night in Vietnam on our part. No untoward incidents of any kind. I think we had a good night. (*Chuckle.*) It's all I can say. (*Chuckle.*)
> **LBJ:** Mmm. Okay, that's it, then.
> **Sit Room:** Right, sir.

Chuckling at the president is obviously not the ideal approach, but it's clear when listening to the recording that this Sit Room officer was nervous. It's easier to speak to someone in authority when you actually have news to report. And apparently this officer wasn't the only one to lose his composure when having no real news to pass along, because in 1966, Sit Room director Art McCafferty circulated a memo addressing the issue:

> Even though it is a quiet period and nothing unusual is occurring, it is not a good practice to start your briefing with the

statement "everything is quiet, nothing is going on." It would be good practice to remember that the person you are briefing would like to make that judgment himself. Therefore, please keep in front of you at all times a few items from the press or cables that you can talk from.

In the interviews I did, I often asked whether people remembered any funny or unusual moments in the Situation Room. But when I asked Tom Johnson that question, he said, "I do not recall a single one. They were very serious. This was not a place for laughter."

"LYNDON JOHNSON ESSENTIALLY used the Situation Room in Vietnam like Franklin Roosevelt used the Map Room during World War II," LBJ Foundation president and historian Mark Updegrove told me. "That's where he saw troop movement. That's where he met with his generals and essentially charted the progress of the war. He spent a great deal of time in the Situation Room... [It] was one of the most important rooms in the LBJ White House."

While JFK wasn't often in the Sit Room, LBJ was there *all the time.* He spent so many hours there, in fact, that he had a chair moved down from the Oval Office so he'd be more comfortable. "That's just quint-essentially LBJ," Updegrove said, then added with a laugh, "That's the least of the requests that LBJ made of his White House staff." The library still has that aqua-blue upholstered chair in its collection.

It also has the famous Khe Sanh model, a tabletop 3-D terrain rendering derisively dubbed "LBJ's sandbox." The Battle of Khe Sanh was a fierce clash in 1968 in which the North Vietnamese tried to overrun a U.S. military installation. Fearing that Khe Sanh could prove to be his Waterloo, Johnson demanded constant updates on how the fighting was going. LBJ's critics had long accused him of micromanaging the war, so when the White House released a photo of the president and Walt Rostow hunched over the Khe Sanh model, appearing to move little pieces as if on a chessboard, the image added fuel to the fire.

President Johnson spent hours in the Sit Room tracking the war in Vietnam. When the White House released this photo of aide Walt Rostow showing him a 3D model of Khe Sanh, critics dubbed it "LBJ's sandbox." (L–R: George Christian, President Johnson, Robert Ginsburg and Walt Rostow) | *LBJ Library photo by Yoichi Okamoto*

"I think that's a pretty fair criticism," Updegrove told me. "It goes back to Lyndon Johnson's psychology. Lyndon Johnson micromanaged his White House... This is somebody who got into the details of every piece of legislation that came across his desk. That's why he was master of the Senate." But those skills didn't naturally translate to the office of the presidency. "He brought that instinct to being commander in chief, much to his detriment," notes Updegrove.

I asked Tom Johnson whether he believed LBJ micromanaged the war from the Sit Room. Did he actually choose bombing targets there? Or was that a myth?

"Recommendations would be made to LBJ normally by [USAF head] General McConnell or [Joint Chiefs of Staff chair] Bus Wheeler," Tom told me. "LBJ would think carefully. What he did was to approve or disapprove. He so wanted to avoid a situation where we might have accidentally bombed one of the Russian tankers or one of the Chinese tankers in Haiphong Harbor or Hanoi Harbor or accidentally flown over Chinese territory." The president worried constantly about such mistakes, fearing they would provoke direct retaliation from the U.S.S.R. or China. Tom Johnson remembers LBJ remarking dryly that "It would be my luck that the pilot who accidentally drops a bomb down the smokestack of a Soviet carrier will be a young Texan from Johnson City, Texas."

So, what was LBJ actually doing during all those hours in the Situation Room? What happened in those meetings?

"There was always an agenda prepared, usually by the NSC adviser Walt Rostow," Tom Johnson told me. "The agenda was often very brief…and he frequently went off the agenda into other topics." Tom showed me a photo from his personal collection, a shot taken in the Sit Room where LBJ has his press secretary George Christian and Walt Rostow on his right, Tom Johnson and defense secretary Clark Clifford on his left, and Bromley Smith at the opposite end of the table. The conference table is covered with papers, a large ashtray sits in the center, and a telephone is at LBJ's left hand. Behind the president, two maps of Vietnam have been taped on the wall.

"When we gathered, that's basically the way it looked—not only in the room, but the way in which people sat in it," he told me, before pointing out "young Tom Johnson with his pencil, taking notes as quickly and accurately as I could." In those pre-laptop days, the way the world's most powerful man kept track of his most secret discussions was by having a young aide write furiously by hand as everyone was speaking. Tom's official title was deputy press secretary, but "one of my most important roles, assigned to me by LBJ himself, was notetaker," he said.

"I actually studied something called Speedwriting," Tom recalls. He'd take the notes by hand, then pass them to Connie Gerard in the White House press office. She would type them up, and return them the next morning with LBJ's notes.

President Johnson preferred two methods for getting his information: reading briefs and talking on the phone. He even went so far as to cancel the daily in-person briefing of the type that McGeorge Bundy had started for President Kennedy, opting instead to receive a series of written reports throughout the day. In the fall of 1965, Bromley Smith compiled a list of five daily reports LBJ was receiving:

7 a.m. daily:	Situation Room summary of crises
8:30 a.m. to 9 p.m. daily:	Spot reports, typed cables from the field, action and information memoranda
7 p.m. M-F, 2 p.m. Sat:	CIA intelligence brief
7:30 p.m. to 8 p.m. M-F:	State Department evening report
10:45 p.m. daily:	Situation Room summary of latest developments

Famously, President Johnson had multiple TV sets in the Oval Office, the residence and at the ranch. But the number of TVs was dwarfed by the number of telephones—seventy-two at the LBJ Ranch alone. As Updegrove told me, "The telephone was practically an appendage for LBJ. He was on the phone constantly...It allowed him to connect with people on an immediate-term basis.

"If you look in LBJ's Oval Office, not only does he have the phone at the desk—which has a very long line, by the way—he also has a phone under the table between the couches and the sitting area, so he doesn't have to go back to his desk," he said. And of course, he used the phones not only to talk, but to record conversations. "Six hundred ninety-three hours of taped conversations," Updegrove said.

I suggested to Tom Johnson that with all the phones and TVs and the taping system, Johnson was a technophile for his time. "Oh, God knows what he'd have been like if he were alive today," Tom replied. "He had two tickers, AP and UPI, in the bedroom…He would so much want to stay ahead of the press that [he would] read it as it literally was coming across the ticker."

The technology used in the Sit Room was cutting edge, though in the 1960s that wasn't saying much. Art McCafferty hoped to make some upgrades in 1965, expanding the complex to make room for new communications systems. As recounted in Bohn's *Nerve Center*, McCafferty "needed space for three new systems—the new LDX [Long Distance Xerography], the secure fax that became so important to all Washington operations centers; a new-generation secure telephone system; and a more secure teleconferencing system." Yet the cost of relocating offices to enable that expansion—about a half-million dollars—was ultimately deemed too high. So chief of staff Marvin Watson instead approved a smaller project, adding a shielded communications enclosure at a cost of $28,000.

There was one piece of technology, however, that outranked all others in terms of cachet and importance. Though it wasn't located in the Situation Room, its first official use in the summer of 1967 would send President Johnson hustling down there to formulate a response.

From LBJ's memoir, *The Vantage Point*:

Just before eight o'clock on the morning of June 5, 1967, the telephone rang in my bedroom at the White House. Bob McNamara was calling with a message never heard before by an American President. "Mr. President," he said, "the hot line is up." ...

I was informed that Chairman [Alexei] Kosygin was at the Kremlin end. He had agreed to wait until I was on hand before sending his message. I went quickly to the Situation Room, joining Rusk, McNamara, and Rostow. Kosygin's message began to arrive in a matter of minutes.

In the popular imagination, the hotline is a bright red phone sitting on the president's desk. In reality, it's a basic teletype machine that spools out messages like a fax. Chairman Kosygin sent his message—the first real use of the hotline in its nearly four years of existence—as Israeli forces attacked Egypt, marking the start of what became the Six-Day War. His missive was brief but pointed:

Dear Mr. President,

Having received information concerning the military clashes between Israel and the United Arab Republic [Egypt], the Soviet Government is convinced that the duty of all great powers is to secure the immediate cessation of the military conflict.

The Soviet Government has acted and will act in this direction. We hope that the Government of the United States will also act in the same manner and will exert appropriate influence on the

*Government of Israel particularly since you have all opportunities
of doing so. This is required in the highest interest of peace.*

The Vietnam conflict was agonizing for Johnson, but the prospect of
war in the Middle East terrified him. "Trouble in that area," he wrote,
"was potentially far more dangerous than the war in Southeast Asia."
And now, it was happening. Relations between Israel and its neigh-
boring Arab states had long been strained, and a conflict over shipping lanes had intensified, with Israeli forces launching air strikes and
ground incursions into Egyptian territory.

Down in the Situation Room, President Johnson discussed possible
courses of action with Rusk, McNamara and Rostow. How would the
Soviets respond? Would this war spread throughout the Middle East?
Could it spiral into nuclear conflict?

While they focused on the substance of the message, the hotline
operator on our side asked the Soviet operator how the president
should address Kosygin. In Communist Russia, the proper form of
address would be "Comrade," so that's what the operator conveyed. But
when Johnson opened his response with "Comrade Kosygin," the Soviets were confused, wondering whether LBJ was mocking them by using
a Communist term. As Soviet ambassador Anatoly Dobrynin later
relayed to U.S. ambassador Llewellyn Thompson, he quickly figured
out what had happened and no harm was done. But the possibility of
miscommunication, while lessened by having a teletype hotline rather
than a voice line, still clearly existed.

The history of the hotline—also known as MOLINK, for Moscow
Link—is a colorful one. On March 20, 1960, *Parade* magazine editor
Jess Gorkin published a full-page open letter to President Eisenhower
and Premier Nikita Khrushchev. While today, *Parade* exists only as an
online tabloid, it was for decades a popular Sunday newspaper insert

with tens of millions of readers nationwide. Gorkin, a World War II veteran who'd served in the Office of War Information, was deeply concerned about the possibility of accidental nuclear conflict. In his open letter, titled "Re: Accidental War," he urged the two leaders to establish a 24/7 hotline:

> An accidental war might be triggered by mechanical failure, human error, and innocent misunderstanding of orders or plain ignorance...Contact between you today, even on the most urgent matters, must wait on the cumbersome, slow-moving machinery of diplomacy, wholly unsuited to the lightning emergencies of the space age...
>
> Must a world be lost for want of a telephone call?

Around that same time, the State Department's director of policy planning, Gerard Smith, wrote a memo expressing a similar sentiment, and the idea began to gain traction in Washington. But it wasn't until the Cuban Missile Crisis, when President Kennedy and Nikita Khrushchev found their communications delayed by having to go through diplomatic channels, that the hotline was fast-tracked into existence.

The Washington-Moscow Direct Communications Link, a clunky typewriter-style machine connected to Moscow via thousands of miles of underground cables, went live on August 30, 1963, with a message recognizable to anyone who's ever studied touch-typing in English. U.S. operators sent the following: "THE QUICK BROWN FOX JUMPED OVER THE LAZY DOG'S BACK 1234567890"—a sentence that uses all letters of the alphabet and numbers. A short time later, the Soviets one-upped the Americans with their first transmission, an ode to the beauty of the sunset in Moscow.

From that point on, each side sent twelve test messages a day to ensure the hotline was functioning. Using the GMT time zone, the Soviets sent messages on odd hours, the Americans on even ones. The hotline became "a kind of minicultural exchange," Lieutenant Colonel June Crutchfield told the *New York Times* in 1973, with each side choosing literary passages to send their counterparts. The Soviets sent excerpts from Turgenev and Chekhov, while the Americans avoided potentially embarrassing excerpts such as text from *Winnie-the-Pooh*, as a passage about a cuddly, pantsless bear might give offense to a country with a bear for a mascot.

For years, the two sides sent such innocuous messages back and forth as tests. So when Kosygin sent his missive on June 5, 1967, it was a historic moment: the first use of the hotline for its intended purpose.

There was another notable detail. A line prefacing Kosygin's message made clear that the Soviets had no idea where the U.S. teletype machine was actually located. "The Chairman of the Council of Ministers, Kosygin, wishes to know whether President Johnson is standing by the machine," the missive began. Never mind the fact that it was coming through at 7:47 a.m., an hour when the president was unlikely to be hovering by the hotline or anywhere else. The machine, as it turns out, wasn't in the White House at all. It was—and still is—at the National Military Command Center at the Pentagon.

Bob McNamara was incredulous that the "direct line" between leaders wasn't actually direct. In a later interview with Walt Rostow, he described learning this fact on that June 5 morning. A duty officer at the Pentagon called McNamara to report that Kosygin wanted to communicate with the president. "He asked what response he, the duty officer, should make," McNamara recalled. "I said, 'Why are you calling me?' 'Well,' he said, 'the hotline ends in the Pentagon.'" In his six-plus years as defense secretary, McNamara had never heard this.

"So I said to the duty officer, in shock and surprise, 'We spend 80 billion dollars a year on the defense budget,'" McNamara recounted. "'And we better find some way, having spent 80 billion dollars, to get that damned line patched over to the White House.'" Eventually, the Pentagon did install another terminal in the WHCA communications center, located in the basement of the East Wing. In the years before computers became ubiquitous, the WHCA staff forwarded the incoming messages to the Situation Room via pneumatic tube.

It's no surprise that the Soviets assumed the hotline machine was in the Oval Office or Situation Room. Similarly, the Americans believed the Soviet hotline sat in the Kremlin. But in the summer of 1973, in a lengthy interview with U.S. journalists, Leonid Brezhnev revealed that it was actually located in the Communist Party Central Committee staff headquarters building, several blocks from the Kremlin.

Regardless of where the machines were physically located, there's no disputing that they improved communications between Johnson and the Soviet leadership. During the Six-Day War, LBJ and Kosygin exchanged a total of twenty messages (interestingly, none came from Brezhnev himself). On the U.S. side, the receipt of a message was followed by a scramble to get an accurate translation into English, which Rostow's secretary, Lois Nivens, would then type up and distribute to those in the Situation Room.

LBJ rarely left the Sit Room during the Six-Day War, finding it easier to simply stay there rather than hurrying in and out. "During some very trying days," he wrote in *The Vantage Point*, "the room served as headquarters for the U.S. government." When he headed down to the Sit Room at 6:40 a.m. on June 6, the second day of the war, Lady Bird decided to deliver a little cheer there. She went to the White House mess and helped the Navy cooks prepare scrambled eggs, then served them herself to Johnson and his team.

"That's so much a reflection of Lady Bird Johnson," Mark Updegrove remarked about this story. "She knew that LBJ was down there early in the morning with intelligence officers, and she thought about the fact that they might not have been nourished at that point…I think Lady Bird Johnson thought it was her primary duty, and rightfully so, that she should take care of the president. And she was worried about him."

On June 10, 1967, six days into the war, tensions were still extremely high. Jordan and Syria had joined the fighting, and more than twenty thousand Arabs had been killed, with hundreds of thousands more displaced from their homes. Kosygin messaged President Johnson through the hotline at 8:48 a.m. to warn that, if Israel didn't back down, the Soviet Union would send its own military forces to the Middle East:

> A very crucial moment has now arrived which forces us, if military actions are not stopped in the next few hours, to adopt an independent decision. We are ready to do this. However, these actions may bring us into a clash, which will lead to a grave catastrophe…
>
> We propose that you demand from Israel that it unconditionally cease military action in the next few hours. On our part, we will do the same. We propose to warn Israel that, if this is not fulfilled, necessary actions will be taken, including military.
>
> Please give me your views.

This opened a flurry of messages between the two sides, with President Johnson insisting that the U.S. was doing all it could with Israel and urging the Soviets to intervene with Syria. In six carefully worded exchanges sent over a period of three hours, Johnson and Kosygin walked the tightrope of pushing each other for action while maintaining respectful and civil dialogue. While the U.S. and U.S.S.R. were unquestionably adversaries in most ways, in this case they both wanted the same outcome: peace. Their real-time communication via the hotline ended up paying off; just before noon, Johnson learned that the fighting had stopped.

LBJ later wrote about the exchanges, and the role of the hotline, in *The Vantage Point*:

> Kosygin's messages later in the morning became more temperate. Israel and Syria moved to a ceasefire. The tension in the Situation Room subsided...
>
> The hot line proved a powerful tool not merely, or even mainly, because communications were so rapid. The overriding importance of the hot line was that it engaged immediately the heads of government and their top advisers, forcing prompt attention and decisions. There was unusual value in this, but also danger. We had to weigh carefully every word and phrase. I took special pains not only to handle this crisis deliberately but to set a quiet, unhurried tone for all our discussions.

THE ORIGINAL HOTLINE teletype machine is on display at the LBJ Library, complete with a message from Kosygin to Johnson curling out of the top. In October 2011, Mark Updegrove gave a tour of the library to Mikhail Gorbachev, who was in Austin to give a lecture. The former Soviet leader paused, then started reading Kosygin's transmission aloud in Russian. "The hair on the back of my neck raised when I saw

Mikhail Gorbachev reading the transmittal from the Soviets about the Six-Day War," Updegrove recalls. As rudimentary as the technology was, it's still capable of causing goose bumps when you consider its place in history.

A story Tom Johnson told me about the Six-Day War is a reminder that even the most advanced communications systems can be foiled by actual events:

"Well, I have a lot of memories, starting with the fact that I went to bed, my wife and I in our apartment then, which was in Alexandria, Virginia," he told me. "About two a.m., I guess, my White House phone—I had a separate phone—rang. And it was Helen Thomas." Thomas, of course, was the famously fiery, diminutive UPI reporter who covered ten U.S. presidents in a fifty-seven-year career. "She said, 'We have a report that war has broken out in the Middle East'...and I said, 'Hold it, Helen.' So I went to my other phone, called the Situation Room. The Situation Room officer said, 'Mr. Johnson, we don't have that.'"

With one phone at each ear, Tom told Helen Thomas that the White House had no information on any war. He was about to hang up when the duty officer exclaimed, "No, it's coming in now. The flash is coming in now." Tom laughs at the memory. "That's not what was supposed to happen with this incredible alert system that the Pentagon and the White House and CIA had," he says. "It was UPI that advised us that the Six-Day War was breaking out. That is a fact."

From television to hotlines to newfangled fax machines to Helen Thomas, there were numerous ways to get information to the Situation Room. The pace was hectic and the room was the heartbeat of the Johnson administration—which, when it came to Vietnam, might have been part of the problem. No information the Sit Room could provide would salvage a flawed strategy. Data was not a substitute for judgment. It could not tell us who exactly we were fighting, how to win, or even why we needed to defeat them.

Richard Nixon would inherit both the room and the war. And he was determined not to repeat what he believed were his predecessor's mistakes.

Chapter 3

"All hell has broken loose"

———◆———

Richard Nixon hated the Situation Room. During five and a half years as president, he almost never set foot in there. And he wasn't present for one of the most dangerous moments of the entire Cold War—a night when a group of White House advisers, facing the possibility of direct conflict with the Soviet Union, had to make decisions for a president who was holed up in the residence, incapacitated by scotch, sleeping pills and depression.

The time was October 1973. The Watergate scandal had been raging for more than a year. White House counsel John Dean had flipped on the president, providing damning testimony against him in televised Senate committee hearings. Presidential aide Alexander Butterfield had exposed the White House tapes, which Nixon had secretly been making since 1971. And Vice President Spiro Agnew—a corrupt man whom Nixon cynically saw as impeachment insurance, since no one wanted him to ascend to the presidency—was days away from being turned out of office while under threat of a tax fraud indictment. With the president mired in these disastrous domestic problems, a tinderbox exploded on the other side of the world.

Just after six a.m. EDT on Saturday, October 6, Henry Kissinger, who was serving as both secretary of state and national security adviser, was awakened at his Waldorf Astoria Towers suite in New York City by assistant secretary of state Joseph Sisco. Egypt and Syria were planning to launch surprise attacks on Israeli forces in the Sinai Peninsula and Golan Heights on Yom Kippur, the highest holy day of the Jewish year.

Quickly, methodically, Kissinger went into action. He called Soviet ambassador to the U.S. Anatoly Dobrynin, Egyptian foreign minister Mohammed el-Zayyat and Israeli chargé d'affaires Mordechai Shalev, among other critical players. Nearly three hours would go by before he sent a memo to the Situation Room with updates for the president.

TOP SECRET / SENSITIVE / EXCLUSIVE EYES ONLY
TO: THE WHITE HOUSE SITUATION ROOM
FROM: SECRETARY KISSINGER

PLEASE PASS THE FOLLOWING TO THE PRESIDENT FOR DELIVERY AT 9:00 A.M., WITH INFORMATION COPY TO GENERAL HAIG.

AT 6:00 A.M. THIS MORNING, I WAS NOTIFIED THAT THE ISRAELIS HAVE WHAT THEY CONSIDER TO BE HARD INFORMATION THAT EGYPTIANS AND SYRIANS WERE PLANNING TO LAUNCH A COORDINATED ATTACK WITHIN SIX HOURS

It's worth noting that, rather than calling Nixon immediately and gaming out a response together, Kissinger simply forged ahead on his own. In the memo, Kissinger recounts the numerous calls he's already made and informs the president that he has alerted U.S. diplomatic posts in the Middle East. He then declares what the next steps should be.

> I HAVE DIRECTED [DEPUTY NATIONAL SECURITY ADVISER] BRENT SCOWCROFT TO CALL A 9:00 A.M. WSAG [WASHINGTON SPECIAL ACTIONS GROUP] MEETING...ON THE BASIS OF THE INFORMATION WE HAVE, I BELIEVE THE ISRAELI FEARS OF POSSIBLE ATTACK ARE JUSTIFIED. HOPEFULLY, WE WILL BE ABLE TO GENERATE SUFFICIENT PRESSURE SO THAT COOLER HEADS PREVAIL.

As Kissinger directed, WSAG immediately convened in the Situation Room—one of many such meetings the group would have there during what would become known as the Yom Kippur War. Normally, Kissinger would helm these meetings, but on this day he was in transit from New York. President Nixon was also out of town, in Key Biscayne, Florida. Yet even if he had been in the White House, Nixon would not have gone down to the Sit Room. He simply never did, even if there was a war breaking out.

Nixon's absence wasn't especially notable on this day, as WSAG struggled to get a handle on what was happening in the Middle East. That he wasn't there two and a half weeks later, when the war threatened to burst into a nuclear conflict, is an astonishing reflection of just how incapacitated he had become.

———◄◦►———

"I DON'T RECALL any stories that Nixon came down, ever," cryptologist Sarah "Sally" Botsai told me. I had been thrilled to find Dr. Botsai, a spry and still-sharp woman in her eighties who served in the Sit Room under both Nixon and Ford. She was the first woman from the National Security Agency ever to be detailed to the Situation Room, but when I asked if that felt like a high point in her career, she shook her head. "I've never really been seized by being the first, because there were many women who contributed great things who were just never heard of," she told me. She displayed this same plainspokenness and humility throughout our interview, even as she told some extraordinary stories about the Sit Room.

Botsai served as an analyst during the Nixon administration. She spent her days preparing briefs for the president and the national security adviser. To my surprise, she said that her 1973 Sit Room workspace had a computer.

"They were just in the beginning," she told me. "The information would come from the intelligence community, and of course, we had the TVs on to get outside information." The space was "very compact. We had secure phones, we had outside phones. And there was a middle room, kind of an L-shaped briefing room with the conference room next door." In that room, "they had an LDX machine [that] was the size of a small refrigerator," she recalled with a laugh.

In fact, the Sit Room was updated the year Botsai arrived. As described in a 1977 *New York Times* article: "The quarters were remodeled in 1972. Silent computer terminals supplanted clattering teletypes. Wallboard hid the plumbing. Two huge safes, with rotating trays of top secrets, were built into one long wall. A dropped ceiling and gold carpeting added to a hushed atmosphere that makes the L-shaped room resemble a corporation's computer center."

"The duty officers would send messages to me from their station about five feet away," Botsai told me. "And then I would decide which ones—which messages and bits of information—should go in the noon notes and the evening notes, [which] would be sent up to the Kissinger office." Her most important task was preparing the morning notes. "I would come in at five o'clock in the morning and hope that the MACV [Military Assistance Command, Vietnam] overnight report would show up in time for us to get it in the morning brief...and we would put that package together along with the President's Daily Brief and send it upstairs, we hoped, by eight o'clock. Because that's when Kissinger came in."

Henry Kissinger was a central figure in the Nixon White House—by late 1973, arguably as central as the president himself. He often carried briefs personally to Nixon to discuss them. And he, rather than the president, led the Sit Room meetings in which advisers charted the United States' course of action.

Why was Nixon so averse to that room? Kissinger offered one theory in his memoir *The White House Years*: "Nixon was convinced that President Johnson had suffered from the 'Situation Room syndrome,' meaning that he had succumbed to the melodramatic idea that the world could be managed, in crisis, from this room." LBJ's obsession with the Sit Room had ultimately done more harm than good. So Nixon went in the opposite direction.

When I asked Kissinger recently to expand on this idea, he told me, "The Situation Room is in the basement of the White House, so the action taken there is out of proportion to its appearance." He laughed dryly. "It's a very simple room...you can get information very rapidly to the decision-makers. But when you're in it, you are happy to get out of it...And on the other hand, it defines your status. Otherwise you wouldn't be there."

I asked whether the room's mystique might lead people to believe they had more control over events than they actually did.

"Well, that's a good point," he replied. "I hadn't thought of it that way. But it's of course true that the orders you give in the Situation Room are bureaucratically implemented very quickly. Whether they *work* is what is to be determined."

Not everyone buys Kissinger's "Situation Room syndrome" theory, at least as it pertains to Richard Nixon. Garrett Graff, the author of *Watergate: A New History* among many other books on contemporary American history, suggested other reasons why Nixon might have avoided it.

"My gut is that Nixon wouldn't trust the Situation Room as a space," Graff told me. "[He] didn't trust the National Security Council staff." He pondered for a moment. "Nixon sees his own White House as hostile territory. I don't think you saw a lot of [him] going down into the Situation Room in part because they were all enemies out to get him, just like everyone else who was an enemy out to get him." The Sit Room was not home turf for Nixon; it was the national security establishment's space. Nixon wanted to be in rooms where he was controlling the conversation and where he could tape what was being said.

Of course, by the time of the Yom Kippur War, Nixon was in control of very little—including his own behavior.

ON OCTOBER 11, five days into the war, Brent Scowcroft and Henry Kissinger had this exchange over the telephone:

> **Scowcroft:** The switchboard just got a call from 10 Downing Street to inquire whether the president would be available for a call within thirty minutes from the prime minister. The subject would be the Middle East.

Kissinger: Can we tell them no? When I talked to the president he was loaded.

It was not yet eight p.m. A war was raging. Israel believed its very survival was at stake. Prime Minister Golda Meir had been pleading for a meeting with the president, while the Arab nations were begging the Soviets for help. Global stability hung in the balance. And the president of the United States was too drunk to get on the phone.

"Nixon is, at this point, disintegrated," Tim Weiner, author of *One Man Against the World: The Tragedy of Richard Nixon*, told me. "He has been deeply insomniac for most of his presidency. He's now drinking heavily. Every night he would have a highball or three as soon as the sun went down. And he had very low tolerance for alcohol. One drink and he'd be drunk—but then he'd have three."

Nixon's world was crumbling. Just the day before, Agnew had pleaded no contest and resigned to avoid jail time. Michigan representative and House minority leader Gerald Ford was the consensus choice in Congress to replace Agnew, precisely because he *wasn't* impeachment insurance. Special prosecutor Archibald Cox was close to securing the tapes that would seal Nixon's fate. And with Nixon struggling to save his presidency, the Soviet Union seized the moment. By airlifting military supplies to Egypt and Syria, they hoped to tip the balance of power in the Middle East. The Yom Kippur conflict was now a superpower showdown.

Nixon hid. Literally. He had set up Room 180 in the OEOB, across the alley from the West Wing, as a second office, and he began spending the bulk of his days there.

But why? The Oval is the world's most famous office. It symbolizes the president's solitary power. And the light is sublime. Anyone who's ever worked in the West Wing jockeys to be as close to it as possible.

So why was Nixon exiling himself to the executive branch equivalent of Siberia?

Perhaps *because* the Oval was where everyone else wanted to be. Nixon may be the most introverted man ever to win the White House—most comfortable alone, jotting his thoughts on a legal pad while sitting in the favorite chair he'd moved down from New York. Room 180 "was a literal hideaway," said Graff, "somewhere he could go and put on the record player and play 'Victory at Sea.'" It was also—unlike the Oval—a place where Nixon felt comfortable drinking. He kept a supply of his favorite liquor, Ballantine's scotch, there. And he began indulging in it earlier and earlier in the day.

As the war intensified, with Nixon holed up in his hideaway, the Situation Room was a hive of activity. Kissinger convened the WSAG meetings there. And the Sit Room staff was, as always, busy collecting and synthesizing reams of information for the president and his advisers.

"That was one of the busier times," recalls Sally Botsai. "The information, the paperwork and the computer information exploded. We had all sorts of things coming in. And you have to decide how much you're going to give to the people upstairs, because you don't want to overwhelm them with tactical details, but you have to be able to give them an overview of the most important issues going on."

"Kissinger needed to be briefed a lot," Botsai told me. And the Sit Room had other tools for assessing the war's progress. "I remember once, DIA [Defense Intelligence Agency] made a model of several of the mountain passes on the Sinai Peninsula," she recalled. "You had a little piece that you attached to your eye so you could kind of fly through the device. It was a three-dimensional mock-up of the mountain passes, made of papier-mâché or something. And so Kissinger could just look through this device...and it gave you the impression you were flying through the passes." Botsai then confessed with a smile that she stole a look through the viewfinder herself when Kissinger wasn't around.

Despite the stress of synthesizing huge volumes of information during a time of war, Botsai recalls the atmosphere in the Sit Room as more communal than competitive. "We tried to work for one another," she told me. "If somebody was overloaded, we would help out. It was a very collegial, relaxed but dedicated group of people." That said, the specter of Nixon's troubles hung over the room. Watergate was always there.

"No matter how many crises we had," said Botsai, "it was always in the background."

And then, in the midst of the war, it boiled over.

On Saturday, October 20, Kissinger engaged in some of his famous "shuttle diplomacy," flying to Moscow to meet with Leonid Brezhnev. Hours later, Nixon blew up his own government by ordering his attorney general, Elliot Richardson, to fire Archibald Cox. Richardson refused, and before the night was over, he and deputy attorney general William Ruckelshaus would resign, and solicitor general Robert Bork would fire Cox—an infamous chain of events that became known as the Saturday Night Massacre.

"All hell has broken loose," White House chief of staff Al Haig reported to Kissinger in a call. The U.S. government was destabilized. Preparations for impeachment hearings went into overdrive. And as Cox himself declared on the night he was fired, "Whether ours shall continue to be a government of laws and not of men is now for Congress and ultimately the American people" to decide.

On the other side of the world, Kissinger had managed to negotiate a cease-fire, which went into effect on Monday, October 22. It would prove to be short-lived. The very next morning, the Israelis once again launched attacks. And the Soviets were livid.

The hotline clattered to life at eleven a.m. Washington time on October 23, spitting out a missive from Brezhnev to Nixon.

> Israel has flagrantly violated the Security Council decision on the cease fire in the Middle East. We in Moscow are shocked that the understanding which was reached only two days ago has in fact been ruptured by this action by the Israeli leaders. Why this treachery was allowed by Israel is more obvious to you.

Brezhnev clearly held Nixon accountable for Israel's breach. Two hours and ten minutes later, Nixon replied via hotline, taking responsibility but getting in a little dig, too:

> I want to assure you that we assume full responsibility to bring about a complete end of hostilities on the part of Israel. Our own information would indicate that the responsibility for the violations of the ceasefire belongs to the Egyptian side, but this is not the time to debate that particular issue.

Despite the sniping, when the sun set over the Potomac River on Tuesday night, October 23, "calm seemed to have been restored," as Kissinger wrote in his memoir *Years of Upheaval*. The cease-fire had been reinstated, with both Israel and Egypt pledging to adhere to it.

"Haig had told me Tuesday night that Nixon was 'down, very down' over Watergate," Kissinger wrote. "Eight impeachment resolutions had that day been submitted to the House of Representatives Judiciary Committee. But I knew that whatever happened in his personal tragedy, Nixon would be firm and acute in the complicated diplomacy ahead of us."

If only that were true. On the following night, an extraordinary series of directives would come out of the Situation Room. President Nixon didn't even know this was happening.

WHEN KISSINGER ARRIVED at the White House at eight a.m. on October 24, he received a message from an Egyptian intelligence source that the Israelis had once again broken the cease-fire. The Soviets couldn't abandon the Egyptians and Syrians, their closest allies in the Middle East, so they warned the Israelis that more attacks would trigger the "greatest consequences." If the U.S.S.R. entered the fighting itself, all bets were off—especially since U.S. intelligence had just discovered that Soviet ships heading toward Israel were carrying nuclear weapons.

The temperature was rising. All day long, messages flew between the Middle East, Moscow and Washington. Kissinger furiously worked the phones, trying to buy time to create a diplomatic solution. But with conflicting reports on what was happening in the war zone, and multiple players angling for their own outcomes, the situation was volatile. In the midst of trying to defuse this ticking time bomb, Kissinger got a call from a distraught Nixon, who was consumed by the prospect of impeachment. "They are doing it because of their desire to kill the president," he told Kissinger. "And they may succeed. I may physically die."

This appears to be the last direct communication Kissinger had with Nixon that night. Al Haig became the messenger, running up and down the stairs in the White House, supposedly to shuttle information to the president. The implication is that Nixon was alert and engaged. But there's no indication Nixon was involved in any decision-making. In fact, he was almost certainly unaware of it.

"We don't know if Nixon was awake, asleep, capable of a response," Tim Weiner told me. "Haig does not mention this in his duplicitous memoirs, and to my knowledge, he never talked about it...We simply don't know what, if anything, transpired between Nixon and Haig." That said, Weiner goes on, "There is no evidence that Nixon was capable of rational thought that night. My best guess is that he had another drink and maybe took a Nembutal and conked out."

We do know that Haig was acting in place of the president. Former NSC staffer William Lloyd Stearman actually goes even further, saying that "Al Haig *was* the president of the United States" as Nixon disintegrated—an assessment that sheds a bit of light on Haig's most infamous moment, his declaration after President Reagan was shot that "I'm in control here." He'd been down the road with an incapacitated president once before.

Nixon, according to Kissinger, had "retired for the night" by 9:30 p.m. Shortly thereafter, Brezhnev sent the president another missive. This one carried an ultimatum.

I have received your letter in which you inform me that Israel ceased fighting. The facts, however, testify that Israel continues drastically to ignore the ceasefire decision of the Security Council. Thus, it is brazenly challenging both the Soviet Union and the United States...

I will say it straight that if you find it impossible to act jointly with us in this matter, we should be faced with the necessity urgently to consider the question of taking appropriate steps unilaterally.

Haig thought the Soviets were bluffing, but Kissinger believed they were issuing a direct threat. The United States needed to take strong, immediate action in response. "Should I wake the president?" he asked Haig. "No," came the reply. Decisions had to be made with or without Nixon, so Kissinger convened his group in the Situation Room to formulate a response.

Piss-swisher.

That unforgettable term appears in the first sentence of one of the more remarkable documents ever recorded of a Sit Room meeting: "At 2230 I received a call from Larry Eagleburger advising me that we had just received a real piss-swisher from Brezhnev regarding the Arab-Israeli Conflict."

The writer was Admiral Thomas Moorer, chairman of the Joint Chiefs of Staff. The "piss-swisher," military slang for a pot stirrer, was the Soviets' ultimatum letter. And when the advisers—including defense secretary James Schlesinger, CIA head William Colby, NSC military assistant Jonathan Howe, Haig, Scowcroft and Kissinger—gathered in the Sit Room to game out a reply, Moorer was taking notes. His memo, declassified in 2007, charts what happened over the ensuing five-plus hours.

Kissinger opened by distributing copies of the letters exchanged between Brezhnev and Nixon over the previous few days. He noted that as of four thirty that afternoon, negotiations had seemed to be on track. So, why had the Soviets pivoted to issuing threats? Had this been their plan all along? Were they playing some sort of high-stakes game?

Haig was now persuaded that the Soviets might launch an attack in the Middle East within hours. The question, he said, "was whether or not this was a rational plan or a move of desperation" on their part. In Moorer's recounting, Haig then suggested that "the Soviets realized that they were losing and that they are now trying to capitalize on what has happened this weekend in Washington, which has served to weaken the president." Schlesinger agreed, saying that the Soviets were "influenced by the current situation the president finds himself in."

Kissinger went a step further. "If the Democrats and the U.S. public do not stop laying siege to their government," he declared, "sooner or later, someone will take a run at us. Friday, the president was in good shape domestically. Now the Soviets see that he is, in their mind, non-functional."

The principals wondered out loud about how the Soviets would exploit the power vacuum. Would they launch their own attacks against Israeli forces? "Why shouldn't they go in there?" Kissinger noted to Haig before the meeting. "They have a cripple in the White House." Now Kissinger's team had to deal with that prospect, or something worse—even a direct confrontation with Soviet forces.

Brezhnev's letter was aggressive, so Kissinger felt the U.S. response should be as well. "The overall strategy of the Soviets now appears to be one of throwing détente on the table since we have no functional president," he declared. "We must prevent them from getting away with this...When you decide to use force, you must use plenty of it." The group debated how to respond most forcefully, formulating a multipart plan with one shocking component: With President Nixon passed out upstairs in the White House, the men in the Sit Room decided to raise military alertness to DEFCON 3.

A quick primer on the Defense Readiness Condition, or DEFCON, scale: It consists of five stages of alertness, with 5 being the lowest or "normal" readiness. DEFCON 4 is a slightly heightened state of alertness, with increased security and intelligence measures. DEFCON 3 is high alert, with military forces on standby. DEFCON 2 is the last step before war. And DEFCON 1 is war. In 1973, the United States had only been above level four on one occasion, reaching DEFCON 2 during the Cuban Missile Crisis. So the step taken by Kissinger and the others that night was huge, particularly in the absence of Nixon's assent.

DEFCON 3 set the entire American military into action. From Moorer's memo:

We took the following actions:

- Set DEFCON III;
- Moved *John F. Kennedy* from West of Gibraltar into the Med;
- Moved *Roosevelt* from the vicinity of Sicily to join *Independence* South of Crete;
- Got the Amphibious Ready Force underway from Suda Bay;
- Alerted European Forces;
- Alerted the 82d Airborne Division;
- Recalled 75 B52s from Guam.

Moorer warned Kissinger that the move to DEFCON 3 was sure to be leaked. And so it was, at about three a.m. Washington time on

October 25. The meeting in the Sit Room was still going on at that time, with the group drafting a reply to Brezhnev—ostensibly from Nixon, though he wouldn't see it before it went out at 5:30 a.m. Meanwhile, the news about DEFCON 3 accomplished what Kissinger had hoped, causing the Soviets to back down.

How does a national security adviser, even one as preternaturally self-confident as Henry Kissinger, decide to take such a critical step with the president incapacitated? For one thing, he believed he was doing what the president would have done. "Nixon and I, we had a tendency—we were not in favor of escalation," Kissinger told me. "But we felt that if we escalated, we should escalate to a point very close to what the other side would tolerate in order to prevent [nuclear war]."

Moorer's memo ends with this item: "At 0400 [4:00 a.m.] we went to bed to await the Soviet response." The most consequential Sit Room meeting without a president had ended. But what Kissinger didn't know at the time is that his counterparts in the U.S.S.R. were dealing with a situation that mirrored his own. Soviet documents released years later detailed how Brezhnev was also in a downward spiral, fueled by alcohol and sleeping pills. When the Kremlin was issuing its ultimatum to the U.S., Brezhnev was out of commission, secluded in his dacha outside Moscow. In this game of nuclear chicken, neither leader was in charge.

◀◉▶

THE DEFCON 3 gambit worked. Less than twenty-four hours after news of it leaked, the Yom Kippur War ended. Remarkably, the process led by Henry Kissinger in the Situation Room succeeded despite the president, not because of him. But President Nixon's troubles were, of course, far from over. By the late summer of 1974, it was clear that his presidency would not survive Watergate.

"In the days before Nixon resigned, you could walk outside and see the taxpayers, the American people, looking through the fences of the White House with these puzzled, sad looks on their faces," Sally Botsai recalls. "It was really sad to see that." She continued to work her regular shifts in the Situation Room, and on August 8, 1974, she was there when word came down that Nixon would give a televised speech that night announcing his intention to resign.

"I decided I couldn't make it home in time to watch," Botsai told me. "So I was just going to stay down there. At about seven o'clock or so, there was a Secret Service guy stationed near the West Wing side door. He said, 'If anybody needs to use the restrooms or get a cup of coffee, now's your chance, because we're going into lockdown.'" And it wasn't just the Sit Room that went on lockdown that evening—it was the entire White House. "The people in the press office were indignant about being closed down," Botsai says. "They were hyperventilating." Though the agent hadn't specified the reason for the lockdown, she learned why after the fact: President Nixon wanted to take one last, lonely walk through the White House, without having to see—or be seen by—anyone.

The following day, August 9, 1974, Botsai attended Nixon's farewell speech to White House staff in the East Room. The president, his upper lip sweaty and eyes misty, approached the podium to a sustained standing ovation from cabinet members, White House employees and Sit Room staffers. He gave an emotional speech, surrounded by his family, as people in the room wiped their eyes.

"It was just a very sad occasion," she told me. "And then you could see when the helicopter was on the Ellipse. You could see Henry Kissinger from the balcony, waving goodbye to him as they stepped onto the helicopter to go out to Andrews." After Nixon and his family flew off, Botsai went back down to the Situation Room to continue her shift.

Gerald Ford was sworn in as the thirty-eighth president of the United States at noon that same day. Shortly thereafter, as Botsai recalls, "General Scowcroft came down to the Sit Room and said, 'Proceed as usual. Nothing will change. We'll just carry on as we have.'" No one knew yet how the new president would use the room—or whether, like Nixon, he'd use it hardly at all. Either way, the men and women staffing it would, as Botsai said, "serve the taxpayers . . . and protect the nation. We took our job seriously."

Chapter 4

S.O.S.

———◆———

*M*AYDAY. MAYDAY.

The international distress call came from a U.S.-flagged cargo ship, the S.S. *Mayaguez*, in the Gulf of Siam on the afternoon of May 12, 1975. The ship's message was succinct and shocking: "Have been fired upon and boarded by Cambodian armed forces...Ship being towed to unknown Cambodian port."

Just twelve days had passed since the fall of Saigon, when images were beamed around the world of Vietnamese evacuees clamoring to board helicopters and crowding into boats to escape. After nearly two decades of fighting in Southeast Asia, the United States had finally retreated in humiliation. And now, without warning, the Communist Khmer Rouge had seized a U.S. container ship and its crew. As Henry Kissinger would later describe it, "We thought we were at last free to turn to healing the nation's wounds when Indochina suddenly reached out and, like a drowning man, dragged us back into the vortex."

It was 3:18 a.m. in Washington, D.C., when the *Mayaguez* sent out its Mayday call. President Gerald Ford was asleep in the White House residence, but on the other side of the world, a chain of events was set in motion to alert him to the crisis.

John Neal, an employee at the Delta Exploration shipping company in Jakarta, Indonesia, picked up the Mayday signal. He then relayed the information, which included latitude and longitude coordinates, to the U.S. embassy in Indonesia. The ambassador prepared a message to be sent via the Critical Intelligence Communications System, or CRITICOMM—the warning system launched during the Eisenhower administration to instantly alert key players in Washington to crisis events. Nearly two hours after the ship first radioed its Mayday, the CRITICOMM alert went out to the Joint Chiefs of Staff, the NSA, the Defense Intelligence Agency, the CIA, the State Department and the White House.

The Situation Room received the message at 5:14 a.m. Washington time. Right away, the duty officers had to make a decision: Should they wake the president? Or could this wait until he was already up?

Deciding when to alert the president and other top officials to unfolding events is a crucial Sit Room function. But how do you know when it's the right time to do so?

"I SWEAR ALMOST every night there's something that happens that you can wake somebody up over," Jim Reed, who served as Sit Room director under President Clinton, told me. "You don't want to be an alarmist and wake up senior decision-makers every night with things. Frankly, there's not much they can do about it that night anyway. When you get the first reports of anything, they tend to have incomplete information. You hate to bother people . . . when you don't have answers to all the obvious questions they're probably going to have."

To wake? Or not to wake? Gayle Smith, the NSC's senior director for African affairs under Clinton, described the difficulty of making that snap decision.

"In my sixth week, I got a call at 3:43 in the morning," she told me. "They said, 'Ms. Smith, this is the Situation Room. We have simultaneous explosions in our embassies in Dar es Salaam and Nairobi. Would you like us to wake up the president?' And I'm lying in my bed, looking up at the ceiling, saying, *Huh. Two explosions at once, and they're calling me? Okay.*" Smith kicked the decision up the line, directing the Sit Room to conference in national security adviser Sandy Berger and counterterrorism coordinator Richard Clarke, who ultimately chose to wake the president. "I think we as a staff erred in the direction of 'better to wake somebody up and let them know than not,'" Smith says.

It's a delicate dance: If you wake the president, he might be annoyed or even angry. But if you choose *not* to wake the president, the consequences can be problematic. Whenever a crisis breaks overnight, the White House press corps's first question is: "When did the president know?" Answering that he slept through it is an invitation to criticism—even if there was a perfectly good reason for that decision.

Bob Kimmitt, who served on the NSC staff under presidents Ford, Carter and Reagan, described such an episode with President Reagan in 1981. Libyan leader Muammar Gaddafi had claimed the Gulf of Sidra as his territorial waters, declaring a "Line of Death" beyond which Libyan forces would fire on intruding aircraft or ships. Reagan wasn't buying it. In meetings with the NSC, he ordered ships and aircraft to be sent into the restricted area, a direct challenge to Gaddafi.

"A three-star admiral dressed in beautiful Navy whites, who was the director of operations on the joint staff, got up and gave a very detailed briefing on the operation," Kimmitt told me. The admiral described each possible Libyan reaction, followed by how U.S. forces would respond. It was a thorough briefing, and at the end, President Reagan had one question: "If a Libyan plane shoots at you, turns around, and is able to get back into Libyan airspace…can you still take him out?" The admiral responded, "Yes, sir. Because he has indicated that he is a threat."

"Good," said the president. "I want your pilots to be able to chase the Libyans back to their hangars if needed."

On August 19, 1981, this exact scenario played out. In what became known as the Gulf of Sidra incident, two U.S. F-14 Tomcats shot two Libyan Su-22 fighter jets out of the sky. Reagan happened to be in California, and because of time zone differences, word of the shootdowns came in the middle of the night. The Situation Room notified Reagan's close aide Ed Meese, who was in Los Angeles with the president. But Meese chose not to wake him, deciding instead to inform him in the morning, six hours after the shootdowns.

At the White House press briefing that day, deputy press secretary Larry Speakes explained that the president only wanted to be notified of incidents "when decisions are required." In this case, the pilots had followed predetermined rules of engagement, and the admiral had briefed the president on exactly what would happen. But the *Washington Post* still questioned whether POTUS had been asleep at the wheel: "Meese's decision not to notify Reagan immediately raised once again a question that has popped to the surface from time to time in the Reagan administration: Who is in command?"

The personality, quirks and desires of the sitting president also come into play. It's hard to imagine a crisis in which President Clinton would *not* want to be involved, for example. But during John Bolton's time in the Trump administration, he often let the president sleep through late-night events. When there was a missile launch in North Korea, he would convene conference calls with cabinet secretaries and Pentagon brass. "We'd go through tracking [the missile], and then it would turn out it was already in the ocean and not a threat," recalls Bolton. "I don't know how many times that happened, but invariably at the end I'd say, 'Okay, well, I'm not gonna tell the president until tomorrow morning.' So we'd all just go back to bed."

Bolton acknowledged that "another president—a George H. W. Bush, maybe Scowcroft would have woken him up. But I'm not gonna call Trump at three in the morning and tell him, 'Well, there was a missile launch, but nothing happened.'"

One of Bolton's predecessors, Zbigniew Brzezinski, didn't have that luxury. On June 3, 1980, toward the end of the Carter administration, Brzezinski faced the ultimate test in deciding whether to wake the president. At 2:26 that morning, he was jolted awake by a phone call from military aide Bill Odom, who told him that 220 Soviet nuclear missiles were hurtling toward the United States. Knowing that the president had a seven-minute window to order retaliatory strikes, Brzezinski told Odom to confirm the information and call back. Odom did, reporting that now it appeared that 2,200 missiles were on the way—enough to cause a nuclear holocaust.

Brzezinski believed that Washington, D.C., was about to be obliterated. He chose not to wake his wife, reasoning it was kinder to let her die in peace. But as he prepared to phone President Carter, Odom called one more time to say that other warning systems weren't showing any incoming missiles. The "attack" was a false alarm.

Marc Gustafson, senior director of the Sit Room under President Biden, says that deciding when to wake your principals is "where you have the most growing pains" in a new administration. When I spoke with him in late 2022, he said, "Our team is always refining that process and trying to figure out, 'Do I wake up the national security adviser when this happens? And who else should I call?'" These are difficult decisions, and they weigh heavily on the minds of those tasked with making them.

"I got called multiple times at night," recalls Kevin Dunay, Sit Room director under both George W. Bush and Barack Obama. "Only 10 percent of the time did I actually push that information…and there were times I'd make that decision and I'd never make it back to sleep. I'd just stare and think, 'God, I hope I didn't screw up,' you know?"

IN THE CASE of the *Mayaguez,* neither President Ford nor Henry Kissinger was advised until hours after the ship was captured. The Situation Room informed deputy national security adviser Brent Scowcroft at 7:30 a.m. on May 12, and Scowcroft told the president ten minutes later in the Oval Office. Kissinger found out at his regular 8:00 a.m. staff meeting at the State Department—and he was *not* happy.

Staffers were going around the table giving Kissinger updates when the deputy assistant secretary of state for East Asia, Owen Zurhellen— who was actually filling in for his absent boss that day—informed him that Cambodians had captured the *Mayaguez.* Kissinger's bushy eyebrows shot skyward. "How can that be?" he demanded, referring not only to the capture, but "to the fact that I should be learning of it in such an offhand fashion," as he wrote in *Years of Renewal.* "The hapless Zurhellen, having himself been informed only two minutes before the meeting, replied truthfully: 'It's beyond me.'"

And this was just the beginning. To the consternation of all involved, information flow and accuracy became a major problem during the

Mayaguez crisis. Where was the ship? And where had the Cambodians taken the thirty-nine crewmen? In four contentious NSC meetings over the next two days, the president's closest advisers would argue vehemently about what exactly was going on in the Gulf of Siam. As President Ford wrote in his memoir, *A Time to Heal*: "All day Monday we received contradictory reports." First the *Mayaguez* was steaming toward mainland Cambodia. Then she was anchored offshore. Then she was heading toward shore. Then she was anchored. Finally, she was reported dead in the water near the mainland.

As the NSC tried to confirm details and debated what to do, the specter of a previous ship seizure hung over the room. Seven years earlier, North Korean forces had captured the U.S.S. *Pueblo*, killing one crewmember and whisking eighty-two others away to a Pyongyang prison camp. For eleven months, the North Koreans interrogated and tortured the Americans, parading them in front of cameras for propaganda purposes, and there was little that President Johnson could do about it. "I remember the *Pueblo* case," Vice President Nelson Rockefeller announced at one NSC meeting, echoing the national rallying cry made famous while that crew was in captivity. President Ford was determined not to allow anything similar to happen to the *Mayaguez* crew.

The conflicting reports about the ship were troubling. Yet far worse was the confusion over where the crewmembers were. Early in the morning on Tuesday, May 13, Navy reconnaissance pilots reported seeing them on Koh Tang Island, a speck of land thirty miles off the Cambodian coast. Desperate to keep the Khmer Rouge from transporting them to prison camps on the mainland, Ford convened the NSC in the Cabinet Room at 10:22 a.m.

At that meeting, the president expressed frustration at the slow flow of information. "I am very concerned about the delay in reports," he told JCS acting chairman General David Jones. "We must have the information immediately. There must be the quickest possible communication to me." The problem was, even when the information came, it was often wrong. General Jones declared that the crewmembers were on Koh Tang, but it was later discovered that none of them ever set foot on the island. Instead, they had been put aboard a Thai fishing boat, which had orders to deliver them to the mainland.

President Ford had to choose a course of action quickly. As Vice President Rockefeller put it, "The longer we take, the worse it gets. If the Communists do not think that you will react strong and fast, they will keep on doing this." Kissinger and General Jones urged the president to act aggressively. So, toward the end of the meeting, Ford enumerated a four-point plan: (1) stop boats from leaving Koh Tang Island, (2) stop boats from coming to it, (3) retake the *Mayaguez,* and (4) send a thousand-strong Marine detachment to invade the island. He added one more detail that would prove to be crucial. Though U.S. forces would rely on aircraft to stop the boats, the president instructed that "you do not sink them, necessarily," but instead simply take "preventive action."

In Kissinger's estimation, Gerald Ford was a leader who "would settle on goals in one or two crisp meetings," and "afterward he would permit himself no second thoughts." But late that night, in the third NSC meeting, Ford would make a decision that caused him a great deal of second-guessing and stress.

WHEN PRESIDENT FORD convened the NSC in the Cabinet Room at 10:40 p.m., his spirits were low. Three hours earlier, the NMCC had informed him that a U.S. Air Force helicopter en route to assist with the Koh Tang invasion had crashed in Thailand, killing all twenty-three Americans aboard. Efforts to resolve the *Mayaguez* crisis diplomatically were going nowhere. And the fighting had begun, with U.S. military aircraft firing on several Cambodian patrol boats that had tried to sail from the island to the mainland.

Then, a dramatic scene took place. As Ford described it in *A Time to Heal*:

> While we were debating what further steps to take, a message was hand delivered to the Cabinet Room from the Situation Room. It was from the pilot of an Air Force A-7 attack aircraft flying over the scene. A Cambodian vessel had just left Koh Tang and was headed toward Kompong Som [on the mainland]. The pilot had made one pass. He was about to sink the ship with his 20-mm cannon when he thought he recognized Caucasians huddled on the deck below.

Imagine this moment. The U.S. pilot has already fired on two boats, sinking one. He has fired riot control agents—tear gas—at a third vessel in an effort to stop it. As he flies in for the kill, he *thinks* he sees white faces on the deck, but he isn't sure. And so he radios his superiors, who communicate to the Situation Room, who pass a note to the president in the Cabinet Room to ask what to do.

This exchange, from the NSC meeting transcript, captures the consternation in the room:

> **Ford:** Did the pilot try riot control agents?
>
> **Scowcroft:** They were tried and they did not work. Now the pilot is not sure what to do next.
>
> **Schlesinger:** He is not certain that there are Caucasians on board . . .

Hartmann (Robert Hartmann, counselor to the president):
How can the pilot tell whether the men are Caucasians?

Schlesinger: By a number of signs, such as their size and the color of their skin.

Scowcroft: It is not an easy identification. It is very tough.

Schlesinger: I would think that avoiding bargaining chips is less of an objective than not being in a position where the Cambodians can say that [we] killed our own men.

Ford: What do we do? Should we let them go into port?

Accidentally killing the American crewmen would be a human tragedy and a political disaster. Almost no one in the room wanted to take that risk. But then Kissinger commented dryly that it might have been better to do so:

Kissinger: We have a pilot who thinks there may be Caucasians. It would have been a much better position for us to take that we will simply hit anything that leaves the island.

Ford: Right.

Kissinger: Now we are debating with the pilot.

This was an extraordinary moment—and a whole new level of micromanagement. Thanks to satellite communications, a pilot in midair, nine thousand miles away from the White House, could ask the president more or less directly what to do. Never again would it take hours, or even days, to get information from fields of battle on the other side of the world. Yet as miraculous as this advance was, it had drawbacks. Was it really useful to have the president of the United States focused on whether a pilot should shoot at a particular boat? One shudders to think what might have happened if Lyndon Johnson had been able to communicate directly, in real time, with our fighters in Vietnam. He might never have left the Situation Room.

The group continued to debate, with Kissinger insisting that the pilot should sink the boat. "I think we should go ahead with the island, Kompong Som, and the ship all at once," he told the president. "I think people should have the impression that we are potentially trigger-happy." As the minutes ticked by, Scowcroft pressed Ford for an answer, saying, "I have got to get the word out. What should I tell them?"

"Tell them to sink the boats near the island," Ford replied. "On the other boat, use riot control agents or other methods, but do not attack it." Admiral James L. Holloway III nodded and walked out, heading for the Situation Room to pass along the order.

This sequence of events unsettled Ford. As he later wrote:

> Once I've made a decision, I seldom fret about it, but this one caused me some anxiety. If the pilot had been right, crew members were on their way to the mainland where we would have a far more difficult time effecting their recovery. My concern increased during the night as new reports flowed into the Situation Room. Several other patrol craft had attempted to leave the island. When they had ignored our planes' signals to stop, they had been destroyed. Suppose those vessels had carried crew members from Mayaguez below their decks? There was no way to tell, and that possibility was awful to contemplate.

As it turned out, the boat was in fact the Thai fishing vessel that held all thirty-nine American crewmembers. Ford's decision had saved them.

Unfortunately, many other American lives would be lost before the *Mayaguez* crisis was over.

———◄◦►———

PRESIDENT FORD CONVENED the fourth and final NSC meeting at 3:52 p.m. on Wednesday, May 14. With the crisis now in its third day, and a contingent of Navy ships entering the Gulf of Siam, it was time to launch military actions. But how much force to use? Was the goal simply to regain the *Mayaguez* and her crewmembers? Or was it important to punish the Khmer Rouge as well?

Ford and Kissinger advocated a more hawkish approach, including bombing the mainland. "My recommendation is to do it ferociously," Kissinger said. "We should not just hit mobile targets, but others instead." Schlesinger, however, felt such bombings would be a step too far. These were the kinds of decisions that determined whether cities were destroyed and whether innocent people lived or died. The men went around and around, and when there was a momentary lull in the discussion, a new voice piped up.

"Has anyone considered that this might be the act of a local Cambodian commander who has just taken it into his own hands to halt any ship that comes by?" Heads swiveled to look. Who on earth was talking?

It was David Hume Kennerly, the twenty-eight-year-old White House photographer. White House photographers, who attend nearly every presidential meeting, are supposed to be flies on the wall. They snap and don't speak—but not this time. What was the *photographer* doing injecting his views into a top secret NSC meeting? The people in the Cabinet Room were among the most powerful in the world. No outsider would dare interrupt them, particularly as they debated U.S.

military action. The absolute chutzpah of this young man was stunning. And then he went on.

"Has anyone stopped to think that he might not have gotten his orders from Phnom Penh?" Kennerly asked. "If that's what has happened, you know, you can blow the whole place away and it's not gonna make any difference. Everyone here has been talking about Cambodia as if it were a traditional government, like France. We have trouble with France, we just pick up the telephone and call. We know who to talk to. But I was in Cambodia just two weeks ago, and it's not that kind of government at all. We don't even know who the leadership is. Has anyone considered that?"

I had never heard this story—and never heard of anything remotely similar happening during an NSC meeting. So I tracked down Kennerly to ask him about it. Now in his mid-seventies, he explained why, as such a young man, he'd felt emboldened to speak. And in the process, he gave me some insight into Gerald Ford's character.

"I was the only one in the room who had ever been in the Cambodian war," Kennerly told me. "So, I mean, it wasn't like I'm some schmuck from Iowa who's never been out of the capital." In fact, Kennerly had already won the Pulitzer Prize for Feature Photography in 1972 for his images taken in the war zones of Vietnam and Cambodia. Believing he had knowledge that the NSC members did not, he felt a moral imperative to speak up. "A lot of people wanted the U.S. to take this heavy action because we'd lost the war in Vietnam," he told me. "And I'm not gonna make the Cambodian people pay for us losing the Vietnam War ... If you bomb Phnom Penh, or around Phnom Penh, it's not going to do any good. And it's going to kill a bunch of innocent people."

Kissinger did not write about this moment in his memoir, but it is safe to surmise that he was supremely annoyed at the photographer's interjection. "A lot of people got pissed off," Kennerly told me.

"Fortunately, my boss was not one of them." His boss—meaning President Ford—welcomed Kennerly's input. And ultimately, based in part on the photographer's words, he called off the B-52 strike that Kissinger was arguing for.

"I felt that what Kennerly had said made a lot of sense," Ford wrote in his memoir. "Massive airstrikes would constitute overkill." Instead, within the hour, he ordered more limited surgical strikes against specific mainland targets. Kennerly was vindicated, though after the meeting, Ford pulled him aside and said, "Next time you're going to speak out, just hand me a note."

The fact that Ford not only welcomed Kennerly's views, but acted on them, speaks volumes about the kind of president he was. He didn't put on airs. He didn't care about titles or the usual Washington chess moves. He was a regular guy who—let's face it—probably never expected to be in the White House. He's certainly the only POTUS who was never elected president *or* vice president, only finding himself in the nation's highest office because Agnew, then Nixon, resigned.

Like Nixon, President Ford almost never used the Situation Room for meetings. Yet his reasons for avoiding it were different from Nixon's, who felt paranoid that the Sit Room was the NSC's domain. It's possible, as Ford biographer Richard Norton Smith speculates, that Ford preferred working in the Oval Office and the Cabinet Room as a way to establish his legitimacy as president. But more likely, he simply found those rooms more spacious and comfortable. "The one time he even referenced it, [he said] he didn't like the room," Kennerly told me. "It was confined and kind of gloomy and dark, he said."

In fact, Kennerly says Ford only went into the Sit Room once during his entire presidency, on the night before Saigon fell. But oddly enough, he and First Lady Betty Ford traipsed through the Sit Room complex often. In their bathing suits. On their way to the White House's new outdoor swimming pool.

In the mid-1970s, after covering up the indoor pool to accommodate a new press briefing room, the White House installed an outdoor one on the South Lawn. An avid swimmer, Ford had suggested joining the local YMCA rather than spending the money, but he was delighted when the pool was built anyway. Unfortunately, the only way to get to it was by walking across the lawn outside the mansion. This created awkward scenes of the First Couple trudging across the grass in their swimsuits, towels or robes—not a particularly distinguished look, though Ford didn't seem to mind.

For the sake of privacy, a new indoor passage was created. "The White House installed an exterior door in the rear wall of the communications vault of the Situation Room complex," according to Michael Bohn. That door led to a staircase, which led right up to the pool. So, the Fords would cut through the Sit Room complex on their way to swim—a more private route in some ways, but less so in others.

"The duty officer said that Gerald Ford used to come down at night to go swimming," recalled Dr. Sally Botsai, who served under both Nixon and Ford. "He had to go through our section, and through the back room where the LDX machine was." This made for some uncomfortable moments for the staffers, she said. "Sometimes the duty officers had only a few moments to clean up the place, shoving all the magazines, half-eaten sandwiches and trash into desk drawers, putting their shoes on and running combs through their hair."

Not that "regular guy" Ford would have cared. Long before No Drama Obama, Ford set the standard for a calm and rational approach to the presidency. "I think it was in his DNA," Richard Norton Smith told me. "He just shied away instinctively from a somewhat artificial, media-fed crisis atmosphere that is so much a part of life in Washington."

Which is why it's so surprising that the most memorable photograph from the *Mayaguez* crisis is of the president wearing a tuxedo, pipe in hand, gesticulating excitedly as other tuxedoed men laugh heartily. David Hume Kennerly shot it in the Oval Office, less than eight hours after daring to speak out at that pivotal NSC meeting.

————◄O►————

AT 7:07 P.M. on May 14, seeing the U.S. military buildup in the gulf, the Khmer Rouge broadcast a statement saying they would release the *Mayaguez*. The message wouldn't be translated and relayed to Ford until more than an hour had passed, and in the meantime, the assault began.

From the start, it didn't go well for the Americans. There were far more Khmer Rouge forces on the ground than our intelligence sources had believed, and they were heavily armed. As eight U.S. helicopters approached the island, a barrage of gunfire exploded from below. The first helicopter went down just six minutes into the fighting, and two others crashed soon after. Only 110 Marines actually made it onto the island, and they immediately began searching for the thirty-nine *Mayaguez* crewmembers—who of course were not there. A-6 and A-7 aircraft took off from the U.S.S. *Coral Sea*, dropping bombs on storage facilities on the mainland. And back in Washington, President Ford put on a tuxedo for a dinner with the Dutch prime minister Johannes den Uyl.

For the president, other duties don't stop for war, assault or crisis. On this day, he not only dealt with the *Mayaguez* situation, he also met with a group of Michigan businessmen in the morning, with labor leaders from New York at 2:00 p.m., and he even squeezed in a visit to his dentist. The Dutch prime minister's visit had been planned long in advance, and Ford didn't want to embarrass him by canceling it. So from 8:22 p.m. until just before eleven p.m., while helicopters crashed and bombs fell on the other side of the world, Ford hosted a "stag dinner" for den Uyl in the State Dining Room of the White House.

It was, as Kissinger put it, "one of the most bizarre and tense evenings of my experience in government." Ford received news of the Khmer Rouge's broadcast from the Situation Room just as the dinner was starting, and he and Kissinger excused themselves to discuss how to respond. A hasty decision was made to continue the bombing raids, and Ford returned to the dinner. But Kissinger, Scowcroft and chief of staff Donald Rumsfeld popped in and out regularly, to check with the Sit Room on events in Cambodia.

Sally Botsai was on duty in the Sit Room that night, "and they were all running around with tuxedos on, looking very smart," she recalls. "I was monitoring the phone from the NSC-NMCC feed, which was monitoring the operation as it was going on...I wanted to be close enough to the Kissinger-Scowcroft office so that if something happened, I could just hand [the information] over to them."

"That was a very unusual type of situation," she told me. "We normally didn't have that in real time." I remarked that it seemed like a dramatic scene, with Kissinger and Scowcroft hustling through, but she shook her head. "Everything's dramatic to the point that it just becomes normal," she said, which seems a pretty apt description of the Sit Room.

The dinner ended just before 11:00 p.m., and Ford, Scowcroft, Kissinger, Rumsfeld and a handful of other aides quickly assembled in the Oval Office. Minutes later, the phone rang. It was Defense Secretary Schlesinger, with news that the U.S.S. *Wilson* had intercepted a

Cambodian fishing vessel. On deck was a group of men waving white flags—the *Mayaguez* crewmembers, all of them safe and sound. The crisis was over.

"I dropped the phone into its cradle and let my emotions show," Ford wrote in his memoir. "'They're all safe,' I said. 'We got them all out. Thank God. It went perfectly. It just went great.' Kissinger, Rumsfeld and the others erupted with whoops of joy."

President Ford spent hours in the Sit Room after Cambodian forces captured the S.S. *Mayaguez*. When the crisis ended, he and his aides, dressed in tuxes for a dinner, let their emotions show. (L–R: Bud Mc-Farlane, Brent Scowcroft, Donald Rumsfeld, Henry Kissinger, Gerald Ford) | *Ford Library photo by David Hume Kennerly*

David Hume Kennerly captured the scene on film. The image is striking, the relief palpable. But despite what Ford said in that moment, it hadn't gone perfectly, or even great. Thirty-eight Marines died during the assault. Three others were captured or left behind on Koh Tang, and their exact fate remains unknown. The names of these forty-one men are etched into the Vietnam Veterans Memorial wall, considered the final casualties of the Vietnam War. Ford did acknowledge the deaths in his memoir, writing that "this was a high toll, and I felt terrible about it." Rumsfeld, too, was troubled by it, and when the photographer made public the photo of everyone laughing in the Oval, he "got pissed off at me," Kennerly said.

President Ford changed out of his tuxedo and into a business suit to announce the release of the crewmembers. By now it was the early morning hours of May 15, and he was exhausted. "I'm going home and going to bed," he announced to his advisers. As the men filed out of the Oval Office, most did the same.

It was left to Brent Scowcroft to do what he'd done before. He walked back down to the Situation Room, where the buzz of activity continued into the night. "He took it upon himself to come down and thank us," Botsai recalls. "That's the first and only time I think anybody ever did that." The duty officers, advisers and staff simply nodded, then turned their attention back to their work.

Chapter 5

CLOSE ENCOUNTERS

————◆————

*May 8. We had a session in the Situation Room con-
cerning a parapsychology project where people can
envision what exists at a particular latitude and longitude, et cetera.*

—*Jimmy's Carter's White House Diary, page 426*

J UST BEFORE ONE p.m. on Thursday, May 8, 1980, an NSC staffer
named Jake Stewart made his way into the Situation Room for a
private briefing with President Jimmy Carter. Stewart, a trim, clean-cut
U.S. Navy captain, had been serving since 1978 in the NSC's Defense
Coordination cluster, with a portfolio that included defense budget,
military programs and arms control. But on this day, he would be briefing the president on a very different type of program.

According to the White House Daily Diary, the official log of the
president's activities, the two men were joined by four other people: chief

of staff Hamilton Jordan, White House counsel Lloyd Cutler, assistant for national security affairs Zbigniew Brzezinski and First Lady Rosalynn Carter. Yet as Stewart recalls it, only he, the president, the First Lady and Brzezinski were in the room that day. Either way, the presence of any First Lady in a Situation Room meeting was exceedingly unusual, though Stewart himself won't say so. "I didn't do any private Sit Room meetings with the president other than this one," he told me in a recent interview. "So I didn't know what was normal or not."

Stewart's task was to brief President Carter on a top secret project called Operation Grill Flame. Launched in October 1978, Grill Flame, later known as Stargate, was a U.S. Army program that explored the use of parapsychology to gather intelligence. Rumors had been swirling for years that the Soviet Union had a robust parapsychology program, and eager not to be left behind on any intelligence front, the CIA and Defense Intelligence Agency worked with the Stanford Research Institute to create one in the United States.

A group of "remote viewers"—essentially, psychics—were recruited and stationed at Fort Meade, Maryland, where they plied their enigmatic craft in complete secrecy in two unmarked buildings. They spent their days attempting to use extrasensory powers to gather information about situations and events across the world, with a success rate that varied according to whom you asked. To skeptics, such as future CIA head and secretary of defense Robert Gates, the program was "bogus." To believers like U.S. Army chief warrant officer Joseph McMoneagle, who was Grill Flame's first remote viewer, the team provided useful data between 30 and 55 percent of the time—an excellent average in baseball, and not bad in the field of intelligence, either.

Jake Stewart was a believer. He and his Defense Coordination colleagues had received a briefing on Grill Flame, and "it really piqued my interest," he recalls. Specifically, he was stunned to learn about one of the program's most astonishing successes. In the late 1970s, a remote viewer named Rosemary Smith had somehow managed to pinpoint the exact location of a downed Soviet Tu-22 bomber in the heavily canopied rainforest of Zaire (now the Democratic Republic of the Congo). Sitting at a desk in Maryland, Smith had sketched a map and a flight path, described the terrain, and claimed to have "seen" the pilot bailing out of the plane—all details that proved correct. Even more surprising, she worked with map technicians to provide latitude and longitude coordinates that turned out to be precisely where the plane went down.

Stewart had come away from the briefing impressed. His colleagues were not. "I was the only one that attended that briefing that had any interest in following up," he told me. "The other guys, maybe they were busier than I was." With his colleagues focused on such projects as SALT II, NATO and arms control issues, Stewart took charge of Grill Flame. He believed the project was providing useful intelligence, and he wanted to help those who were working on it. "It was a very tough road for them. The environment for this kind of stuff is exceedingly mixed and exceedingly hostile," he recalled. They faced "a nasty mix of politics and antagonisms," since most people were skeptical about paranormal psychology.

And yet, as it turned out, two very important people in the Carter administration weren't skeptical at all. In fact, Jimmy and Rosalynn Carter were extremely open to the idea of the paranormal.

Jimmy Carter grew up Southern Baptist in the pinprick, red-clay town of Plains, Georgia. Baptized at eleven, he was steeped in the rhythms and rituals of the church, fully embracing the concepts of being "born again" and filled with the Holy Spirit. His younger sister, Ruth Carter Stapleton, became a well-known charismatic faith healer, claiming to speak in tongues and partake in "miraculous healings." To a nonbeliever, such notions seem mystical and esoteric. To Carter, they were foundational. And they appear to have opened his mind to other kinds of inexplicable phenomena as well.

In 1969, while standing with a group of people outside a Lions Club in Leary, Georgia, Carter saw what he would later describe as "a kind of green light...It didn't have any solid substance to it, it was just a very peculiar-looking light. None of us could understand what it was." In another interview, he added more details: "It got closer and closer to us. And then it stopped, I don't know how far away, but it stopped beyond the pine trees. And all of a sudden it changed color to blue, and then it changed to red, then back to white...and then it receded into the distance." Carter wasn't sure what exactly he'd seen, but he was intrigued by the possibility that the object originated from outer space. Later, at a Southern Governors Conference, he said, "I don't laugh at people anymore when they say they've seen UFOs, because I've seen one myself."

Rosalynn Carter was also curious about paranormal phenomena. In December 1976, just a month before her husband's inauguration as president, she was introduced to the famous Israeli psychic Uri Geller at an event in Mexico City. Geller, who had ties to both Mossad and the CIA, impressed the future First Lady with his spoon-bending and mind-reading skills, and she came away from the experience convinced that he had special powers. Upon returning to the United States, she eagerly relayed the details of the encounter to her husband, and early in his presidency, Jimmy Carter took a lengthy meeting with Geller to discuss possible intelligence applications of paranormal psychology.

All of this formed the backdrop to the Situation Room meeting of

May 8, 1980. Zbigniew Brzezinski, who was himself agnostic about paranormal phenomena, decided for a multitude of reasons that the time was right for the president and First Lady to learn about the Grill Flame program. He asked Jake Stewart to prepare a briefing. "And so I wrote up a brief of what had been found in the research," Stewart recalled, "and what I thought of it and how its value might manifest itself to us in current situations."

Stewart delivered his brief to the president and First Lady, who sat side by side across the table from him. Neither said a word, just taking in the extraordinary information Stewart was revealing, including the tale about locating the plane in the Zaire rainforest. When he finished, the president "looked at me and he didn't say anything. He was of sober mien, like he always was—he's seldom funny, or amused, or anything like that." And then Carter did something surprising.

"He wrote on a piece of paper, the old, white, three-by-five sheets with 'White House' on them," said Stewart. "He wrote one word: 'Hostages?' Carter shoved it silently across the table to me and said, 'Can you do anything?'

"And I said, 'I don't know. Do you want me to try?' And he just nodded. And I said, 'Yes, sir.'"

This remarkable Sit Room exchange came 186 days after Iranian militants had seized the U.S. embassy in Tehran, taking hostage more than sixty American diplomats, military personnel and civilians. More crucially, it came just two weeks after the Desert One mission, also known as Operation Eagle Claw, to free the fifty-two Americans who remained in captivity. Rather than culminating in a heroic rescue, Desert One was a debacle, a botched effort that killed eight U.S. servicemen in the Iranian desert.

By the time of the May 8 meeting with Jake Stewart, President

Carter had been agonizing for more than six months over how to end the hostage crisis. With his election-day showdown against Ronald Reagan approaching, he was mired in political problems. The economy was moribund. Inflation was soaring, and Americans were weary of long lines at the gas station. Carter's singular big gambit to free the hostages in Iran had just ended in catastrophe.

How had he gotten here? And was it possible this Grill Flame program could actually help him resolve the situation in Iran?

THE IRAN HOSTAGE crisis had started on November 4, 1979. Enraged at the U.S. government's attitude toward the Iranian revolution, and catalyzed by the fact that we'd given refuge to the deposed shah of Iran, a group of young militants—mostly college students— scaled a fence and stormed the U.S. embassy in Tehran. Initially, the students intended the takeover to be short and mostly symbolic. But when Iran's supreme leader Ayatollah Ruhollah Khomeini voiced support for the action, the students dug in, demanding the return of the shah as a condition for releasing the Americans.

The situation in Tehran quickly consumed Jimmy Carter's presidency. "Once the hostages were taken, Carter made it the number one issue in the U.S. government," recalls Gary Sick, a Middle East expert who served in the NSC under presidents Ford, Carter and Reagan. "And it remained that, really almost until the hostages were released." As Sick described it in an interview with me, this was "our first televised foreign policy crisis, and our first real exposure to Islamic politics...We didn't have a playbook to operate from, but it was the number one issue on everybody's mind, and Carter kept it that way."

Gary Sick, shown with President Carter on Air Force One, argued for a bold plan to rescue the hostages in Iran. | *Courtesy of the Jimmy Carter Library*

Sick himself had been jolted awake between four and five a.m. on November 4 by a call from a Situation Room duty officer, who informed him that the embassy had been taken over. After a brief conversation, Sick "got up and dressed in the dark, then drove through the empty streets of the capital listening to the bulletins coming in on the radio," as he wrote in his book *All Fall Down: America's Tragic Encounter with Iran.* "Unshaven and a bit bleary-eyed, I had no reason to suspect that this pre-dawn shuttle was to become a routine part of my life for the next fourteen months."

And yet, that's what happened. Nearly every morning for months to come, a group of high-level officials and staffers called the Special Coordination Committee (SCC) gathered in the Sit Room to discuss the unfolding crisis. Zbigniew Brzezinski led these hour-long meetings, using agendas prepared by Gary Sick. Which meant that Sick had to get to the Situation Room before dawn each day to assess new developments and, with the help of Sit Room staff, quickly boil down thousands of pages of information for the one- to two-page agenda.

"I was just one person," recalls Sick, "and the amount of classified information that was flowing into the U.S. government at that point was unbelievable. I mean, the whole U.S. government was focused on this one thing, so everybody that had anything to report got very high attention. It [all] came into the Situation Room, and the hardworking folks there prepared a notebook for me. And I would arrive at sunrise and have my little notebook there to look through.

"It was often about five hundred to a thousand pages," Sick went on. "But I could go through it very fast. Because you were looking for particular types of information, anything that was new or unusual—and believe me, you really get to be a speed-reader in a situation like that. I calculated at one time that, at least one day that I was operating, I got ten thousand pages of stuff in my office. And obviously, you can't read ten thousand pages in a day. But I could skim it."

This was the 1970s, the days just before personal computers and the Internet made sourcing and organizing information so much faster and easier. Sick relied not only on these vast reams of paper, but on "listening to the radio," he recalls. "I had a portable radio right beside my desk, and I had it set to go off every hour on the hour, knowing the news would hit the radio faster than it would almost anyplace else."

In the end, despite the Herculean efforts of the Sit Room staff to funnel him information from a multitude of sources, Sick recalls that "the stuff that I found most useful during that period of time, and which I mostly read at home, were [from] the Foreign Broadcast Information Service, which actually carried full texts of speeches that Khomeini, [Iranian political figure Ebrahim] Yazdi [and other] people made... They'd be talking to a group, and these were broadcast, and people in Cyprus took those and turned them into really good English very fast."

To Sick, these speeches, which were printed out on colored paper according to region (green for China, orange for Eastern Europe, etc.), provided more valuable insight than any secondhand reports could. "You could tell what these people were thinking. And so when there was a change in thinking, it would show up in these documents," he says. "It wasn't that I didn't look at the other stuff... [but] I was thinking intentions, and for intentions, you can't do better than get a politician and let 'em rant on for two hours."

After whittling the mountain of available material down to molehill size, Sick would type the daily agenda on his "little IBM Selectric" typewriter, he recalls. "I would make myself a copy, and I'd deliver it to Zbig's office by eight thirty... I found that if I had something to say to Brzezinski or to the president, I could type it out faster than I could give it to a secretary to type for me, put in the correct format, make the appropriate number of copies, etc. etc.," he says. "I could type it and be over there in fifteen minutes." Not as fast as today's instantaneous emails, but "amazingly enough, you get quite a lot done."

One such memo would change the course of not only the hostage crisis, but ultimately the entire Carter presidency.

IN EARLY APRIL 1980, a group of senior State Department officials paid Sick an unofficial visit. "They quietly came across the street and talked to me," he told me. "Clearly, they were not supposed to. The secretary of state [Cyrus Vance] doesn't like his people going out and making offers and initiatives that he didn't have anything to do with and didn't agree with. But they came and said, 'Look, we've been through this long enough. If negotiations were gonna get anywhere, they would have happened by now. So if you've got anything on the burner, this is the moment to do it.'"

There was indeed something on the burner. In the early days of the crisis, President Carter had directed the Joint Chiefs of Staff to come up with a plan for a possible rescue mission. Over the ensuing months, a Joint Task Force honed the details, identifying commanders and training personnel in secret locations. It was a complex mission, involving multiple locations and aircraft, and the president preferred not to put it into action if there was any chance of ending the crisis diplomatically. But now, what Sick was hearing was that negotiations were at a dead end. So he decided to act.

"The next day, I wrote a memo to Brzezinski which started out saying, 'The hawks are flying' and that people were really beginning to get antsy," he told me. "This was an issue that people were tired of, and they thought it was time to do something, either strike or cut bait." Sick typed up the memo on his trusty Selectric, then hand-carried it to Brzezinski's office. "Within minutes, he called me back to his office. He said, 'Make this a memo from me to the president,' because he clearly was in favor of this." Sick typed up a new memo, from Brzezinski to Carter, and once again walked it over.

"I handed it to Brzezinski and I never saw it again," he says. "I gave it to him, and he gave it to the president."

Sick's original memo appears to have been lost to history, but the one from Brzezinski to Carter can be found in the Carter Library archives. Dated April 10, 1980, the memo opens with the subject line "Getting the Hostages Free," followed by four pages of single-spaced argument for why Carter should launch the rescue mission that became Desert One. "It is now clear that the diplomatic option is closed," the memo states, before outlining two possible courses of action—either "graduated pressure" on the Iranian government or a "rescue operation." It concludes with a strong recommendation to take the latter course.

"I am struck by the evaluation of some of those closest to the situation," Brzezinski's memo stated. "My staff assistant, Gary Sick, who has been living with this issue day and night for the past five months, has personally and privately urged me in the strongest terms to adopt this course of action, and has proposed this memo...In my view, a carefully planned and boldly executed rescue operation represents the only realistic prospect that the hostages—any of them—will be freed in the foreseeable future."

The memo was apparently persuasive, because the next day, April 11, 1980, President Carter met with the NSC in the Cabinet Room. "Gentlemen," he announced, "I want you to know that I am seriously considering an attempt to rescue the hostages." He went on to ask the opinions of those gathered, saying, "Before I make up my mind, I want to know your reactions." Brzezinski, unsurprisingly, spoke forcefully in favor of moving ahead with the mission. Vice President Walter Mondale, CIA director Stan Turner, press secretary Jody Powell and Hamilton Jordan also spoke in favor of it. And although Carter claimed he hadn't made a decision yet, saying that he would "think and pray about it over the weekend," Jordan believed the president had already made up his mind.

There was only one problem, but it was a serious one. And it would lead to an extraordinary secret meeting in the Situation Room a few nights later—one of the rare times that Carter met with the NSC in that room.

Secretary of State Vance had missed the April 11 meeting, as he was on an ill-timed vacation in Florida that week. When he learned that President Carter planned to approve the rescue mission, Vance went ballistic. Back in D.C., he laid out his objections privately for the president, who then called an NSC meeting in the Cabinet Room on April 15 so Vance could air his views to the full group. As recounted in Hamilton Jordan's *Crisis*, Vance spoke forcefully against moving forward, declaring:

> I have serious doubts that the mission will work. We would have to get into Iran undetected, move into Tehran, scale the compound wall, and remove all the Americans. I cannot imagine that all this could be accomplished without harming some of the hostages or rescuers. Consider the best outcome and suppose everything goes according to plan and everyone gets out alive. Several hundred Americans live in Tehran. Suppose the militants seize them next? What will we do? We'll be back where we are now.

President Carter responded coolly to Vance's comments, and he gave no indication that he was reconsidering forging ahead. But it's possible that Vance's impassioned objection did give him pause. According to Jordan, defense secretary Harold Brown "sensed that Carter wasn't completely comfortable with the details of the mission," so he "suggested a secret meeting of the foreign policy group with the leaders of the rescue team."

That meeting would take place the following night, April 16, in the Situation Room.

As DEADLY SERIOUS as the topic was, the secret Sit Room meeting started off on an incongruously light note. When President Carter met the leader of the Delta Force team that would carry out the mission, a stocky, crew-cut U.S. Army colonel named Charlie Beckwith, he noticed the colonel's distinctive Southern accent. "Chargin' Charlie" Beckwith, it turned out, was not only from Georgia, he'd grown up in Schley County, mere miles from Carter's hometown of Plains.

"You're my neighbor!" the president exclaimed. "Who are your folks?" As the two men bantered about people they knew in common, defense secretary Brown slid a note across to Hamilton Jordan that said, "You've got to hand it to the Pentagon for finding a good ole boy to head up the mission."

The meeting started at 7:36 p.m. and went past ten p.m. During those two and a half hours, mission commanders Colonel Beckwith, Lieutenant General Philip Gast and Major General James Vaught described point by point how the action would unfold. Sitting around the crowded table, listening intently, were Brzezinski, Vance, Jordan, Brown, deputy director of the CIA Frank Carlucci, Joint Chiefs of Staff chair General David Jones and President Carter. In *Crisis*, Jordan recounted a key moment:

> Beckwith described in detail the plan to enter Iran at night in transport planes, which would rendezvous in the desert with the helicopters. The team would be flown to an overnight resting place in the mountains and then be driven by CIA-recruited Iranians in old Iranian trucks to a warehouse near Tehran. The next night, in the same trucks, the team would enter the city.
>
> "And then, Mr. President," Beckwith said, "we go over the wall and get our people out."

According to Jordan's account, the president ended the proceedings by telling the commanders, "I am impressed with your planning for this mission... I will make my decision in the next few days. If we go, you know that you'll have my full support." Beckwith replied that he hoped the president would give them the green light. "We want to do it and think we can," he said. Carter replied, "That will be a factor in my decision, Colonel. That I think you believe you can do it is very important to me."

And then, closing the meeting on the same light note on which it had started, the president added, "Also, Colonel, the fact that you are from Schley County, Georgia, is not a disadvantage."

The mood in the room was one of eager anticipation. It seemed obvious that, barring any unexpected developments, the rescue mission was a go. And every man in the room had expressed his support for it—except for one.

As they walked out of the Situation Room that night, Hamilton Jordan asked Cy Vance whether he felt any better after hearing the detailed plans. "I feel a little better," Vance replied. "But generals will rarely tell you they can't do something. This is a damn complex operation, and I haven't forgotten the old saying from my Pentagon days that in the military anything that can go wrong will go wrong."

His words would prove unhappily prescient.

The following night, April 17, Vance informed President Carter that if the mission went forward, he would have no choice but to resign. As Vance would later write in his memoir, *Hard Choices*, "I knew I could not honorably remain as secretary of state when I so strongly disagreed with a presidential decision... Even if the mission worked perfectly, and I did not believe it would, I would have to say afterward that I had opposed it, give my reasons for opposing it, and publicly criticize the president. That would be intolerable for the president and for me."

Vance delivered his formal letter of resignation to Carter on April 21, three days before the rescue mission took place. The two men agreed to keep the resignation secret, so as not to distract from the upcoming mission. It was, Vance wrote, "one of the most painful days of my life, as I am very fond of Jimmy Carter."

But there was much more pain to come.

ON THE MORNING of April 24, 1980, six C-130 transport planes took off from Masirah Island, a speck of land in the Arabian Sea just off the coast of Oman. Their destination was Desert One, a desolate stretch of sand and salt flats in central Iran that lay almost sixty miles from the nearest town. The C-130s were carrying more than a hundred men, as well as five motorcycles, a Jeep and enough fuel to replenish eight RH-53D Sea Stallion helicopters that had just lifted off from the U.S.S. *Nimitz*, anchored off the southernmost coast of Iran. This was the first step of the rescue mission; at Desert One, the helicopters would load up with the Special Forces teams, then fly to Desert Two, just outside Tehran, for the raid on the embassy compound the following night.

Ordinarily, for a mission of this magnitude, the president and his advisers might be expected to huddle in the Situation Room. But President Carter was desperate to keep information about the operation from leaking out, so he instructed Brzezinski, Jordan, Cutler and Mondale to follow their usual schedules for the day.

Carter himself undertook an agonizingly routine slate of meetings that morning, including sit-downs with members of Congress and one with Hispanic leaders about a planned anti-inflation program, all while waiting nervously for news from the Middle East. Meanwhile, down in the White House basement, the Situation Room staff was busy tracking another crisis: the mass exodus of Cuban refugees that became known as the Mariel boatlift. Another reminder that presidents don't get to pick and choose when global crises occur, and that their attention is almost always pulled in multiple directions at once.

For the hostage rescue mission, the White House had turned to a brilliant young cryptologist and self-described "tech guy" named Gary Bresnahan to connect the principals in Washington with Major General Vaught and Colonel Beckwith in the field. Bresnahan was "one of those secret guys that no one's ever heard of," Richard Clarke told me. "He worked for every administration and made the Situation Room work." The son of a truck driver and a mother who collected welfare, Bresnahan had grown up in Boston "on the wrong side of the tracks," he told me. He enlisted in the Army, studied cryptology, and went on to serve in the Situation Room under seven presidents. He's simultaneously the Zelig of the White House and the MacGyver of the Sit Room.

Bresnahan could have connected Vaught and Beckwith via satellite phone directly to the White House, but Carter preferred to have the information flow through General Jones, who was at the National Military Command Center in the Pentagon. "We went through the Pentagon to get to the field," Bresnahan told me. "Whereas nowadays we'd go right to the field."

The conversations between General Jones and President Carter were recorded, so we know exactly how the president received news of the unfolding catastrophe in Iran. As State Department files note, even the recordings were obtained in an unusual way: "Because of secrecy requirements, normal recording capabilities were not used. Instead, a portable cassette recorder was connected to the secure instrument provided for dedicated point-to-point contact. The recorder required manual start-stop for each transmission, and therefore had no electronic means of establishing the time for each call."

The mission went sideways right from the start. The six C-130s made it safely to Desert One, which the commanders had believed would be an empty stretch of sand. But to everyone's shock, a passenger bus full of Iranians pulled up to the landing spot, followed by a couple of trucks. Upon receiving updates from those on the ground, General Jones placed a call to the president, who was understandably confused.

> **Carter:** David, just as a matter of intent...do you recall why we decided to land just adjacent to a highway?
>
> **Jones:** It's not a highway, sir, it's that little road...the only place we've been able to find, so for that we could land the 130s...and we looked and looked and looked and it's the only place we found. We looked at another one and hoped to land there, and...we just did not find any place to land.

The mission was still on, but this was only the beginning of the troubles.

Although eight Sea Stallion helicopters had taken off from the *Nimitz*, only six of them made it to the landing spot. One developed a rotor blade problem two hours into the flight, and the pilots were forced to set down and abandon the craft (another helicopter landed and picked up the crew). The remaining helicopters then flew into a haboob—an intense dust cloud that arose out of nowhere, so thick that it blinded the pilots and disabled the navigation instruments on one of the helicopters. Those pilots chose to return the damaged craft to the *Nimitz*, rather than continuing on with limited navigational abilities.

Six was the absolute minimum number of helicopters needed to fulfill the rescue mission. There was no more margin for error.

At this point, General Jones attempted in a call to reassure Vice President Mondale.

Mondale: Hi, Dave. I'm here alone. Are you worried about this latest stuff?

Jones: You're talking about the two choppers down?

Mondale: Yeah.

Jones: Well, I am. I don't consider it as of now a "go/no-go." It is of concern, but not to the point of determining an abort.

Mondale: Okay. Thank you, David.

But the bad news kept coming. A third helicopter had experienced partial hydraulic failure on the way to the landing site, and while the crew had flown on, hoping the chopper could be repaired on the ground, there was no replacement hydraulic pump on-site. The aircraft was unsafe to fly, which meant there were now only five usable helicopters. And so, with extreme reluctance, Beckwith and Vaught relayed to the Pentagon that the mission would have to be aborted.

At 4:45 p.m. Washington time, Defense Secretary Brown called Brzezinski. "I think we have an abort situation," he said, then explained the situation. Brzezinski argued strenuously that Beckwith and Vaught should consider continuing the mission with five helicopters, then walked to the president's private study to inform him of the possible abort. Carter was stricken, muttering, "Damn. Damn." Ten minutes later, the president himself got on the phone with Secretary Brown, to ask directly if the commanders believed there was any way to continue the mission. Told that Beckwith believed they should abort, Carter said simply, "Let's go with his recommendation." And then he put his head in his hands and sat for a moment, clearly devastated by this turn of events.

Carter then turned to the small group of advisers who had joined him in the study—Mondale, Powell, Jordan, Brzezinski and Warren

Christopher. "At least there were no American casualties," the president said softly, "and no innocent Iranians hurt."

And then the phone rang again.

Carter: David?

Jones: Yes sir. The news is not as good as I indicated to you a few minutes ago. A RH-53 [helicopter] getting... trying to get out of Desert One ran into a C-130. The only report we have is there's some burns and injuries to people... our people.

Carter: This was on the ground?

Jones: On the ground, is the report... on the ground there at Desert One. Still sketchy report. And some burns and injuries and people... we assume in the 130, but we haven't got whether it's in the 130 or the RH-53... We have no idea how many or how serious. We will try to get that as soon as we can.

Minutes later, another call:

Jones: I just got a report from General Vaught. He's on the other phone but let me just give you a rundown. He believes that all Americans who are alive are off the ground. That is his report.

Carter: All Americans what?

Jones: He said who are alive. There are some who evidently were fatalities there. Here is his report. He said it's unsure until they sort it out... In the EC-130, when the helicopter hit it up in that part, the pilot is believed missing and presumed dead. And some passengers... the passengers, most got out, but there may have been some trapped in there. And they haven't been able to make an exact accounting. They just went around and made sure that everyone they could get ahold of got aboard and got them out. They don't believe that anybody remained, except fatalities, but the accounting is very, very poor.

In the end, eight U.S. servicemen died at Desert One, most from burns suffered as they were trapped inside the C-130 that had been struck by a helicopter. In a horrifically sad turn of events, the rest of the mission team had to evacuate for their own safety, leaving the aircraft in flames, and later, the charred bodies of the men to be discovered and displayed as war trophies by the Iranian government.

THE FAILURE OF Desert One effectively ended Carter's presidency. It would also haunt the Situation Room for decades to come, hovering like a specter over planning sessions for later military missions. Several people who would go on to play major roles in future administrations had formative experiences during the hostage crisis, and they would never forget the pall that the failed mission cast over the administration and the country.

Bob Gates, who would go on to spend time in the Sit Room under seven presidents, was CIA head Stan Turner's executive assistant during Desert One. "I wasn't involved in the preparation," he told me, "but I was a witness to it all." Years later, when Gates was involved in planning the raid that took out Osama bin Laden, he remembered keenly the lessons of the earlier mission. "All I could think about as we were planning and thinking about bin Laden was those helicopters going down, and the disaster in the desert, because it started with a helicopter crash." Gates would join several others in arguing successfully for the addition of more helicopters in the Abbottabad raid—an inclusion that would prove extremely fortuitous when one of the helicopters went down during that mission.

Anthony Lake, who would later serve as national security adviser under President Clinton, was an aide to Cyrus Vance during Desert One. "I remember Vance privately saying to me that as he looked around the table, probably in the Situation Room"—most likely the April 16 meeting—"that while he was not in combat, he was the only one there, except for the military [men], who'd actually served in the military during a war. And he knew how screwed up things can get in an operation that depended on so many different steps."

Lake told me he disagreed with Carter's fundamental approach to the hostage crisis. "If you're bargaining to buy a horse, you don't walk up to the guy who owns the horse you want to buy and say, 'That is the most beautiful horse I've ever seen in my life, and I've got to have it,' and then try to talk down his price. Similarly, if somebody takes hostages, you increase the price by saying, 'This is the most important thing in the world to me'"—which he felt Carter had publicly done.

I asked Lake if he felt like the centralization of foreign policy inside the White House had been counterproductive in the case of the hostage crisis.

"Yes, I think you're right," he said. "Of course, you care a great deal, and can show you care. But you don't try to make it a central, public issue...You do it in a way that doesn't build it up. It just made him look weaker." Better to "blame the State Department if it doesn't work, and claim credit yourself if it does, in political terms. But you just don't make such a huge public issue out of it."

Nearly two decades later, as national security adviser to President Clinton, Lake would learn some hard lessons in the limits of that strategy. The fact that the failed Black Hawk Down mission in Somalia was outsourced to the Pentagon did not shield the White House from blame when eighteen Americans lost their lives in 1993. Lake also amended his views on centralizing foreign policy decision-making through the Situation Room, acknowledging that solving the crisis in Bosnia required presidential leadership and White House control.

"I bought a used sailboat once," Lake told me. "And in the cockpit, someone left up a little brass plate that said, 'In an emergency, consider doing what the captain suggests.'"

◄○►

As we now know, two weeks after the Desert One debacle, Jake Stewart briefed Jimmy and Rosalynn Carter in the Situation Room about Grill Flame, the U.S. Army's parapsychology program. The president ended that meeting asking whether the "remote viewers" might be able to help with the hostage situation. Stewart replied that he would try, believing that the president was giving him free rein to do "whatever I could" to help end the crisis.

Stewart soon learned that the Grill Flame program was already deep into working the problem. "I saw it written down someplace, that in total they did 272 remote viewings," he told me. In one of those sessions, a woman identified only as "Nancy S." was reported to have had a rather extraordinary experience as she attempted to envision a far-away "target." As recounted in Annie Jacobsen's book *Phenomena*:

> Nancy S. was conducting Remote Viewing (RV) Session CCC84 when she broke down. The tasker noted, "Admin note 0300 Hours in Iran," or at 3:00 a.m. local time, Nancy S. reported she was having trouble getting the target she'd been sent to, which was a building in Tehran code-named India. Instead, she saw "an attacking force of some kind." She apologized and stated that

perhaps she was "hallucinating." What she saw was "weird and illogical" but "very vivid, horrible. Like a bad dream"...

According to a report declassified by the CIA, she saw "a very boring sequence and all of a sudden you are aware something is amiss and something is very wrong, people are running... with great stealth... and all of a sudden you find you are in an attack"...

The way [Joseph] McMoneagle recalls what happened, Nancy S. reported "a huge explosion... a huge fire she couldn't understand what for." And then she became overwhelmed with emotion and broke down in tears.

The date of this viewing was April 24, 1980. The following day, President Carter delivered a televised speech revealing the Desert One catastrophe to the nation. According to Joe McMoneagle, Nancy S. quit the program in distress soon thereafter.

Another seemingly inexplicable "vision" came from a remote viewer named Keith Harary, who in July 1980 was given the vague directive that "We have a person who needs a description." In a November 2004 article in *Psychology Today* magazine, Harary described what happened next:

Though I hardly understood the process, the question triggered a cascade of impressions about a person in a debilitated state of health. "He seems to be suffering from nausea," I said. "One side of his body seems damaged or hurt." I wondered whether the person I was describing might be some business person or a head of state.

"Where will he be in the next few days?" the monitor asked, again without inflection. I suddenly felt the sensation of sitting on an airplane that was taking off.

"On an airplane," I said.

The target turned out to be the hostage Richard Queen, held by Iranian militants and now desperately ill with multiple sclerosis that affected his nerves on one side.

Jake Stewart received this information from Grill Flame operatives. I asked Jake whether he passed it along to Brzezinski or the president.

"I did not," Stewart told me. "I told Gary [Sick]. I did not tell Gary the source, but people working in the Situation Room don't come out of the category of being dumb or unobservant. They could put things together.

"And Gary said, 'Is it an A-level source?' Because you know, the agencies in the military departments rate sources in a different way. And I said, 'No rating. This is just some special kind of intelligence, one of a kind.'" (Sick doesn't recall that exchange, but he told me, "There was talk of supernatural stories...and people in the agency were looking for paranormal things.")

A few weeks later, the Iranian militants released Richard Queen, who was suffering from multiple sclerosis. "They were worried about a hostage dying in captivity," says Stewart. "They didn't want that bad PR." And as Harary wrote in *Psychology Today*, it was "in part due to my input [that] President Carter dispatched a plane to bring Queen home."

Whether you believe that parapsychology is real or imagined, there's no debating the fact that the U.S. government invested real resources into it for many years. A half-dozen remote viewers worked on the hostage crisis, doing so in absolute secrecy so as not to embarrass the Carter administration. In the interest of keeping the program as dark as possible, Stewart took his briefing report with him when he left the Sit Room on May 8. But later, Lloyd Cutler informed him that the First

Lady wanted a copy of it. "I went up to his office, talked to him briefly, gave it to him, and I guess he gave it to Rosalynn," Stewart recalls.

Why take the chance to pursue such a controversial program? Because it was a tool in the toolbox, and as long as word didn't get out, the downside was minimal. A secret CIA memo dated March 16, 1981, acknowledges as much. Written by Grill Flame project manager Murray Watt, the memo places the success rate of remote viewing as being between a JCS estimate of "37% of the reports as having some correlation/use" and Watt's own slightly higher figure, 45 percent. The final paragraph of the memo concludes:

> One must keep in mind the relative low cost of this project versus the information gained. The data/information provided to the user apparently was information that could not be obtained through normal intelligence collection channels. The degree of success appears to at least equal, if not surpass, other collection methods.

"Zbig wanted the hostage crisis solved and the hostages back," Jake Stewart told me. "If he could do something at no cost, no embarrassment, he would be apt to do it."

But unfortunately for Carter, not even extrasensory assistance could get the hostages released before the end of his presidency.

———◀◯▶———

ON THE MORNING of January 20, 1981, Jimmy Carter was a disheveled mess. He had spent the last two days of his presidency frantically trying to finalize a deal to free the hostages, camping out in the Oval Office, barely sleeping, desperately hoping he could end the crisis before Ronald Reagan took the oath of office. As the clock ticked down toward the inauguration, Carter reluctantly, at the insistence of the First Lady, tore himself away from the Oval Office, going up to the residence to put on a rented suit for the ceremony.

Gary Sick was in the Situation Room that day. "I was the liaison point between the intelligence people who, by that time, knew—if a plane moved in Iran, they knew where it was, they knew it was moving. We had improved our intelligence pretty significantly by that time," he told me. "I was in a little room that was just adjacent to the main part of the operation center...and I had headphones on, and I was listening to direct feed from NSA about what was going on."

As the Carters and Reagans rode to the Capitol together in the presidential limousine, Sick "had a direct line to [Carter]. I called him twice between the time they left the White House until they got up to Capitol Hill," he recalls. "And he was getting rather annoyed with me, but I was getting this stuff directly from intelligence, and he had really, in effect, sacrificed his entire presidency to this cause. And so I thought he deserved to know what was going on. Whether he passed them on to Reagan, I have no idea."

I asked Sick if he remembered what the updates were. "They were technical," he replied. "'The hostages have moved from this place to that place.'" I asked whether the scene in the Sit Room was at all like the familiar scene from the bin Laden raid three decades later, when top officials gathered in the small conference room to receive real-time updates from the field. "Yeah, we weren't so sophisticated," Sick said. "It was just me."

During the inauguration, "the communication stopped," Sick recalls. "He didn't have a receiver with him of any sort, and...he had other things on his mind. So I stopped the updates. But I was watching, and I was aware—I was getting the standard news feed stuff, and I was aware when we changed presidents . . . I was in my little cubby hole there, following this stuff minute by minute."

The fifty-two hostages were released minutes after Ronald Reagan was inaugurated. For years, rumors abounded that there was a back-channel deal to ensure they remained captive while Carter was president, though a 1993 congressional investigation concluded: "There is no credible evidence supporting any attempt or proposal to attempt, by the Reagan presidential campaign—or persons representing or associated with the campaign—to delay the release of American hostages in Iran." Then, in 2023, a new twist. Former Texas lieutenant governor Ben Barnes confirmed that the rumors were at least partly true, revealing that he had accompanied former governor John Connally on secret missions across the Middle East to persuade the Iranians to wait until Reagan was sworn in.

Now ex-president Jimmy Carter would learn the bitter truth at the end of the inauguration. He wrote in his *White House Diary* simply that he "was informed" while walking off the inaugural platform that the hostages had flown out of Iranian airspace. But Gary Sick recalls being the one to tell him, or at least to give him the details, in a phone call to the vehicle taking him to Andrews Air Force Base.

"I was in touch after the ceremony. Carter got in a car and headed to Andrews, where he was gonna take a flight back to Plains," Sick told me. "And in the car, I got him again and gave him an update on where we were. I think he knew at least as soon as anybody else, as soon as anybody in the government, in the world maybe, that the hostages actually were on the plane.

"And so in effect, the thing was over. At that point, there was nothing," Sick went on. "Reagan was now in charge. I was still working for the NSC, but things had changed."

This was a deeply discombobulating moment for Sick. And it was about to get more so.

"I suddenly said, 'I've got nothing else to do. You know, I'm done,'" he told me. "And so at that point, I took off all the stuff, put it all down, waved to the boys in the Situation Room, and went out into the West Wing of the White House.

"And while I had been in there, they had changed every picture. As I walked out of the room, there were these huge photos of Ronald Reagan on the wall, staring down at me, and I was astonished," he said. "I went in that morning with all the Carter pictures up. When I came out, the pictures had all changed."

For his part, Jimmy Carter has always steadfastly insisted that he was ecstatic that the hostages were free, regardless of the timing of their release. When I interviewed Carter on ABC in 2015, he told me, "I'd say that was probably the most happy moment of my life."

"Of your life?" I asked.

"Yes. I think it was," he said. "Maybe, except marrying Rosalynn. But you know, yes."

Gary Sick was more equivocal.

"You know, the objective was to get 'em out safe, and they got out safe," he told me. "Looking at the hostage crisis, I would not give a single name of success or failure. It was a process that we went through, and it was an extraordinary process. And you can argue that it was not done the right way. And we could talk about that forever, but it is what it is."

Chapter 6

THE HELM IS
RIGHT HERE

———◆◆———

AT 2:27 P.M. on March 30, 1981, President Ronald Reagan
walked out of the Washington Hilton hotel into a slate-gray D.C.
afternoon. Suddenly, shots rang out. Bodies fell, Secret Service agents
whipped out their weapons, and agent Jerry Parr heaved Reagan into
the presidential limousine. None of the six bullets fired by assailant
John W. Hinckley Jr. initially hit Reagan, but one ricocheted off the
limo, striking him in the left side of his chest.

"Get out of here! Go! Go! Go!" Parr shouted. The car sped away,
leaving behind pandemonium: Three men lay on the ground, bleeding
profusely, while a scrum of others piled on top of Hinckley. Realizing that the president had been hit, Parr directed the limo to rush to
the George Washington University Hospital emergency room. Four
minutes after Hinckley pulled the trigger, Reagan walked into the ER
under his own power—and then he collapsed.

Had the bullet hit his vital organs? Would the president need surgery,
or be otherwise incapacitated? Was he dying? Where was Vice President

Bush? Instantly, an ordinary Monday turned into a day of confusion and panic, not just at the scene of the shooting, but in the White House, too. And more specifically—and unusually—in the Situation Room.

We know this because national security adviser Richard Allen, who convened the president's top aides in the Sit Room, did something no one had ever done before. He brought in a small tape recorder, placed it on the conference table, and hit the record button to capture the scene for posterity. He did this in full view of everyone, and no one objected. As a result, we have recordings and transcripts of some of the most dramatic and chaotic hours in the history of the Situation Room.

The recording starts at 3:24 in the afternoon, less than an hour after the shooting. At that moment, staff director David Gergen, treasury secretary Don Regan, White House counsel Fred Fielding and several other aides were in the room. Two minutes later, secretary of state Al Haig walked in. He would be followed by defense secretary Caspar Weinberger, attorney general William French Smith, presidential assistant Richard Darman and others. Vice President Bush wasn't present. He was flying from Dallas back to Washington, and there was, incredibly, no secure voice connection (though messages could be sent) between his plane and the White House.

From the start, the conversation in the Sit Room was frenzied, with everyone talking over each other as they tried to sort out who would release information to the public.

> **Allen:** [Chief of staff James] Baker says they are controlling the press over [at the hospital] . . . He wants us to put [the information] out, but not any more than that. Who would do it? You? Is Al [Haig] talking to the vice president?
>
> **Gergen:** I'll write it out.
>
> **Unidentified:** They're going to bring a statement back in.

Allen: Oh shit, it looks like they got Jim [Brady] right smack in his head. Is it? Oh my God! Oh Jesus, God in heaven.

Press secretary James Brady had taken a bullet to the forehead, and information would continue to trickle out about his condition, as well as Reagan's, over the next few hours. Gary Bresnahan was dispatched to the hospital to set up secure communications; he would spend the next three nights there. Back at the White House, the group monitored television news reports, and much of the information broadcast was incorrect—some of it, disastrously so.

With Jim Brady grievously wounded and deputy spokesman Larry Speakes and Reagan aide Ed Meese at the hospital, the men in the Sit Room debated who should be the lead communicator at the White House. Haig very quickly assumed a posture of control.

Haig: Let's everybody stay together on—nobody do anything. Gergen cannot be playing public relations without everybody knowing it, and we will decide here what the hell we're doing. That's the best way. Always!

And later:

Haig: We'll be on a straight line with the hospital. So anything that is said, before it's said, we'll discuss at this table. And any telephone calls that anybody is getting with instructions from the hospital come to this table first. *Right here!*

There was immediate concern about who was in control of the "football"—the black briefcase containing the codes for launching nuclear strikes. The football always travels with the president, though

Air Force aide General Godfrey McHugh was a close friend of both John and Jacqueline Kennedy. He was also the man who, on April 7, 1961, brought the idea of a "Situation Room" to JFK. *Robert Knudsen. White House Photographs. John F. Kennedy Presidential Library and Museum, Boston*

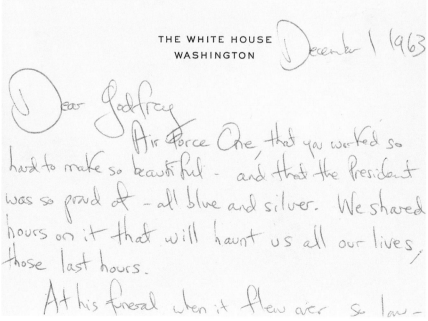

THE WHITE HOUSE
WASHINGTON

December 1 1963

Dear Godfrey
Air Force One, that you worked so hard to make so beautiful - and that the President was so proud of - all blue and silver. We shared hours on it that will haunt us all our lives, those last hours.
At his funeral when it flew over so low -

McHugh remained close with Mrs. Kennedy after the assassination. In this handwritten note, she reminisces about their shared experience on that terrible day.

Prototype Situation Room sketches from the early 1960s envisioned a sleek, high-tech space.
Courtesy John F. Kennedy Presidential Library

The actual room, built hastily over one week in 1961, was far less impressive. *Robert Knudsen. White House Photographs. John F. Kennedy Presidential Library and Museum, Boston*

The cramped file room, adjacent to the conference room, felt more like a middle-school library than the nerve center of the White House. *Robert Knudsen. White House Photographs. John F. Kennedy Presidential Library and Museum, Boston*

The secretary's office, outside the conference room. When JFK first saw the complex, he dismissed it as a "pigpen." *Robert Knudsen. White House Photographs. John F. Kennedy Presidential Library and Museum, Boston*

Young Tom Johnson (center right, with glasses), takes notes furiously by hand during a crucial Sit Room meeting. (L–R: press secretary George Christian, national security adviser Walt Rostow, President Lyndon Johnson, deputy press secretary Tom Johnson, defense secretary Clark Clifford, NSC head Bromley Smith) *LBJ Library photo by Yoichi Okamoto*

The MOLINK— essentially a glorified teletype machine— provided the first direct link between the White House and the Kremlin. *LBJ Library photo by Jay Godwin*

Henry Kissinger, serving as both secretary of state and national security adviser to President Nixon, took extraordinary nuclear steps in the Sit Room—without the president's knowledge. *Wally McNamee / Getty Images*

Nixon hated the Sit Room, preferring instead to sip scotch and listen to jazz alone in his "hideaway"— room 180 in the Old Executive Office Building. *Courtesy Richard Nixon Presidential Library and Museum*

Intelligence analyst Sarah "Sally" Botsai, who served under Nixon and Ford, was one of the first female staffers in the Situation Room. *National Security Agency*

President Ford had an unusually close relationship with his White House photographer, twenty-eight-year-old David Hume Kennerly. Kennerly shocked Ford's national security team by volunteering his thoughts during a crucial meeting about the *Mayaguez*. *Bettmann / Getty Images*

The 1980 Desert One mission was intended to rescue U.S. hostages in Iran. Instead, its catastrophic failure would lead President Carter down an unexpected path. *AP Photo*

In an extraordinary meeting, NSC staffer Jake Stewart briefed President Carter on a top-secret U.S. Army psychic program called Operation Grill Flame. Carter requested help from the psychics to solve the Iran hostage crisis. Here, Zbigniew Brzezinski pins a medal on Stewart. *Courtesy Jake Stewart*

President Carter slept in the Oval Office during the final days of his term, agonizing over the hostage crisis. *Courtesy of the Jimmy Carter Library*

On the day John Hinckley Jr. shot President Reagan, the Sit Room devolved into confusion and panic. National security adviser Richard Allen taped five hours of chaotic conversation; his recorder and cassette tapes are visible on the table. *Courtesy Ronald Reagan Presidential Library*

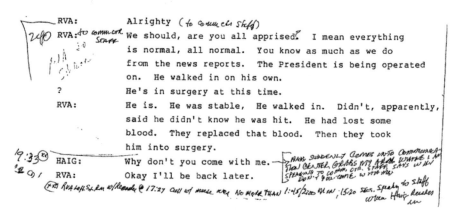

Allen marked up the resulting transcripts, though he stopped before finishing the task. We may never know who was speaking in some parts of these historic tapes. *Courtesy Ronald Reagan Presidential Library*

Secretary of State Al Haig's infamous declaration, "As of now, I am in control here," had its roots in a Sit Room conversation with David Gergen. *Courtesy Ronald Reagan Presidential Library*

backups exist. But where were those? And with Reagan in the hospital, who was in charge of the nuclear codes? Haig, unsurprisingly, wanted them within reach.

> **Haig:** Cap, is the—the football is near the vice president, so that's fine.
> **Allen:** We should get one over here. We have a duplicate one here.
> **Haig:** Get the football over here.
> **Allen:** There is one at the military aide's office.

The longer the crisis went on, the less certain people were about what was happening.

> **Haig:** The important thing, fellows, is that there are things that always generate a lot of dope stories. Everyone and everybody is running around telling everybody everything that they can get out of their gut.
> **Unidentified:** That's right.
> **Haig:** And I think that it is God damn important that none of that happens! The president, as long as he is conscious and can function…
> **Allen:** Well, just let me point out to you that the president is not now conscious.

The president was at that moment in surgery, under general anesthesia. With Vice President Bush still in flight, discussions intensified about who was in charge.

> **Gergen:** Al, a quick question. We need some sense, a better sense of where the president is. Is he under sedation now?

Haig: He's not on the operating table.

Gergen: He *is* on the operating table.

Haig: So the helm is right here. And that means right in this chair for now, constitutionally, 'til the vice president gets here.

Gergen: I understand that. I understand that.

Gergen didn't understand it, of course. He knew that constitutionally, the helm was nowhere near Alexander Haig, since the order of succession is the vice president, then the Speaker of the House, then the president pro tem of the Senate. But no one wanted to wrangle with the pugnacious Haig, who was already puffing up like a rooster. Let him say what he wanted; everyone knew the order and it wasn't worth fighting over. Until Haig impulsively decided to go public with it.

Larry Speakes, who had returned to the White House from GW Hospital, was briefing the press corps when a reporter asked who was running the government. "I cannot answer the question at this time," Speakes replied. Hearing this, Haig went ballistic, pulling Richard Allen out of the conference room into another part of the complex. Allen grabbed the tape recorder and brought it with him.

Haig: He's turning this into a God damn disaster!...

Allen: Oh, Jesus Christ Almighty, Almighty. Why is he doing that?

Unidentified: They want to know who's running the government...

Haig: We'll assemble them.

Haig then charged into the press room and up to the podium. He gave a statement intended to calm the waters, announcing that the cabinet was in the Situation Room, the president was stable, and no alert measures were needed. He invited the reporters to ask questions, and when one asked who was making decisions for the government, he uttered these now-infamous words:

Haig: Constitutionally, gentlemen, you have the president, the vice president, and the secretary of state, in that order. And should the president decide he wants to transfer the helm to the vice president, he will do so. As of now I am in control, here in the White House, pending the return of the vice president and in close touch with him.

"I was astounded," Allen would later recall, "that he would say something so eminently stupid."

Haig had been in the Nixon White House when the president was incapacitated by alcohol. He'd taken charge in that moment—and he clearly believed he should be in control now. He was a classic alpha male, a former Supreme Allied Commander of NATO and a four-star Army general who was used to issuing orders and having them followed. But he was far out of line in this instance, and his bumbling attempt to take charge only added to the stress and confusion roiling the Situation Room.

While Haig was still at the podium, Weinberger received an intelligence update. Four Soviet submarines were patrolling the waters off the East Coast—more than the usual number, and at a closer distance. In fact, one of the subs was close enough that if it launched a missile, it could destroy Washington in less than eleven minutes. Was the assassination attempt part of a Soviet plot to distract from an impending attack? The identity of the assailant was known, but no one knew anything about him or why he had shot the president. As had happened when Kennedy was assassinated, fears grew that the Kremlin might have had a hand in the shooting.

So even as Haig was publicly asserting that "no alert measures [were] necessary at this time or contemplated," Weinberger was in the Sit Room issuing orders for the Strategic Air Command to raise its alert level. When Haig learned about this, he was not happy.

> **Haig:** I said up there, Cap...I'm not a liar. I said there had been no increased alert.
>
> **Weinberger:** Well, I didn't know you were going up, Al...
>
> **Haig:** I had to, because we had the question already started and we were going to be in a big flap.
>
> **Weinberger:** Well, I think we could have done a little better if we had [agreed] on a specific statement to be handed out.

The two men began bickering. Haig seemed less concerned with the actual alert level, or the reality of the Soviet submarine presence, than about whether he had been properly consulted.

> **Haig:** Well, we had just discussed that here at the table, and we said we were not going to increase alert...
>
> **Weinberger:** [O]nce you get the additional information which I got about the one sub being closer than is normal, but not closer than they've been before, then it seemed to me prudent to save three or four minutes.
>
> **Haig:** Yeah, but I think we could have discussed it.
>
> **Weinberger:** Yeah, well, you were not here. I didn't know that you were going to make any statement...

Haig: Well…we did talk about it and everyone agreed there wouldn't be an increased alert.

Weinberger: I didn't know you were going up! I didn't have the information about the sub at that time. This stuff is coming in every three or four minutes.

The squabbling continued off and on, until Allen finally pulled Weinberger and CIA head William Casey into his private office. Once again, Allen brought the recorder with him.

Allen: Jesus Christ. I didn't know he was going to make any God damn statement up there, Cap, and sorry I wasn't up there like a watchdog. Shit, I thought he was going to pull Speakes off, I didn't know that Speakes had gone up to make a statement…

Weinberger: Rumors are unfortunate, but it's better to have a God damn rumor that you can deny later than—

Allen: I don't appreciate carrying the turf battle over into this sort of thing, so when George [Bush] is here it will be fine, but you have the command authority now, as I understand it.

Not all of the talk in the Sit Room was contentious, and not all was focused on matters of strategy or government. There were moments of humanity, such as when the group was told—erroneously—that James Brady had succumbed to his injuries.

Allen: We just learned Jim Brady has died.

Don Regan: You better get a statement ready on that…

Allen: And we better just have a moment of prayer in silence for Jim Brady.

Seven seconds of silence passed. It was, predictably, Haig who broke it. He asked a procedural question about who would release a statement on the death.

> **Haig:** Now, is that going to be put out [at the hospital]?
> **Gergen:** I'm trying to reach them right now . . .
> **Haig:** We certainly have an obligation here to say something.
> **Allen:** I think that . . . Jesus . . . God in heaven . . . poor
> fellow . . . That's a hell of a loss.

Richard Allen continued taping into the night, ultimately capturing five hours' worth of Situation Room conversations. These were later transcribed into four lengthy documents, and the chaotic nature of the scene is apparent on every page. All are typewritten, but the first two also have detailed handwritten notes, as Allen tried after the fact to sort out who was talking.

As provided by the Reagan Library, the third document has no names at all, with every speaker labeled simply as "Voice"—though it is possible to identify some speakers when others call them by name. The fourth identifies only Vice President Bush and, toward the end, Dr. Dennis O'Leary, whose televised comments on the president's condition were audible on the tape. Incredibly enough, no one ever went back to the third and fourth transcripts to decipher who else was speaking. Perhaps for this reason, it appears that, before now, no one has ever written about what was said in them.

———◄O►———

AT THE START of the third transcript, Vice President Bush was approximately a half hour away from arriving at the White House. By now, the Sit Room was hazy with smoke, as people anxiously drank coffee and puffed on cigarettes. An unidentified voice asked, "Cap, got something to [unintelligible]?" Cap Weinberger responds with this, about the vice president:

> **Weinberger:** I guess we should give him some recommendations on whether or not he should make a statement, 'cause he's not going to be seen. He's been smuggled aboard, he's going to be smuggled into a hangar at Andrews, and he's going to be smuggled all the way in here, so nobody knows if he's alive or not.
>
> **Voice:** I think, I think that probably something should happen, but he should not go over to the hospital...
>
> **Voice:** It's even critical now in its succession that we not have them both in the same place.

It still wasn't clear whether John Hinckley had acted alone. Was Vice President Bush potentially a target, too? And the Soviet angle was still concerning:

> **Voice:** If the Soviets were ever going to make a move in Poland, this might be a damn good time to do it.

On the domestic front, the president was scheduled to sign a dairy bill the following day. Failing to do so would throw that industry into disarray, disrupting production and raising prices. What would happen if he didn't sign? Were there other ways of making the bill into law?

> **Voice:** During the Eisenhower years, there were certain things that Ike could approve by nodding...

Voice: But usually it's the definitive things that require the signature of the president that he can't acquiesce, he can't delegate...

Voice: He may be able to sign tomorrow. It sounds odd, but he may—

Voice: Even if he can sign the thing—

Voice: He has the legal shift of his authority.

Voice: Well, that's a little more sticky. I mean, either he's president or he isn't; he can't shift authority.

This led to a surreal discussion: Would the president need to sign a paper declaring himself incapable of signing a bill?

Voice: He's temporarily incapacitated.

Voice: Yeah, but it isn't necessary for him to do anything other than delegate authority to sign one bill if it's indeed the last day.

Voice: On that, if I may say, that requires a signature. If he can sign that, he can sign the bill.

Attorney general William French Smith—identifiable because whoever spoke before him used his name—became agitated at the uncertainty. He jumped in to try to clarify the president's position.

Smith: The idea that the president can sort of shove off certain of his powers and not all of it is a mistake. It can't be done. He is the president or he isn't, and there are two specific procedures that should be followed in the event that he becomes disabled. And I think it's important for everybody to know what those are. And it's a little gruesome to think about it...but the fact of the matter is, we're in the condition now where we have to think about it.

And then it was back to the dairy bill, with someone—my guess is Haig—noting that if the president did manage to sign it, "they'll want to know exactly how his hand moved, and his signature, and his thumb, and so on and so forth. Historic signature."

Amid more back-and-forth about a transfer of power, the president's condition and the vice president's expected time of arrival, another strikingly humane moment came when thoughts turned to the family of Jim Brady.

> **Voice:** Does anybody know who's really close to Sarah Brady?
> **Voice:** Pat, my wife, is.
> **Voice:** Pick her up and go over to the hospital and get her cleared through the Secret Service...
> **Voice:** Just pass it through the Secret Service that Pat should be admitted and taken to Sarah.
> **Voice:** They've got a two-year-old that somebody ought to take for the night.

Shortly after this exchange, Vice President Bush at last entered the Situation Room. The group quickly brought him up-to-date on events—in particular, military alertness and the position of the Soviet submarines.

> **Voice:** [We] left everything on DEFCON 5, which is the normal non-alert condition. PAC is always on DEFCON 4... There was one Soviet submarine within [REDACTED] minutes 57 seconds of missile length of Washington.

At this point, someone realized that not everyone in the Sit Room had top secret, or "code word," clearance.

Voice: Anyone without Codeword clearance?

Voice: If you don't have it then you ought not to be in on this.

Voice: Yeah, a lot of people don't have Codeword...

Voice: If you don't have Codeword clearance, please excuse
   yourselves for a minute...

Voice: I think we need to make sure that we don't break the law
   right here in the Situation Room.

With the non-cleared parties out of the room, the briefing continued. Eventually, the team discussed the vice president's schedule for the following day, which included meetings with the NSC and the cabinet, and a working lunch with Dutch prime minister Andreas van Agt.

Vice President Bush's response provided the first moments of calm in what had been a long, chaotic day. He urged everyone to leave the Situation Room, to restore a semblance of normalcy:

Bush: I'd like to see us, when we finish this round, not meet in this
   room. I mean, go upstairs, unless we're waiting for something
   extraordinarily sensitive, because it gives the signal that we're
   all sitting around on the edge of something, which of course
   we could understand everybody doing up to a couple of hours
   ago...It seems to me that as soon as we get into the most normal
   condition possible, and everybody do his job, the better it is.

More than four decades after these recordings were made, many of those who were in the room are dead, and the memories of those still living have faded. I had hoped to listen to the tapes myself, to try to identify the speakers, but they remain classified. So even though we have this unprecedented record of one of the most significant days in the Situation Room's history, it remains incomplete.

————◄○►————

ELEVEN MONTHS AFTER John Hinckley tried and failed to take the president's life, Ronald Reagan sat in the Situation Room and saw himself killed.

The date was March 1, 1982. President Reagan faced a screen in the Sit Room, watching as the world as he knew it was destroyed. This was day one of a classified four-day exercise meant to assess the U.S. government's readiness in the face of a nuclear attack. Code-named Ivy League, the drill involved more than a thousand people in multiple locations, and it included actual helicopter evacuations of key personnel to offsite bunkers. In the course of the exercise, images flashed onto the Sit Room screens depicting Soviet warheads blowing Washington, D.C., to smithereens. And the "president"—played in the exercise by former secretary of state William Rogers—was killed in the conflagration.

All U.S. presidents since the 1950s had received briefings on how nuclear conflict might play out. As McGeorge Bundy recalled: "There was a practice, developed in the Eisenhower administration, of an annual mock nuclear war … They would run the war and see how our warheads did against their warheads and how many million casualties this produced." Though Eisenhower found the exercises unsettling, he ran them several times during his presidency.

When Kennedy went through a similar drill, he too found it disturbing. Walking back to the Oval Office afterward, he remarked bitterly to Dean Rusk, "And we call ourselves the human race." For his part, Rusk recalled the words of Kennedy's Soviet counterpart. "Khrushchev put it very well one time," he noted, "when he said that in the case of nuclear war, the living will envy the dead."

Even though all presidents received nuclear briefings, Ivy League was the biggest and most complex since Eisenhower's time—and the first to be headquartered in the Sit Room. The exercise was extremely detailed, tracking an escalation of fighting that started in the Korean peninsula and then spread across the globe. Reagan watched in horror as red dots, representing Soviet nuclear strikes, bloomed ominously across the United States. "While he looked on in stunned disbelief... more red dots wiped out the survivors and filled in the few holes in the sea of red," aide Tom Reed recalled. "In less than an hour, President Reagan [saw] the United States of America disappear."

Before the destruction was complete, another event shocked him. Part of the exercise involved determining the U.S. government's response to an attack. When officials ordered retaliatory missile strikes, "killing" millions of Soviet citizens, Reagan's perception of nuclear weapons changed forever. The consequences of decisions he might one day be forced to make became all too real.

Reagan was "a very intuitive learner, he learned by experience, and by these firsthand encounters that really terrified him," Will Inboden, author of *The Peacemaker: Ronald Reagan, the Cold War, and the World on the Brink*, told me. Seeing the "president" killed had a big effect on Reagan, Inboden went on. "It brought home for him that this is not just some abstraction. This would be *me* who's gone." The experience shocked and distressed the president. More important, it deepened his determination to eradicate the threat of nuclear war.

Reagan had been crusading against Communism for decades. In 1977, he summarized his strategy in four words: "We win, they lose." In the 1980 campaign, he railed against Jimmy Carter for believing that détente was still possible. And three months before the election, when adviser Stuart Spencer asked him why he wanted to be president, he said simply, "To end the Cold War." This was a tall order, as relations with the Soviets had been frigid for more than three decades, and they weren't getting any warmer. Five days after Reagan made this pronouncement, the Summer Olympics opened in Moscow—without the United States, which was boycotting the games.

Another clue to Reagan's state of mind can be found in the diary entry he wrote on Saturday, April 11, 1981, the day he was released from the hospital following the assassination attempt. "Whatever happens now," he wrote, "I owe my life to God and will try to serve him in every way I can." The specter of nuclear conflict terrified him, but to Reagan, the battle against Communism was more than simply an effort to avoid war. It was a holy battle of a God-fearing nation versus a godless one.

Reagan gave full voice to that belief in a speech to the National Association of Evangelicals on March 8, 1983. After opening with a folksy joke about a politician arriving at heaven's pearly gates, then musing on the greatness of America and the importance of traditional values, Reagan turned his attention to the U.S.S.R. "Let us pray for the salvation of all of those who live in that totalitarian darkness," he said. "Pray they will discover the joy of knowing God. But until they do, let us be aware . . . [that] they are the focus of evil in the modern world."

Then, he went further:

> I urge you to beware the temptation of pride—the temptation of blithely declaring yourselves above it all and label[ing] both sides equally at fault, to ignore the facts of history and the aggressive impulses of an evil empire, to simply call the arms race a giant misunderstanding and thereby remove yourself from the struggle between right and wrong, and good and evil.

This address, which became known as the "Evil Empire speech," set the tone for Reagan's approach to the Soviet Union. At the time he delivered it, the American public's fear of the Soviet threat was intensifying. Leonid Brezhnev had recently died, vaulting former KGB head Yuri Andropov to power. In U.S. schools, children were drilled on what to do in case of a Soviet nuclear attack. And two weeks after delivering his Evil Empire speech, Reagan announced a new research program—the Strategic Defense Initiative (SDI)—to construct a space-based defensive shield against incoming missiles.

The fall of 1983 was a frightening and destabilizing time. In September, a Soviet Sukhoi fighter jet shot Korean Air Lines Flight 007 out of the sky, killing 269 people. A few weeks later, only the stoic forbearance of a Soviet colonel prevented the false alarm of a U.S. missile attack from triggering a nuclear apocalypse. In late October, Hezbollah suicide bombers killed 241 U.S. personnel at the Marine barracks in Beirut. Two days after that, U.S. forces invaded the island nation of Grenada to help overthrow its Communist government, in the biggest commitment of American ground troops since Vietnam. The U.S. military was also deploying Pershing II and ground-launch cruise missiles in Europe, and in November, the Soviets put their nuclear forces on alert in response to a major NATO military exercise, Able Archer.

Not since the Cuban Missile Crisis had Cold War tension been so terrifying. But most of those thirteen days unfolded behind closed doors. The events of autumn 1983 were escalating mostly in public. And Americans' fears of a Soviet attack reached their frenzied peak on November 20, 1983. That was the date ABC aired a movie called *The Day After*.

It's difficult to remember in these times of TikTok, YouTube, multiple streaming outlets and hundreds of cable channels, but in 1983 the release of a made-for-TV movie on one of the "big three" broadcast networks (ABC, NBC and CBS) could dominate the national conversation. One hundred million people, out of a total U.S. population of

233 million, tuned in on a Sunday night to watch Lawrence, Kansas—and the rest of the country—thrown into a nuclear winter by a Soviet attack. Viewers were left stunned by graphic scenes of death and mayhem, and even President Reagan admitted that the film had shaken him, writing in his diary that it was "very effective and left me greatly depressed."

The geopolitical lines were drawn, and the specter of nuclear war cast a horrifying shadow over everyday life. At the beginning of 1984, the "Doomsday Clock"—the symbolic indicator of how close humanity is to self-induced catastrophe—was advanced from four minutes to three minutes before midnight. As President Reagan's first term wound down, it felt like nothing could stop the inevitable trajectory into global war.

Yet all that would, surprisingly, change in Reagan's second term. And the Sit Room—or in one strange case, a parallel version of it—was right at the center of the action.

UNLIKE NIXON, FORD and Carter, President Reagan spent a lot of time in the Situation Room. He held meetings of the National Security Planning Group (NSPG) there at least once a week, sometimes more. Created as an offshoot of the National Security Council, the NSPG handled crisis management of sensitive matters, which meant attendance was kept tighter than usual. "Very often, it meant meetings in the Sit Room with no plus-ones," former NSC executive secretary Bob Kimmitt told me. "So it would be just the cabinet officers and others at the table."

Each president's attitude toward the Sit Room reflected his personality. Johnson was a control freak, so he wanted to be in the place where things happened. Nixon was paranoid, so he disliked being in the NSC's domain. Reagan was the type of man who was comfortable in any room he entered. As Michael Bohn wrote in *Nerve Center*, "He was unfailingly polite and greeted everyone warmly. He entered the conference room, sat down, ate a jelly bean, and started the meeting."

While Reagan's comfort was mostly due to his personality, it didn't hurt that the complex was greatly improved during his administration. For the Sit Room's first two decades, all duty officers came from the CIA. Starting with Reagan, they came from the State Department, CIA, NSA and the military branches. This mix of personnel broadened the room's analytical reach. Shifts were cut to twelve hours, with forty-eight hours off in between, and tours of duty limited to two years, keeping the room fresh. The Sit Room became a place where the best and brightest from across the government were chosen to serve. It was a capstone for some careers, and a booster shot for others.

Technology also vastly improved during Reagan's two terms. After years of rudimentary communications—handwritten notes, typewritten reports, telexes, cables, basic fax machines and delivery of paperwork via pneumatic tubes—computers came into wider use. Cables from U.S. embassies could now be screened and forwarded electronically. Basic email was set up for NSC staff. Video teleconferencing was introduced, though it was used only sparsely until the George H. W. Bush administration. In fact, the video teleconferencing (VTC) room set up under Reagan was used so infrequently, Sit Room staff turned it into an informal dining area.

The 1980s was the decade when personal computers began to take hold. The Reagan years saw the release of the Commodore 64, the IBM PC and the Apple Macintosh, while Intel's microprocessing chips made dramatic leaps in speed and power. The commercial Internet was still a few years off, awaiting Tim Berners-Lee's invention of the World Wide

Web and the first browsers. But full connectivity was just around the corner.

Yet even with the improvements, the Reagan-era Sit Room still had its idiosyncrasies. Tired of being asked what time it was in other countries—because pre-Internet, there was no easy way to find out—Bohn bought a large Geochron clock that showed the path of sunlight across the globe. And the staff was constantly scrambling to get whatever paper maps were needed for meetings, as there wasn't enough room in the complex to store them. The digital age was coming, but in certain ways the Sit Room remained resolutely analog.

Many of the changes to the complex felt inevitable, a natural outgrowth of keeping up with the times. Yet one change made under Reagan seemed to come out of left field.

Dismayed at the turmoil in the Sit Room after the president was shot, national security adviser John Poindexter investigated how the complex itself might have affected what unfolded. In a report, he suggested that Reagan's team didn't understand the Sit Room's core function. "They thought it was a…command center set up to facilitate high-level decision-making," Poindexter later recalled. "It was really more of a switching center where duty officers routed incoming information."

Poindexter then recommended building an actual command center. "We needed to supplement the Situation Room and create a place that could take over a crisis while the Sit Room continued to watch the rest of the world," he recalled. This new center would have a bigger conference room, with its own staff and video capability. Unfortunately, there was nowhere to put it in the West Wing—or the East Wing, for that matter. Every square foot in the White House was spoken for. But just across West Executive Avenue, in the Old Executive Office Building, there was plenty of space. So, in 1982, the administration built a new Crisis Management Center (CMC) in Room 208 of the

OEOB—a spacious, lavishly decorated room, with windows overlooking the White House's South Portico and a rich history of serving as the secretary of state's office.

One point that was made repeatedly in the Kennedy-era studies was that the Situation Room should never "usurp the operating responsibilities of any department or agency." Yet by design, the CMC did exactly that. In attempting to remove the crisis-management burden from the Sit Room, Poindexter inadvertently created a monster. This would become apparent shortly, in a damaging and embarrassing way for President Reagan.

Under Poindexter's direction, the CMC became a high-tech command center, even more advanced than the Sit Room. "John Poindexter was probably the tech-savviest guy in the U.S. government," Bob Kimmitt told me, adding that he "pushed right from the start for the NSC to upgrade its technology." Seven Digital Equipment VAX computers were installed in the CMC, then connected to operations centers in the State Department, the Pentagon and other Washington hotspots. The Situation Room received new terminals as well, so staff there could access the same databases.

In 1985, with the help of Gary Bresnahan and the White House Communications Agency, NSC executive secretary William Martin got the first email system set up. "The email system we had for the NSC staff was unique to us," Bresnahan told me. "It was internal. That was the classified one." Because email technology was so new, no one was sure how to categorize it for purposes of recordkeeping. As Martin recalls:

> All paper goes through the executive secretary. And so we had a discussion: What is an email? Is it a piece of paper? Is it a telephone call? How do you handle this new means of

communicating? And so basically the guidance was: It's just a little message. It's not a formal paper which required concurrences and everything else you have to go through.

This decision allowed Poindexter to circumvent normal security controls. He opened backdoor communications with an NSC aide named Oliver North, which was the beginning of the scandal that nearly brought down Ronald Reagan's presidency: the Iran-Contra affair.

Colonel Oliver North was a Vietnam War hero, a career U.S. Marine with a floppy forelock of hair and a hangdog expression that belied an ambitious nature. He had been serving on the NSC staff since the beginning of Reagan's presidency, and he had "built up credibility and goodwill on the NSC staff as a guy who gets things done," as Will Inboden put it. "He played a key role in the *Achille Lauro* hijacking, in eventually capturing the terrorists and bringing them to justice. He put together the Grenada operation, which was controversial, but at least in operational terms was pretty successful."

Kimmitt, who was North's first boss at the NSC, believed North was "the most effective member of the NSC staff." But Kimmitt had a more nuanced perspective than Inboden: "Ollie North would come into my office, steps from the Sit Room, several times a day," he told me. "And he would almost always have the worst idea and the best idea you were going to hear that day. He just needed someone to say, 'Focus on that really good idea.'"

Unfortunately for President Reagan, North spent much of 1985–86 focusing on a very bad idea. An evangelical Christian who, like Reagan, characterized the Cold War as good versus evil, North was willing to break the law to further his vision of the United States' standing in the world.

The Iran-Contra scandal was, in essence, an arms-for-hostages deal with a twist. Hezbollah, an Islamist group with ties to Iran, was holding seven Americans hostage in Lebanon. North's plan was to sell weapons covertly to Iran, circumventing an arms embargo that dated back to the Carter administration, in exchange for the hostages' release. Since the weapons sale was secret, there would be no official accounting of the funding it brought in. So, North decided to use some of it for a cause near and dear to his heart: battling Communists. He diverted money to the Nicaraguan Contras, a right-wing group that was fighting to overthrow the leftist Sandinista government. This broke another law, the Boland Amendment, which prohibited sending aid to the Contras.

North orchestrated all this from the new CMC, turning it into his own little fiefdom. This was unprecedented, illegal and against the entire ethos of the Situation Room. Yet there were those in the Sit Room who knew what he was doing and supported it—tacitly or otherwise.

"The parallel op that was built by Colonel North basically had two factions in the Situation Room," recalls David Sedney, who served as a senior duty officer in the last six months of the Reagan administration. "Those who'd been essentially recruited by and were loyal to North. And the people who I would say were the real professionals." The Sit Room had always been rigorously apolitical and united in its mission, but North used his charisma and anti-Communist zeal to drive a wedge into it. Among the dozens of people I interviewed for this book, no one could remember anything remotely similar happening in the room's sixty-plus-year history.

John Poindexter made the covert missions possible, and North made them operational. But ultimately, President Reagan was responsible.

Yet as revelations dripped out from late 1986 into 1987, Reagan was in deep denial. The Great Communicator, as he was known, retreated from public view for long stretches during this time. He seemed unable to face up to what had transpired on his watch.

The Tower Commission report, issued after a three-month investigation into the scandal, was highly critical of Reagan. "The president did not seem to be aware of the way in which the operation was implemented," wrote authors John Tower, Edmund Muskie and Brent Scowcroft. "At no time did he insist upon accountability and performance review."

On March 4, 1987, a week after the release of the Tower report, President Reagan finally acknowledged what had happened and took responsibility for it. "A few months ago, I told the American people I did not trade arms for hostages," he said in a televised address to the nation. "My heart and my best intentions still tell me that's true, but the facts and the evidence tell me it is not." It was a strange summation of an unprecedented situation.

Some of Iran-Contra's peripheral aspects were also unprecedented. The first administration in history to use email became the first to suffer an email scandal. North and Poindexter tried to destroy evidence of their backdoor channel by deleting thousands of emails from their NSC computers. But NSC staffers saved backups of their systems, and the Tower Commission made extensive use of the damning emails in building its case.

But while some NSC staffers felt duty-bound to expose North's corruption, others remained under his sway even after he resigned in disgrace. David Sedney told me that after North was barred from the White House, "one of my colleagues in the Situation Room admitted openly and proudly that he had let Ollie North back in" to destroy evidence. North and his secretary, Fawn Hall, had fed so many documents into the CMC shredder that they broke it; after that, they came down to the Situation Room to finish the job. The Sit Room shredder, nicknamed the Alligator, was extremely thorough, reducing documents to something resembling "angel hair pasta," according to Michael Bohn. North and Hall threw the shreds into the garbage—which apparently gave one enterprising Sit Room staffer an idea.

"He recognized the significance of what he was seeing," Bohn wrote, "and took the bag home with him...and started selling the shredded documents, just like you buy the shredded dollar bills at the Bureau of Engraving." The staffer, whom Bohn never named, was apparently fired, as he never saw the man in the office again.

Iran-Contra nearly destroyed Reagan's presidency. In one month, his poll ratings plunged more than 20 percent, the most precipitous drop in modern presidential history. Just 28 percent of Americans believed he was doing a good job in foreign policy. Before Iran-Contra, Reagan had ridden high on his folksy appeal, cruising to reelection in 1984 with the slogan "It's morning again in America!" Now, with just two years left in his second term, he ran the risk of being remembered as a damaged, polarizing, relatively inconsequential president.

As he hit bottom, Reagan realized he needed to refocus his efforts. So he returned to the goal that had animated him from the beginning: ending the Cold War. Fortunately for him, the perfect counterpart for this mission had ascended to power in the Soviet Union.

BEFORE HIS DEATH in November 1982, Leonid Brezhnev led the U.S.S.R. for eighteen years, a period that was remarkable for its relative political stability. But the twenty-eight months that followed were turbulent. Two more Soviet leaders—Yuri Andropov and Konstantin Chernenko—rose to power, then died before settling into the office. Weary of this funereal succession of doddering old men, the Politburo unanimously selected an energetic fifty-four-year-old named Mikhail Gorbachev.

Gorbachev quickly established himself as a new kind of Soviet leader. With his twin policies of perestroika (economic restructuring) and glasnost (openness), he seemed eager to transform the Soviet Union from within. At first, President Reagan wasn't sure what to make of him. Gorbachev seemed less antagonistic to the West than his predecessors—but was he truly a reformer, or was this just an act to get the United States to let its guard down?

From the start, British prime minister Margaret Thatcher believed Gorbachev was truly different. As early as 1984, she declared, "I like Mr. Gorbachev. We can do business together." But Vice President Bush wasn't so sure. He met with Gorbachev in Moscow, where he'd flown for Chernenko's funeral. ("You die, I'll fly" was, he liked to joke, the unofficial motto of his vice presidency, since he attended so many state funerals.) He then wrote a long missive to Reagan, detailing his feelings about the new leader. Bush commented on everything from Gorbachev's demeanor to his confidence, to his birthmark, to his clothing, noting that "his tailor does not rival [White House chief of staff Michael] Deaver's . . . but he beats the hell out of the Penney's basement look that some of his predecessors projected."

Bush urged Reagan to "set up a true back channel totally apart from the wide array of experts upon whom we must depend . . . All normal channels would remain open, but this would be something very special that you could use, in confidence, to establish a truly personal rapport with this new and different leader." His conclusion about Gorbachev was measured, but with a surprisingly colorful kicker:

One has got to be optimistic that Gorbachev will be better to work with, a more permanent addition to the scene and hopefully one who truly will "start anew"; but, after 8 hours of contemplation, there is also the possibility that his attractive personality will be used to divide us from our allies... It will be an interesting trip, but as the monkey said when he was shot into outer space, "It beats the hell out of the cancer research lab."

By the time the Iran-Contra affair decimated Reagan's poll numbers in late 1986, he had already begun to warm to "Gorby," as the U.S. press dubbed him. The leaders had met twice, at summits in Geneva and Reykjavik, and while neither meeting resulted in substantive agreements, they were crucial steps in deepening the relationship. Reagan now believed that Gorbachev could be his partner in ending the Cold War. But with only two years to go before the end of his presidency, he was running out of time.

Reagan would have to move quickly, be willing to take risks and rely on his instincts. And in one crucial case, he'd have to overcome the deep skepticism of his advisers in the Situation Room to make a pivotal move in the chess game of U.S.-Soviet relations.

———◄o►———

PETER ROBINSON WAS a twenty-nine-year-old speechwriter for President Reagan when he got a juicy assignment. The president was planning to deliver a speech at Berlin's Brandenburg Gate in June 1987, and Robinson was picked to write it. In preparation, he traveled with the advance team to Berlin in April to get some ideas.

During his thirty-six hours in the city, Robinson had dinner with a group of Berliners. He asked them whether they had gotten used to the Berlin Wall—the concrete monolith, constructed by the Soviets, dividing East and West Germany. The Germans shared awkward glances, then one man spoke. "My sister lives twenty miles in that direction," he told Robinson. "I haven't seen her in more than two decades. Do you think I can get used to that?" This opened the floodgates. As Robinson described it in his memoir:

> Another man spoke. Each morning on his way to work, he explained, he walked past a guard tower. Each morning, a soldier gazed down at him through binoculars. "That soldier and I speak the same language. We share the same history. But one of us is a zookeeper and the other is an animal, and I am never certain which is which."
>
> Our hostess broke in. A gracious woman, she had suddenly grown angry. Her face was red. She made a fist with one hand and pounded it into the palm of the other. "If this man Gorbachev is serious with his talk of *glasnost* and *perestroika*," she said, "he can prove it. He can get rid of this wall."

Robinson was so moved by the woman's words, he decided to make them the centerpiece of Reagan's speech. But back in Washington, he struggled with the wording. *Mr. Gorbachev—bring down this wall!* didn't sound right. How about...*take down this wall!* Still not right. Then Robinson hit on what he thought was a great idea. "In my first draft," he told me, "the big line was—and I'm not making this up, this is how stupid I was—*Herr Gorbachev, machen Sie dieses Tor auf!*"

He presented this draft to head speechwriter Tony Dolan, who told him, "Peter. When your client is the president of the United States, give him his big lines in English."

Finally, Robinson found the right verb: *Tear down this wall!* The rest of the speech was still a work in progress, but White House communications director Tom Griscom decided to take a section in to the president to gauge his reaction. He, the president, and chief of staff Howard Baker met in the Oval Office, and Griscom handed over a page and a half.

"He read it one time, right through," Griscom told me, "and then he delivered it as if he was standing at [the Brandenburg Gate]...I still remember to this day, hearing those words come out." It was obvious that the president liked it. But the "tear down this wall" phrase made Baker nervous.

In fact, it made a lot of people nervous, including most of the NSC. Over the next several weeks, numerous people fought to remove the phrase. Secretary of state George Shultz wanted it out. An assistant secretary of state called to request its deletion. Deputy national security adviser Colin Powell argued it should be taken out. Embassy officials in West Berlin hated it, feeling it was too confrontational. To diplomats, the idea of one leader using a speech to issue orders to another leader was ludicrous.

The pushback made Robinson nervous. "The one argument I thought they had was that it might put Gorbachev in a difficult position," he told me. "His hard-liners would say, 'You see, Comrade, you have been doing business with President Reagan, and how does he treat you? He embarrasses you in public.'" What if it torpedoed relations between the two leaders? "Who the hell was I, at the age of twenty-nine, to shove in a line that I knew Ronald Reagan would fall in love with?"

Speechwriter Peter Robinson penned President Reagan's most famous phrase: "Mr. Gorbachev, tear down this wall!" | *Courtesy Ronald Reagan Presidential Library*

And yet...Robinson still believed the line should stay. "Look over the Berlin Wall," he says. "You see the Communist East. At the bottom of the wall, you see crosses where people were killed trying to escape...My job was giving Ronald Reagan something to say that was equal to the setting." He didn't want the speech to be, as he called it, "State Department drivel."

At 8:45 a.m. on June 3, 1987, President Reagan and the First Lady departed the White House for the nine-day trip to Europe, which would culminate in the speech at the Brandenburg Gate. The NSC staff wasted no time, gathering in the Situation Room that morning to discuss the speech. Even knowing that Reagan liked the line, and even though it was reinserted every time they took it out, the group once again deleted it. Colin Powell forwarded the new draft to Tom

Griscom with a handwritten note saying, "Please call me and let me explain the rationale page by page before you act on the suggestions."

As a speechwriter, Peter Robinson wasn't at that Sit Room meeting, but I asked him his thoughts on it. Incredibly, he'd never heard about it. "Bastards!" he said, with a touch of melodrama. "They were still at it then? Oh, those sons of bitches. Unbelievable." But while Robinson professed to be shocked, he wasn't really surprised. "I served in a White House where every single member of the senior staff was convinced he was smarter than the president," Robinson said. "So this kind of screwing around just never ended." In fact, Shultz and others never stopped trying to get the line removed, even faxing over a memo to Air Force One on the day the Reagans flew to Berlin for the speech. In the car on the way to the Brandenburg Gate, Reagan joked about all the opposition to the line. "The boys at State are going to kill me," he said, "but it's the right thing to do."

For the most part, the Situation Room is a place where cool heads, an apolitical environment and a wealth of accumulated experience lead to good decision-making. But this was a case in which the smartest, most experienced people in the room *didn't* know best. All the wisdom in the room couldn't measure up to the gut instincts of the one man whose decision would carry the day. "Mr. Gorbachev, tear down this wall!" became the most famous line of Ronald Reagan's presidency. And it paved the way for two extraordinary meetings with the Soviet leader, one in Washington and one in Moscow, that would set the two superpowers on the path to ending the Cold War.

A YEAR LATER, on the third day of the May 1988 Moscow Summit, Reagan and Gorbachev took a stroll through Red Square. Their talks were progressing well, and the mood was buoyant, with the president at one point even throwing his arm around Gorbachev's shoulders. Seeing this, ABC's White House correspondent Sam Donaldson asked him, "Do you still think you're in an evil empire?"

"No," Reagan replied. "I was talking about another time and another era." In the eight years since candidate Reagan had told Stuart Spencer he wanted to end the Cold War, the relationship was clearly thawing. But would it be enough?

In January 1989, when President Reagan gave his farewell address, he came close to declaring American victory in the Cold War. He extolled "a satisfying new closeness with the Soviet Union," then offered this warm view of his counterpart: "President Gorbachev is different from previous Soviet leaders. I think he knows some of the things wrong with his society and is trying to fix them. We wish him well."

Yet he tempered this rosy assessment with another signature line from his presidency: "It's still trust but verify."

The Berlin Wall was still standing. But not for long.

Chapter 7

RIGHT SIDE OF HISTORY

————◆————

I WAS A BACKBENCHER," said Condoleezza Rice, recalling her first meeting in the Situation Room. It was February 1989. George H. W. Bush had just become president, and the newly minted director of Soviet and East European affairs sat along the conference room's wall, furiously scribbling notes as NSC principals discussed "how to deal with this fellow Gorbachev." This was the first of many NSC gatherings that year to discuss the Soviet Union and its rapidly dissolving empire.

"Every meeting was about 'There's been a revolution in Czechoslovakia. Havel's back in power.' Or 'Ceausescu has been executed [in Romania],'" Rice told me. As the months went by, Eastern Bloc countries threw off the Soviet yoke one by one. "It was just dizzying, the speed and thrill of it . . . We were being carried along by history."

Dave Radi, a Navy commander who served under Bush 41 as a Sit Room senior duty officer, recalls this period as "euphoric." A first-generation American whose father arrived at age eight on a boat from Slovakia, Radi "couldn't have dreamed of working in a place like [the Sit Room], because I didn't even know it existed." But as a Navy intelligence officer, he learned about the pipeline from the Pentagon to the White House that sent military staff there for two-year tours. Every day in the room was a "pinch me" moment, Radi says—but the year the Eastern Bloc collapsed was even more special.

The mood in the room was *"Can you believe this is happening?"* he recalls. As one satellite state after another fell, "I remember going up ... to tell General Scowcroft—and I don't know if it was Bulgaria, Romania, it really doesn't matter, whichever one was falling—and he said, 'Can you get me a scorecard? I can't keep track anymore.'"

In Poland, Lech Walesa's Solidarity party swept the elections. In Hungary, the government opened its border with Austria to give East Germans passage to the West. In Bulgaria, Todor Zhivkov resigned after an astonishing thirty-five years as head of state. In Czechoslovakia, the Velvet Revolution propelled playwright Vaclav Havel into power. And in Romania, the brutal Communist leader Nicolae Ceausescu was executed by firing squad. All of this happened in a single year—the same year that the Soviets ended their decade-long occupation of Afghanistan and began building their first McDonald's in Moscow.

The most memorable moment in this democratic tidal wave happened on November 9. Communist party leader Günter Schabowski mistakenly announced at a press conference that "immediately, without delay," East Germans would be free to travel into West Germany. He had misunderstood new government regulations, which were intended simply to open an application process for emigration. But as soon as the words were out of his mouth, people rushed to the wall. Very quickly, crowds on both sides began hammering at it, knocking off chunks and punching holes into the concrete. Just two years after

President Reagan stood at the Brandenburg Gate and challenged Gorbachev to "tear down this wall," the Germans were doing it themselves.

Condi Rice was in the Situation Room during this remarkable time. "One thing that people don't realize is that we received a really dark letter from Gorbachev, almost a warning…that it was happening too fast," she recalls. Gorbachev sent the message to French president François Mitterrand, British prime minister Margaret Thatcher and President Bush. In it, he warned that with "huge numbers of people moving in both directions, a chaotic situation could easily develop that might have unforeseen consequences… [including] not only the destabilization of the situation in Central Europe, but also in other parts of the world."

In the Sit Room, Rice felt something was off about the message. "I remember thinking that somebody else had written that letter," she told me. It sounded like a hostage video written by Soviet hard-liners. And yet, she observed, Gorbachev almost seemed to welcome the reunification.

This was a seismic moment in world affairs, and Rice felt the exhilaration of being in the Sit Room as it happened. "Going into that room when you're on the right side of history," she said, "is pretty thrilling." It's certainly more enjoyable, as Rice would later learn, than being there while on the wrong side of history.

"One of Bush 41's triumphs was the way he handled the Berlin Wall, which was at some level the art of doing nothing," said Bob Gates, who was then serving as deputy national security adviser. In his view, the president wisely sat back and allowed history to take its course, watching as the cycle of events played out. Facing pressure to say more and do more, Bush worked through the dilemmas in his diary. "The press gets all over me," he wrote. "'Why aren't you more excited? Why aren't you leading it?'" But he was more concerned about provoking a violent

Kremlin backlash. "What if there is a big attack—crackdown," he wrote. "It is a reason to be prudent and be cautious and to stop short of the euphoria some are exhibiting." His patience paid off. By the end of 1991, the Soviet Union fell, marking the end of Communist rule over Eastern Europe.

Yet, several thousand miles farther east, the Chinese Communist Party had—despite similar protests and uprisings—managed to hold on to power. They did so through violence and repression, starting with the Tiananmen Square massacre on June 4, 1989. For President Bush, who had served as chief of the U.S. Liaison Office (essentially, the ambassador) to the People's Republic of China, this one was more difficult to sit back and watch. It was personal.

TIANANMEN SQUARE IS a highly symbolic and meaningful place for the Chinese. It stands adjacent to the ornate imperial palace known as the Forbidden City, and it contains significant landmarks such as the National Museum of China and the Great Hall of the People. It's also the final resting place of Communist revolutionary Mao Zedong, whose embalmed body lies in a glass case within a stately mausoleum.

Starting in mid-April 1989, students began gathering on this historic plaza, agitating for political and economic reforms. The protests grew larger over the next seven weeks, with students setting up tents, staging a hunger strike and constructing an enormous statue dubbed the "Goddess of Democracy." As Communist and Socialist dictatorships fell across Eastern Europe, it seemed possible the same would happen in China. But at one a.m. on June 4, army tanks rolled in, and Red Army soldiers opened fire with automatic weapons, killing or injuring thousands of people. The square's concrete bricks ran slick with blood, a scene of carnage that was soon broadcast around the world.

David Sedney was on duty in the Situation Room when the massacre started. "It was night there, but it was also otherwise a slow time for us," he told me. Because of time zone differences, it was midday on June 3 in Washington when the troops stormed the square. President Bush was at his family's summer home in Kennebunkport, Maine, but Sedney knew he would want a play-by-play. The Sit Room staff immediately started sending whatever information it had. "We were passing things through Deputy National Security Adviser Gates," Sedney recalled. "We wouldn't call the president [directly]."

The Sit Room staff knew it would be a challenge to provide President Bush with adequate information, considering his experience and deep knowledge of the country. As secretary of state James Baker put it, "George Bush was so knowledgeable about China, and so hands-on in managing most aspects of our policy, that even some of our leading Sinologists began referring to him as the government's desk officer for China." This led to an unusual moment—one that would never happen today.

"President Bush is calling us when it started, when the tanks are rolling," recalls Dave Radi. "He wanted to know what avenues they were going down." In pre-Internet times, this was difficult information to find, and there was discussion of why the president would even need it. "Somebody said, 'Hey, he was our quasi-ambassador. He rode his damn bike [all over Beijing].'" Unlike other U.S. presidents, this one knew the layout of the Chinese capital intimately, and he wanted to know *exactly* where the troops and tanks and students were moving in real time.

"Up on Farragut Square...there was a store that sold atlases, maps and everything," Radi recalled. "The most brilliant move we made was to run up there and buy a detailed tourist map of downtown Beijing, because it enabled us to be quasi-intelligent in speaking to the president."

The staffers also looked to television for details of the massacre: Nine years after launching, CNN had become *the* resource in the Sit Room for breaking news. Having instantaneous TV reporting was extremely helpful, but it also presented a dilemma. "We're trying to do value-add to what's on TV," Sedney recalled. "People are watching CNN, so you don't want to be reporting what people have already seen . . . So that's where you try and report in reactions of others, and then bring in the intelligence that we might have that would elucidate things that people can't tell from TV."

"You have to be very aware of what's on CNN," Sedney adds, "because that's the main source of information for all policymakers."

It's also how Secretary of State Baker learned about the massacre. Baker called his son Jamie to invite him out for a round of golf, and Jamie said, "I don't think you're going to be playing any golf today."

"What do you mean?" Baker asked.

"Well, I'm sitting here watching tanks roll through Tiananmen Square on CNN," Jamie replied.

Seriously? How was it possible that the secretary of state was learning about an event of such global magnitude from . . . his son? Moments later, a duty officer at the State Department called with the news, but Baker was so stunned by this sequence of events, he wrote about it in his memoir.

Paper maps, CNN broadcasts, hard copies of reports, and new-fangled devices called pagers: These were linchpins of Sit Room technology in the late 1980s. This doesn't seem like a terribly advanced setup, but that wasn't due to lack of know-how on the part of the support staff. Gary Bresnahan was now serving in his third presidential administration, and his technological prowess—and the level of his importance in the White House—were on display a few weeks after the massacre.

While President Bush had demonstrated the "art of doing nothing" when the Berlin Wall came down, he acted more forthrightly in the days after Tiananmen Square. Aggrieved by what had happened in Beijing, and eager to communicate directly with Deng Xiaoping to salvage what had been a relatively good relationship, he wrote a long letter to Deng, which Brent Scowcroft personally delivered to the Chinese ambassador. The missive was filled with emotionally direct appeals: Bush wrote that he was reaching out "in the spirit of genuine friendship" with "great reverence for Chinese history, culture and tradition."

"We must not let this important relationship suffer further," Bush continued, adding that "We must not let the aftermath of the tragic recent events undermine a vital relationship patiently built up over the past seventeen years." The president was clearly anxious about relations between the two countries. Yet he was also aware that he couldn't appear to be placating the dictators. International reaction to the massacre was swift and sharply critical, and Congress endorsed steep sanctions on China. But Bush's gamble of sending such a plaintive letter did pay off. Deng sent his own private reply within twenty-four hours, inviting Bush to send an envoy to meet with him in Beijing.

The meeting would take place under absolute secrecy, so the president needed to have full trust in whoever was making the trip. He chose Brent Scowcroft and Larry Eagleburger. Scowcroft would bring his secretary, Florence Gantt. Never before disclosed, the fourth person to make the trip was Gary Bresnahan.

On June 30, 1989, an unmarked Air Force C-141 took off from Andrews Air Force Base with a crew of six pilots, none of whom were initially told the mission's ultimate destination. The four civilians would make the long flight inside an Airstream trailer–style "comfort pallet" installed in the belly of the C-141. To make absolutely sure the mission remained top secret, a military Stratotanker would refuel the plane in midair, to avoid the possibility of any ground crews recognizing Scowcroft or Eagleburger.

"That was a really unique one," Bresnahan told me, in a comment that could easily apply to the man himself. His job on this mission was to set up and monitor top secret communications between the plane and the president—no small feat in 1989. "I had what they call a patch antenna...You can put a special antenna in there, so you can have UHF Satcom back to somewhere," he explained. To thwart anyone trying to listen in, Bresnahan—who was trained as a cryptologist—created an encryption key.

"We have a generator that can make this stuff," he said. "So I had to make a special key for this trip so nobody else had it—even the people in the White House comms that would normally listen." The only two people who would be able to access this encrypted line were Scowcroft and President Bush. Because the president was in Kennebunkport, someone would have to deliver the encryption key to him.

"I gave it to the WHCA commander," Bresnahan recalled. "He says, 'What's this for?' I says, 'Sir, I'm just the messenger'...Even though I was the one that created it, I had to play dumb," he said with a laugh.

Bresnahan couldn't shake a strange feeling that the carefully laid plan might still fail. If you're using satellites to communicate, when you fly around the curvature of the earth, there comes a point when you have to do an "M-hop"—switching from one satellite to another. "You go over one satellite, you come back down to a ground entry point, go back up to another satellite and get back in," Bresnahan explained. On this trip, that switch would happen through ground-based equipment in Hawaii. If the equipment wasn't functioning properly for any reason, the crucial connection between Scowcroft and the president would be lost.

So, in the days before the flight, Bresnahan decided to send a colleague who specialized in radio communications to take a look. "I said to his commander, 'Hey, I need Billy to go out on a maintenance trip to Hawaii.' He says, 'When you want him to leave?' I says, 'Tomorrow morning.'" And just like that, the commander dispatched the tech from Washington, D.C., to Hawaii. Which turned out to be a good thing, because as Bresnahan had suspected, the equipment there wasn't up to par. "The amplifier in Hawaii was falling apart," he recalls. "So it wouldn't have worked. I was just lucky my intuition said I needed a guy to go to Hawaii to check this out."

As Bresnahan told me this story, I couldn't help but think how incredible the whole scenario was. Here was an Army enlistee, a guy from a blue-collar background who grew up about as far from the halls of power as you can get. He became a crucial part of top secret White House operations. He never told a soul—not family, friends, colleagues or even many of his superiors—about what he was doing. Yet he could just pick up a phone and inform a superior officer that he needed a guy to fly to Hawaii, and it happened—no questions asked.

"Well," Bresnahan said, in his typically understated way, "this commander said, 'There's one thing about Gary—just trust him.' You know? And I don't know what it was. I was lucky. I don't know what the trust was."

It clearly wasn't luck. The trust would endure through the next four presidencies.

ONE OF THE biggest leaps in Sit Room technology actually came about by chance.

Bresnahan had set up a secure video teleconferencing system (SVTS) facility in the back room of the complex, but no one wanted to use it. "It was used by lower-level coordinating committees once or twice," Dave Radi recalls. But mostly "it was where we ate our lunch. Because during my two and a half years, nobody would take technology over being face-to-face."

Richard Clarke, who during this Bush administration was serving as assistant secretary of state for political-military affairs, elaborated on the problems. "No one would use it because they thought the White House was recording. And so we signed an MOU [memorandum of understanding] that that wasn't happening." Then people started worrying that whenever video conferencing did take place, others might actually be in the room, just out of the camera's range. "We began a tradition that you would zoom the camera back at the beginning of the meeting," Clarke said, "so you could see the room and know that there was no one lurking."

People clearly didn't trust the SVTS. Sit Room meetings had always taken place in person—why change it now? Just because a new technology existed, did that mean it was better than doing things the old way?

But then, in December 1989, the NSC got its first glimpse of how useful video technology could be. In the Philippines, army forces loyal to ousted dictator Ferdinand Marcos launched a coup, attempting to overthrow democratically elected president Corazon Aquino. Should the United States intervene? Or wait and see how the fighting unfolded? With U.S. military bases on Philippine soil and a close relationship with Aquino, the Bush administration needed to respond quickly.

Unfortunately, Brent Scowcroft, James Baker and Bob Gates were at that moment flying to the tiny Mediterranean island of Malta for a summit with their Russian counterparts. "We decided there's no point in going to the Sit Room because Brent's not there. And Bob Gates isn't there. So let's just use this video thing," Clarke recalls. "And we ran that crisis exclusively by video—and it worked."

As the group discovered, there were substantial benefits to running Sit Room meetings by SVTS. Instead of everyone having to rush to the White House, they could simply connect via video from their own offices. And being in their own offices meant they had instant access to all the information from their departments.

"At the end of it, everybody said, 'Well, shit—this is the way to do it, because we're all in our command centers,'" recalls Clarke. "If we'd all been in the Situation Room, we would have been cut off from our sources of information." Of course, a large part of the Sit Room staff's job is to gather and sift through information from other departments. But the NSC members liked being able to bring the most critical data to the meeting themselves.

"It really changed the way government did its work," under secretary of state for political affairs Bob Kimmitt told me. "It didn't diminish the importance of the Situation Room...but it dispersed or diffused the conversation to internodal rather than one central 'we've gotta be in that room to have this conversation!'" That said, Kimmitt still believed it was important at times to meet face-to-face. "I think the NSC system works best when modern communication, including video conferences, is supplemented by personal look-the-individual-in-the-eye meetings," he told me.

The Philippines coup attempt marked the beginning of regular use of the SVTS room. Eight months later, when Saddam Hussein invaded Kuwait, video conferencing became a crucial tool in formulating the U.S. response.

"There were an untold number of meetings at the deputies level," John Bolton, who was at that point an assistant secretary of state, told me. "And principals meetings and full NSC meetings that, I think for the first time at a real crisis level, involved a lot of the secure video communications."

Bolton would join the meetings from his post in the State Department's operations center. "It was really only Gates and a few other people who were in the Situation Room," he recalls. The benefit, as he saw it, was the savings in travel time. "How many hours would have been consumed with people traveling to and from the White House?" he asked. "Even just a half mile away at the State Department, it makes a lot of difference than having to drive over, go through the security to get in—I mean, hours are being wasted fooling around with that."

There was another, more subtle strategic benefit: keeping a lid on crisis events. As Dave Radi put it, "Instead of all the black limousines coming in when there's a crisis, let's start using technology, and let's not have [everyone gathering] in the West Wing. Maybe we can mask things for a little bit, to buy us a little bit of time."

Any extra time would certainly be useful whenever a geopolitical catastrophe erupted—as one did on August 2, 1990. Saddam Hussein invaded Kuwait.

"Gates was away on vacation. And Eagleburger was somewhere on vacation in early August. Baker was hunting with [Georgian leader Eduard] Shevardnadze in Mongolia or something goofy like that," recalls Richard Haass, who was then serving as special assistant to the president. "So we had an all-day interagency meeting over at State...and probably about four or five o'clock in the afternoon, we finally said, 'These guys ain't just rehearsing. They're gonna go in.'"

For two weeks, Iraqi president Saddam Hussein had been massing Iraqi troops near the border of Kuwait. Most observers didn't believe he would actually invade, thinking instead that the show of force was meant to pressure Kuwait into settling a financial dispute between the two nations. Much like Vladimir Putin's threat to invade Ukraine in 2022, it seemed like a bluff. But on August 1, "all the warning lights went off," Haass says. "This was the day we realized that what Iraq was doing was not simply coercion, but they were going to invade."

Haass was tasked with persuading the president to call Saddam directly—a last-ditch effort to prevent him from going in. So he and Brent Scowcroft walked over to the East Wing, where they found the president in the medical office getting a massage.[1]

"The president's on the table getting pounded. I'm kind of sitting there, looking every which way," Haass recalls with a laugh. "It was one of those slightly bizarre moments, a little bit more close-up than you really wanted." Bush, Scowcroft and Haass discussed the question at hand: How do you reach Saddam Hussein?

"It wasn't obvious," Haass says. "You had the crazy Iraqi [information minister], Baghdad Bob...So we were debating how to do it." By now it was evening in Washington, which meant it was the middle of the night in Baghdad. "Who the hell's gonna wake up Saddam Hussein at two o'clock in the morning?" Haass says. "This is the way we got the expression 'shoot the messenger'—it's not just an expression!"

As the group continued to debate, Bob Kimmitt called from the

---

1.   In his book with Scowcroft, *A World Transformed,* Bush wrote that he was getting heat treatment for sore shoulders after hitting a bucket of golf balls. But Haass swears he was lying on a table getting a massage.

State Department. It was too late: Saddam had already sent tanks into Kuwait.

"If I remember correctly, Brent and I went down to the Sit Room," Haass told me. They convened an interagency meeting using SVTS. "That was the night we froze not just Iraqi, but Kuwaiti assets, because we didn't want Iraq to get hold of Kuwaiti assets and drain the accounts." This was the start of the Gulf War, a six-month conflict that included the allied military buildup dubbed Desert Shield, followed by the air strikes known as Desert Storm.

"We had what we called the 'small group,'" Haass recalls. "This was a group of a subset of deputies, with no plus-ones. It was Bob Gates chairing as the deputy national security adviser, and Bob Kimmitt from State, Paul Wolfowitz from the Defense Department, Dave Jeremiah from the Joint Chiefs, Dick Kerr from Intelligence and me. And the six of us were kind of the steering group for the crisis." This group met several times a day, using SVTS about half the time, according to Haass.

Then there were the "Gang of Eight" meetings—Bush's war cabinet of Scowcroft, Gates, Baker, defense secretary Dick Cheney, chief of staff John Sununu, vice president Dan Quayle, JCS chair Colin Powell, and director of central intelligence William Webster. Most of those meetings, Haass says, were in the Sit Room—though President Bush rarely set foot in the room himself, choosing instead to meet with the Gang of Eight in the Oval after they'd discussed strategy among themselves. "I can't remember a single meeting with President Bush 41 in the Sit Room conference room," Bob Kimmitt told me.

Yet even though he didn't attend meetings there, President Bush—like LBJ—called the Sit Room first thing every morning, to find out what had happened overnight.

"We did shift change at six a.m.," says Dave Radi, "and typically he would call at 6:01." The White House operator would ask for the duty officer's name, then connect the president. "[I'd] hear the president say, 'Dave!' And at a certain point, he would say, 'Oh, hey! My Navy guy!'... You know, you could just tell that he was still in the rack, trying to figure out what was going on."

President Bush wasn't the only one communicating with the Sit Room before the sun came up. Richard Haass actually began living in the complex a few days after Saddam invaded Kuwait.

"My office was over in the Old Executive Office Building," he recalls. "And I kept getting called to the Oval so often that it just became inefficient. I was spending maybe eighteen hours a day in the office, and it just became easier to be there." For about a month, Haass slept in the complex. Upon waking, he'd immediately ask for whatever new intel had come in overnight.

"They kept feeding me the cables," he said. "The only thing I didn't have time to check was my email. So about a month into the crisis, I realized I had something like ten thousand unopened, unread emails." He deleted them all in a single stroke, without even bothering to read them.

Haass hardly slept for the first few days after the invasion, and his decision to camp out in the Sit Room led to a comical moment. On Sunday, August 5, President Bush was returning to the White House from Camp David. About a half hour before the helicopter was scheduled to land, Scowcroft asked Haass to meet the president, brief him on the latest developments and give him some talking points. Haass was up to the task, except for one problem: He was dressed in shorts and a T-shirt, looking more like a disheveled suburban dad than a high-level White House aide.

He ran around the Sit Room asking the guys on duty for clothes. "I borrowed a jacket, borrowed a shirt. I still kind of looked like a mess," he recalls. Dave Radi helped Haass with his wardrobe, he told me with a laugh, "to make it so that he didn't look like a total buffoon."

Haass hurriedly threw together talking points. "I knew what I wanted to get him to do, but I was so tired, I couldn't physically do it very fast," he says. "Condi [Rice] was with me, and she got frustrated watching me. She said, 'This is pathetic. I can't stand it!' So she yanked me out of my chair and said, 'Just dictate.'" Haass talked out his thoughts while Rice typed them up. "It was the only time in my life I've had Condoleezza Rice as my secretary," he says. She ripped the paper out of the typewriter and thrust it into his hands as he hustled out to the South Lawn to meet the president.

After sleeping in the Sit Room for days, adviser Richard Haass had to borrow clothes from staffers to meet with President Bush. | *George H. W. Bush Presidential Library and Museum*

Bush descended the steps of the helicopter, and Haass handed him what Rice had typed. When he addressed the waiting reporters, Bush declared, *"This will not stand."* Those four words became the most famous of his presidency.

The lines had been drawn. And now it remained to be seen how the Bush administration would function in a time of war.

"WE HAD A rhythm that we set up very soon after Saddam invaded in August of '90," Bob Kimmitt told me. Deputies committee meeting, using SVTS, at 10:30 a.m. Then Small Group meeting in the Sit Room at noon. Gang of Eight meeting in the Oval Office right after that. Then more deputies meetings, policy coordination committee meetings, and finally an all-hands gathering at the State Department at 8:00 p.m.

"From August, certainly through December or early January, that was our rhythm," Kimmitt recalls. "Five days a week."

Kimmitt was doing this at State. Others were doing the same at their own home departments—CIA, Defense, all the major agencies. A huge funnel of information flowed down, all morning long, into the Sit Room and then eventually to the president. Decisions got made. And then that information started flowing out, going back to the departments and agencies. It was like an hourglass, I ventured.

"It is an hourglass," Kimmitt agreed. "And the center of the hourglass was the Oval Office. But just above it and below it was the Sit Room."

In almost every account of the Bush 41 White House, and in multiple interviews I conducted for this book, I heard the same sentiments expressed over and over: Bush's team worked together incredibly well. The Situation Room functioned at peak performance. The decision-making process was efficient and professional. It's difficult to find anyone who has a *bad* recollection of working in the first Bush administration.

According to Richard Haass, it all flowed from the top. "This worked well," he told me, "because Bush 41 assembled really good people who got along." That included one man in particular who was pivotal to the smooth functioning of the administration. "Scowcroft played a critical role," Haass recalls. "Scowcroft had the trust and respect of everybody, whether they agreed or not."

As we've seen, Lieutenant General Brent Scowcroft is one of those key people who keeps popping up in administration after administration. He trained as an Air Force fighter pilot but pivoted to a ground-based career path after crash-landing his jet in 1949. Slight of stature, modest by nature, and possessed of an ability to get along with anyone anywhere, Scowcroft quickly moved up the ranks in a variety of jobs, working for the Joint Chiefs of Staff, teaching at the Air Force Academy and West Point, and serving overseas.

He got a White House job during the Nixon administration, when he was tapped as military assistant to the president. He served as deputy national security adviser under Presidents Nixon and Ford, then as national security adviser under Ford and George H. W. Bush. During the Reagan administration, he served on the Tower Commission that investigated the Iran-Contra affair—which is one reason he was so valuable to subsequent administrations. Bush 41 brought him in as a close friend and alter ego to right the ship. Scowcroft had helped uncover the excesses of Oliver North and the parallel Sit Room, so he was able to use that knowledge to streamline the Bush White House's process.

"If you looked up in a dictionary 'perfect national security adviser,' it would have been Brent," Condi Rice told me. "He was self-effacing. I think he could have walked down the streets in Washington, D.C., and nobody would have known who he was." Scowcroft promised secretary of state James Baker that he wouldn't appear on television or deliver a speech before clearing it with Baker. And unlike the domineering Henry Kissinger, who hoarded private time with President Nixon, Scowcroft, Rice observes, was "great at making sure that the secretaries were not just informed, but had a chance to talk to the president." He was a classic honest broker. To build trust, he held a weekly breakfast with Baker and Dick Cheney—no aides allowed. "He was the gold standard," Joint Chiefs chairman Mark Milley told me.

"My first time I went down there, I kept calling him 'sir,' because I was in the Army and he's a retired *general*," recalls former NSC staffer Jane Lute, who is one of the very few people to have shared with a spouse the experience of serving in the Situation Room (hers is former deputy national security adviser and NATO ambassador Doug Lute). "And [Scowcroft's deputy Bob] Gates was like, 'Will you knock that off?'"

Under the first Bush administration, Lute says, the NSC ran like a well-oiled machine. "It was not only that Brent and Bush 41 had known each other and had worked together," she said, "but that both of them had very deep foreign policy and political instincts."

John Bolton agrees. "That was really the legendary period of how the thing functioned and how it was used," he told me, going on to compare the Bush team to the 1927 Yankees.

"I'm apolitical here. Let's just make that clear," Dave Radi said. "But they were the right men at the right time—men or women—for what was going on, not just with Iraq, but the fall of the Berlin Wall, Tiananmen and everything else."

———◄o►———

Two incidents in the Situation Room give a flavor of how the Bush administration functioned during wartime.

In the first, on October 11, 1990, the NSC core group was meeting to hear General "Stormin' Norman" Schwarzkopf's plan for how to drive Saddam out of Kuwait. Schwarzkopf wanted to send U.S. ground troops straight up from Saudi Arabia into Kuwait, confronting the Iraqi army head-on, what national security professionals call "force on force."

Bush and Scowcroft were, to put it mildly, unimpressed with this plan. In the book they co-authored, *A World Transformed*, Scowcroft wrote simply that he "was appalled with the presentation." John Bolton gave me a more colorful description of the meeting, even though he wasn't personally there; this was how Larry Eagleburger recounted it to him:

> Everybody's sort of sitting there listening, and you know, Schwarzkopf is this big bear of a guy in a small room with a loud voice, a lot of charts...
>
> And then all of a sudden this little voice from little Brent Scowcroft pipes up and he says, "Well, Norm, why are you going force on force?" And he said Schwarzkopf kind of exploded. And then Bush 41 said, "Yeah. Why are you going force on force?" And that was the end of Schwarzkopf Plan A. They had to go back and do Plan B.

This story hearkens back to JFK's advice to "watch the generals and to avoid feeling that just because they were military men, their opinions on military matters were worth a damn." Scowcroft stuck his neck out for his boss, and Bush then pushed back on Schwarzkopf. The two worked in tandem to send the general back to the drawing board.

The second incident took place two weeks later, on October 30, 1990. Once again, the NSC core group was meeting in the Sit Room, this time to decide whether sanctions or military force was the better option for getting Saddam out of Kuwait. With more than 200,000 U.S. troops in the region, we had enough force to go in. But according to Bob Gates, Schwarzkopf now opposed the plan. Basically, his bluff had been called—and when military leaders don't want to do something, they try to make it sound impossible, or a bloodbath in the making, or both.

As Schwarzkopf's second-in-command briefed the group, President Bush asked, "What would it take for you to take the offensive and liberate Kuwait?" Gates described to me what happened next:

> This guy does the usual military thing—and it's a three-star general. And he says, "Well, Mr. President, here's what it would take. Six aircraft carrier strike groups. You would have to move the Seventh Corps out of Germany to Saudi Arabia. They've been there since 1945. They're the two heaviest divisions in the U.S. Army. You'd have to paint 'em all tan [for desert camouflage]...And by the way"—and this is, like, a week before the midterms—"you'll have to activate the National Guard and Reserves."
>
> And to the day I die, I will never forget. Bush stood up. He pointed at Dick Cheney and said, "You've got it. Let me know if you need more." And walked out of the room.

A presidential moment. Bush called the military's bluff, more than doubling the number of troops from 225,000 to half a million, without even hesitating.

President Bush was "very comfortable making decisions," Haass told me. "He didn't need thirteen meetings on an issue. And he was very comfortable with the use of force, maybe because he was a combat veteran."

This was the tough, decisive side of George H. W. Bush. But what many Sit Room staffers remember best is his kinder, gentler side. Unlike some presidents, Bush 41 truly enjoyed interacting with the men and women who worked so hard for him. He didn't approach them as cogs in a machine; he appreciated their knowledge and expertise and spoke with them as equals. Kevin O'Connell, who served in the Sit Room during the Gulf War, recalls that "General Scowcroft and his deputy, Bob Gates, believed that the person with the most knowledge about a situation should be the one talking to the president...For an intelligence officer, it was a pleasure to brief him because he understood everything."

In fact, Bush was so respectful of the Sit Room, he actually asked permission to enter when he dropped by one Saturday early in his administration. The room is equipped with a camera and phone outside the door, and that morning, he picked up the receiver and said, "This is the president. May I come in?" The startled secretary, Gilda Kay, buzzed him in.

For staffers who had served during the Reagan administration, the Bush family's informality was at first jarring. Dave Radi described the difference in demeanor between the two First Ladies. "I had seen Mrs. Reagan a couple of times. And you know, talk about someone who was impeccably dressed. And the unspoken word was, *don't try to talk, don't make eye contact.*" Then, a few weeks into Bush 41, he saw Barbara Bush. "She had come down the steps, dog in tow, with a couple of grandkids. And she was in sweats. And I'm embarrassed to say that my first reaction was, 'Lady, that's not proper dress.'"

But the Bushes treated the White House as their home. They walked the dogs, hung out with their family, and invited friends to movie nights in the screening room. And sometimes, they invited Sit Room staffers there, too.

"On a slow Saturday, Barbara would call over and say, 'Hey, y'all want to watch a movie with us?'" recalls Dave Sedney. "And if we weren't that busy, we'd send somebody over." This made for some incredible memories for staffers. They'd get to watch the movie with President and Mrs. Bush, enjoy some popcorn, and chat with their hosts about what was going on in the world.

Dave Radi says that the president "seemed to get bored on the weekends, especially when he and Mrs. Bush stayed at the White House instead of going to Camp David." Bush would call down to the Sit Room and ask for "funny cables," he recalls. "Hey, I know I appointed some ambassadors that are funny as hell," he'd say. "Bring me some stuff to read!" Radi would carry a stack of cables up to the little study off the Oval Office. Even before he got there, he could hear the president's choice of music wafting down the corridor. "He'd be in that private study blasting the most godawful country and western," Radi says with a laugh.

When Radi's son was born, Bush surprised him with a gift. "We probably were the lowest level of life in the West Wing, but the president brought down a bottle of champagne for me, for my son," he says, still sounding amazed at the memory. And at an NSC picnic the following year, Radi's son apparently decided he was entitled to the president's own beverage as well. "I'm holding my son. The president is drinking," recalls Radi. "The next thing I know, he puts his hand in the president's beer." Radi was mortified, but Bush was unfazed. "He takes his little hand out and says, 'Now, can't a man have a beer?'" Seeing how embarrassed Radi and his wife were, he laughed. "You two calm down! I'm a grandparent."

My favorite story, though, comes from Gary Bresnahan. He was in Kennebunkport, hooking up communications equipment in the attic of the president's house with another technician. Bresnahan sent his colleague back to their hotel to get a piece of equipment they'd forgotten, and the guy seemed to be taking forever. After forty-five minutes or so, Bresnahan finally heard footsteps behind him. He wheeled around and barked, "Where the fuck you been?!" To his shock, he found himself nose to nose with the president of the United States.

"Well, I didn't know I took so long," Bush said, not missing a beat.

Bresnahan laughs. "I'm pissing my pants—I still piss my pants when I tell the story. I literally said the F-word to the boss, right in front of his face."

———◄○►———

THE BUSH 41 team was tight-knit, efficient and superb at handling foreign policy. Yet they learned the same lesson handed to Winston Churchill after World War II: Leaders don't always get rewarded politically for winning a war.

I had a front-row seat to the events that defined—and ultimately defeated—the Bush presidency. In the summer of 1989, I was offered a dream job as executive floor assistant to House majority leader Richard Gephardt. In that role, I would be his shadow, his surrogate and his eyes and ears in the Capitol. There was a bonus, too. Gephardt was planning on running for president in 1992, and I would be in on the ground floor of his campaign.

Gephardt seemed well positioned during the budget fight of 1990. He and his fellow Democratic leaders, Speaker Tom Foley and Senate majority leader George Mitchell, refused to negotiate until President Bush broke his signature "Read my lips: no new taxes" promise from the 1988 campaign. To his credit, Bush agreed to a deal that raised taxes, for the sake of reaching a bipartisan agreement to reduce the budget deficit. But he paid a high price. During the fall of 1990, as he was building an Iraq war coalition abroad, his GOP coalition in Congress was cracking apart.

All that political trouble seemed to be swept away by the swift victory in the Gulf War. By the summer of 1991, Bush was again riding high, with approval ratings near 90 percent. A series of big-name Democrats, including my boss, Gephardt, backed away from challenging him. Which created an opening for Bill Clinton—and me.

I joined Clinton's campaign that fall, getting in *literally* on the ground floor: Our headquarters was a storefront paint shop in downtown Little Rock. From the moment we met, I could tell he was a political genius; in thirty minutes, he mapped out how the primary campaign might unfold, in a manner that matched almost exactly what happened. Clinton hammered Bush on his economic record, declaring that America needed a president who "cares as much about the Middle West as the Middle East." It was a famously rocky campaign, with Clinton having to fight through sex scandals and questions about the draft, but he ultimately cruised to victory on the promise of change after twelve years of Republican presidents.

Back at the White House, Brent Scowcroft gathered the NSC staff in Room 208 of the Old Executive Office Building—the same room where Oliver North had set up his Iran-Contra operation. In an essay she wrote for the book *Transforming Our World*, Jane Lute recalled the scene: He "took in the whole of the room and minced no words," before announcing, "We've all been fired." Scowcroft being Scowcroft, he looked for the silver lining. He told the group that the loss wasn't due to any foreign policy issues, then remarked dryly, "I suppose we can take some satisfaction in that."

Inauguration Day came two months later. I was thirty-one years old and hours away from becoming White House communications director, a role that would prove more demanding and exhausting than I could ever have imagined. We had no idea what we were in for, but that morning at Blair House, as we toiled over Clinton's inaugural speech, I saw in Brent Scowcroft's face how very emotional and draining life in the White House could be—and how difficult it was to leave.

He walked into Blair House to brief the incoming president and deliver the nuclear codes, his final official duty. Then Scowcroft—the stalwart and stoic adviser who had bolstered the morale of Sit Room staffers after the defeats of Bush and Ford and the resignation of Nixon—walked out of Blair House alone in a rumpled raincoat and fedora, tears in his eyes.

Chapter 8

PLEASE HOLD FOR THE PRESIDENT

———◆———

I DON'T REMEMBER MY first time.

At the top of every interview conducted for this book, I asked each person the same question: Do you remember your first time in the Situation Room? It was a good icebreaker, and many people described in great detail their initial impressions and the intensity of their experiences. I always felt a bit sheepish because I don't remember my own. But I like to think I have a good excuse.

I had been to the White House only once before Bill Clinton was sworn in. During the transition, I went to the West Wing to meet with President Bush's press secretary, Marlin Fitzwater, who handed me a bulletproof vest that had been passed down by presidential press secretaries since the 1970s—an ironic nod to the flak we take at the podium. There wasn't time for a full tour, though, so the White House was still unfamiliar territory for me. Then came Inauguration Day, and I entered a whirlwind that wouldn't subside for four years.

THE SITUATION ROOM

As I wrote in my White House memoir, *All Too Human*, "Inaugural week was a manic mix of public celebrations and private chaos." All-nighters revising the president's speech. Then the inaugural ceremony and balls—a time of celebration before my first White House press briefing, where I bombed. To be fair, I had a tough brief: The president's first nominee for attorney general, Zoë Baird, was getting pilloried in the Senate over a tax issue and was about to be dumped. So was Clinton's campaign promise to lift the ban on gays in the military, which faced veto-proof opposition in Congress. And the press corps was livid about a decision (soon to be reversed) restricting their access to the West Wing. It was a harsh welcome to the White House briefing room.

I assume that at some point in those first couple of days I ducked into the Situation Room—maybe when I was grabbing a bite right next door at the White House mess. As just about everyone from that era agrees, the room at first glance was unremarkable and underwhelming. In those days, before being renovated in 2006, it was just a conference room without any high-tech trappings. What makes it special is what's debated and decided there.

By the end of my White House tenure, in December 1996, I had spent dozens of hours either in the Sit Room or in contact with its staff. There were pre-dawn phone calls to the duty officers after an overnight crisis, so I could brief the White House correspondents doing their morning broadcasts from the North Lawn. I would often check back during the day, whenever the latest news broke on CNN, so I could update the president with additional information.

I wasn't a member of the NSC's principals committee, but I did sit in on Situation Room meetings covering a wide range of issues: Russia's economic struggles. North Korea's efforts to build nuclear weapons. A coup in Haiti and civil war in Somalia. Also domestic crises, such as the Oklahoma City bombing in 1995 and the crash of TWA Flight 800 in 1996, both of which spawned multiple conspiracy theories. When I attended those meetings, my job was to offer advice on how to communicate the administration's response, anticipate how Congress would react, and keep an eye on how decisions aligned with President Clinton's past statements and campaign promises.

This was a delicate balancing act for all foreign policy issues. But the one that bedeviled Clinton most during the first term was the crisis in Bosnia.

PRESIDENT CLINTON's U.N. ambassador Madeleine Albright was only four foot ten, but with her colorful scarves and signature brooches, she cut a striking—and often imposing—figure. This was never more true than at a 1993 meeting in the Situation Room, where she let her temper fly. She wanted the United States to bolster U.N. peacekeeping efforts by supporting NATO air strikes.

"What's the point of having this superb military you're always talking about," she snapped at chairman of the joint chiefs General Colin Powell, "if we can't *use* it?" War was raging in the Balkans, and up to that point, the Clinton administration had taken a wait-and-see attitude. But as Bosnian Serbs intensified bloody attacks on their Muslim neighbors, the Czech-born Albright decided she'd seen enough. She wanted the administration to support air strikes against the Bosnian Serbs, to stop the killing. And if she had to embarrass someone to make that happen, she was willing to do it.

The general, who at six two towered over the diminutive Albright, was livid at her blunt critique. "I thought I would have an aneurysm," he wrote in his memoir. "American GIs were not toy soldiers to be moved around on some global game board." His namesake policy, the Powell Doctrine, set a high bar for military action: A vital U.S. interest had to be at stake, and the nation had to be prepared to go in with overwhelming force with public support. In his mind, the situation in the Balkans hadn't cleared the bar.

Jane Lute, the NSC's director of European affairs, was in the room that day. "Colin was not happy," she told me. Then she offered some insight into clashes that often occur between high-level civilians and military personnel over sending troops into combat.

Ever since the 1991 invasion of Iraq, Desert Storm, "the Army does not conceive of, or really talk about, 'boots on the ground,'" Lute told me. Instead, it focuses on "military solutions...in a very complicated system of rotation, preparation, recovery." In her view, most civilians—with the exception of some, such as Albright—are clueless when it comes to war. She recalled one conversation with a civilian aide to President Clinton. "She said, 'We could move a brigade.' I said, 'How big is a brigade?'" The aide couldn't answer. Lute and others referred to this as "the brigade test"—a pretty reliable indicator of who doesn't know what they're talking about with regard to military intervention.

At a later Sit Room meeting, President Clinton asked Lute what *she* thought about the situation in the Balkans. "Jane," he said, "you're in the military. Would you put troops on the ground in Bosnia?" Lute felt her eyes widen as a lower part of her anatomy clenched shut, a reaction she colorfully characterizes as the "eyeball to asshole" ratio. "There's principals in the room—and me," she told me. "And I remembered when Scowcroft said, 'When the president asks you a question, do not say, *Well, Mr. President, it's your decision. He knows that.*'"

Lute knew she had to give the president a real answer, so she said, "Yes, sir, I would. Under two conditions: if we're asked for a capability that only we can provide, or in an emergency where the preservation of

NATO allies, lives and troops are at stake." Clinton took this in. And still the discussions continued.

Between 1993 and 1995, there were countless meetings about Bosnia. Most followed the same script: Albright, national security adviser Tony Lake and the NSC's Europe expert Sandy Vershbow agitated for action. Powell and secretary of state Warren Christopher opposed it. These two camps were locked in a stalemate, with President Clinton caught in the middle.

He was anguished by the killings and had staked out an aggressive stance on Bosnia in 1992, promising to do "whatever it takes to stop the slaughter of civilians." But his top campaign promise was to "focus like a laser" on the economy. The public and Congress were wary of risking American lives in a Balkan civil war—a fear reinforced after the October 1993 Black Hawk Down disaster, when Somalian forces killed eighteen U.S. soldiers after shooting down two helicopters. NATO allies and a newly democratic Russia were also pushing back against the use of force. Given the cross pressures, the noninterventionists prevailed. "Muddling through seemed the safest course from their point of view," Vershbow concluded. They feared that "taking a high-risk initiative could end in embarrassment."

Tony Lake was disturbed by the ongoing, grinding horror of the war. "Clinton hated it. I hated it," he recalls. "And if we were going to solve it, we had to run some risks, come to grips with it." Lake was eager to make something happen. True to form, he would do so behind the scenes.

A national security adviser in the mold of Brent Scowcroft, Lake was ambitious, yet content to be unknown to the general public. He was a proud man but not burdened by an overactive ego. And he was moral without being a moralist. A foreign service officer and veteran of the Carter administration, Lake served because it was in his blood, not because he needed the validation or attention for doing it. He was dry and self-deprecating, a man who kept his focus on the long game. The hamster wheel of the Bosnia situation was driving him crazy, so by summer of 1995, he decided he had to act.

"Do you remember the British queen Mary?" he asked me in our interview. "[She] said that when she died, they would find a C for 'Calais'"—the northern French town she lost in battle—"written on her heart. I always felt like, in the morning meetings with the president, I had a 'B' written on my forehead, for Bosnia." Every time he'd walk into the Oval, he could feel Clinton wincing, knowing that another one of their endless conversations about Bosnia was coming.

Lake recalls that in the more formal Situation Room meetings, it was impossible to get consensus on how to proceed. "So I decided to go smaller still. And rather than continuing to argue it out in the Situation Room with all the formal papers and discussions, I started to have lunches at my little table in my office, with just the secretaries of state and defense and Madeleine." This gave the key people a chance to argue things through.

I asked him why he felt it necessary to switch to smaller meetings about the so-called endgame strategy, involving more military pressure combined with more flexible diplomacy. "So the conversation would become all the more flexible," he told me. In Lake's view, the Situation Room itself was part of the problem of why no consensus had yet been reached.

Lake wasn't the only one who felt that way. David Scheffer, who was serving as a senior adviser to Albright, told me, "I'm gonna be very blunt and succinct when I say this. I think there's a failure far too often in the Sit Room for the big ideas to be presented and even to have any chance of prevailing." He believes that people are hesitant to put forth their big ideas and bold policy concepts in the Sit Room, because "once you do that, you are opening yourself up to all the conventional criticism...that is usually centered [on] minimizing risk and the cost of what you just proposed."

Scheffer felt that this was the situation Albright faced in 1993, when she first began agitating for intervention in Bosnia. "What she was doing was saying, 'Look, the way to break this is with something unconventional: unleashed NATO airpower against a non-NATO force.' And while she was able to do that, once it was shot down, she had to shelve it for a couple of years until the circumstances permitted her to put it on the table again."

The July 1995 Srebrenica massacre forced the issue. Serbian forces killed more than 8,000 Bosnian Muslim boys and men, expelling 20,000 more Muslims in a bout of ethnic cleansing. The scale of the atrocity was not fully known right away, but reports started to come in the first week of July. The U.N. requested more air strikes, and President Jacques Chirac of France pressed Clinton for action in a personal phone call. Clinton finally decided to act, and he did it through the orchestration of Tony Lake.

On July 17, Lake hosted a breakfast meeting in his office. Albright, Christopher, deputy national security adviser Sandy Berger, secretary of defense William Perry and JCS chairman General John Shalikashvili attended. Lake presented his "endgame strategy"—a complex package of bold initiatives intended to end the war. It was "an NSC/ Tony Lake–sponsored effort to think outside the box and develop some options," Sandy Vershbow told me, "even as the formal interagency process kept coming back to muddling through and nothing else but muddling through."

As had happened so many times before, Christopher, Perry and Shalikashvili believed the risks of intervention were too high, and they began urging Lake back toward the stagnant but safe strategy already in play. Just then, President Clinton appeared at Lake's door. He came in and announced that he wanted to change tacks. "I don't like where we are now," he said. "This policy is doing enormous damage to the United

States and to our standing in the world. We look weak." He asked the group to come up with new ideas.

"There was a moment of theater," Lake told me with a smile, "because Clinton wanted to end it, and he knew what I was doing at these lunches. I didn't exactly put him up to this, but during one lunch, he suddenly appeared through the door and said to all of us that he really wanted to bring an end to this."

The consensus view, however, is that Lake *did* put him up to it. "I was there as the notetaker," Sandy Vershbow told me, "so I guess I can say after all these years... it was definitely staged." Clinton and Lake had discussed both the endgame strategy and the casual drop-by in advance. "The president was a willing co-conspirator in staging this surprise appearance," Vershbow says.

"A bit of theater": the pivotal meeting about Bosnia in Tony Lake's office. (L–R: President Clinton, Warren Christopher, Tony Lake, William Perry, General John Shalikashvili) | *Courtesy William J. Clinton Presidential Library*

That drop-by at Lake's office marked a turning point in the discussions. Now, the principals had no choice but to recognize that the president wanted a change in strategy. This was reinforced by their knowledge that American troops would have to go in if the U.N. mission failed. "We needed a new paradigm," says Vershbow. "We couldn't just drift any longer. And so at least their people started working with us, though they still opposed decisive action."

Clinton knew he couldn't let the conflict in Bosnia become a weight around his neck in the 1996 campaign, which was just around the corner. "In the Sit Room, we all knew it was there," recalls David Scheffer. "The elephant in the room." At that time, Clinton also confided in me. We need "to bust our rear to get a settlement in the next couple of months," he said. "Explore all alternatives, roll every die." Otherwise, he feared it might be "dropped in during the middle of the campaign." He'd made his decision, but it would take another tragedy halfway around the world to put it into action.

———◆◇▶———

IN MID-AUGUST OF 1995, assistant secretary of state Richard Holbrooke led a delegation to the region, traveling there with Lieutenant General Wesley Clark and a team of negotiators to present a new peace plan. The Americans needed to get to Sarajevo for meetings, but Serbian president Slobodan Milosevic couldn't—or wouldn't—guarantee them safe passage by air. Instead, the team set off on August 19 in two armored vehicles, planning to traverse a narrow, waterlogged red-clay road over Mount Igman, southwest of Sarajevo.

Holbrooke and General Clark buckled themselves into a U.S. Army Humvee, and the rest of the negotiating team piled into a French armored personnel carrier, or APC. Midway through the drive, as they came upon a U.N. convoy heading in the other direction, the two vehicles carrying the Americans moved to the outer edge of the roadway. Suddenly, the red clay began crumbling beneath the APC. The vehicle slid, then tumbled more than three hundred feet down the side of the mountain. And then it exploded.

General Clark leapt out of the Humvee and scrambled down the mountainside, in a desperate attempt to save the men in the APC. But it was too late. NSC aide Colonel Nelson Drew and special envoy Robert Frasure died in the conflagration, and deputy assistant secretary of defense Joseph Kruzel succumbed to his injuries later that day in a field hospital. A French soldier accompanying the delegation also died.

"I remember racing down the hall at the State Department to tell the ops room," David Scheffer recalls, "and asking for as much detail as I could about it, and reporting to Albright." In the back of his mind, he was thinking about how many months Robert Frasure had spent trying to negotiate peace. "He was a brilliant negotiator, a very articulate individual who produced narratives in his cables that were fantastic to read," he told me. "And then we lost him."

Sandy Vershbow learned of the accident from the Situation Room. "It was a Saturday, and I was at home," he recalls. "I got a call from the Sit Room, from one of the duty officers, saying, 'Okay, we're getting preliminary reports of this road accident.' And we very quickly got more details." Vershbow, too, was devastated at the loss of the three negotiators. But he had other, more complex emotions mixed in as well, because at one point he was supposed to have been on this particular mission. "It was a kind of 'There, but for the grace of God'" situation, he says. "I would have been in that armored personnel carrier instead of Nelson Drew."

For Tony Lake, Drew was not just a colleague, but also a friend. He was the only NSC staffer ever to die in the line of duty, and "while he was in the Air Force, I was kind of his commanding officer," Lake recalls. "I had to drive out to tell his wife that her husband was dead." He brought Sandy Vershbow, Sandy Berger and the Air Force chaplain with him, and the three men stood on the doorstep of their colleague's home. When Lake knocked, Drew's wife opened the door. "She just saw me, saw my face and told her two kids to go back into the dining room," Lake told me. She knew instantly that this particular knock could mean only one thing.

"We told her the bad news," recalls Vershbow, "and she said, 'You've got to solve this for Nelson.' So if there was any need for additional motivation, that was it." In Vershbow's view, the accident "steeled everybody's resolve that failure is not an option. We have to succeed where all previous initiatives have failed."

President Clinton "had already made the decision that he wanted something done," says Ivo Daalder, an NSC staffer at the time. "But now he *really* wanted something done." Four days after the accident, the three diplomats received a memorial service at Arlington National Cemetery. The president decided to seize the moment: He called together all the top-level officials who attended the funeral, pulling them in for a meeting at Fort Myer, an Army outpost adjacent to the cemetery grounds.

A photo of that meeting shows President Clinton sitting in a small, modestly decorated room, addressing the top members of his administration. Tony Lake, General Wesley Clark, chief of staff Leon Panetta, Richard Holbrooke, Warren Christopher, William Perry, Madeleine Albright, General John Shalikashvili—all listen raptly as Clinton exhorts them to find a way to end the war.

"Clinton at that point said, 'Because of what happened, we have to succeed,'" says Daalder. "When members of your staff [die] as a result of the effort, it becomes even more personal and even more direct."

Ending the war would mean their colleagues hadn't died in vain. Intervention wasn't just necessary—now it was urgent. This unscheduled meeting in an unremarkable Fort Myer room would prove to be a turning point in the Bosnian crisis.

One week later, with the support of the United States, NATO unleashed a fierce bombing campaign in an effort to bring the war to a close—exactly the kind of intervention Madeleine Albright had argued for two years earlier. As she had predicted, it worked—which means that if the men in the room had heeded her recommendation in 1993, thousands of lives might have been saved. Instead, those who finally green-lit the aerial assaults took the credit for the decision, however belatedly they made it.

Unfortunately, as I would learn in the course of doing interviews, that's an all-too-common experience for women in the Situation Room.

"I REMEMBER SHE told me a story once," Gayle Smith recalls of Madeleine Albright. "There was a call on a Sunday—a conference call on some crisis. All the men kept talking and she kept trying to break in, and they kept talking over her. She was pushing the buttons on her phone, going 'Hello?! I'm not on mute here. Hello!'" The men ignored her until finally she interjected loudly, pointedly announcing her name and title.

Albright "fought for the space," says Smith. "But then she commanded a respect." She also became a resource for other women, a mentor who understood what they were going through because she had been through it all, too.

Smith, the NSC's senior director for African affairs under Clinton, told me another, more personal story about Albright. "I had lived in

Africa for twenty years, moved back on a Saturday, and started at the NSC on a Monday," she recalls. "You want to talk about interplanetary change? It's like, *Holy shit, how did I end up here?*" Smith was standing outside the Oval Office on her first day, feeling self-conscious about her unconventionally short, spiky haircut, when Albright walked up to her.

"You're the funkiest person in the whole U.S. government!" Albright exclaimed brightly.

"Do you think that's okay?" Smith asked her.

"Totally," Albright said with a big smile. "Just go with it!"

"People had asked me whether I was going to change my hair or dress differently" in the West Wing, Smith recalls. "I said, 'They hired who they hired.' But she was incredibly supportive...She had solidarity with every woman in government."

In the Sit Room's earliest years, no women served there. Dr. Sally Botsai was one of the first, if not *the* first, and she started during the Nixon administration. The number of women grew with each successive administration, and by the time Clinton was in office, "it was male-heavy, but probably about a 60:40 distribution," senior duty officer Bonnie Glick recalls. There were fifteen duty officers in her tenure during Clinton's second term. "There was one officer from each branch of service," she told me. "They were not all men. We had three men, two women...Before my generation in the Sit Room, I think all of the military had been men."

Glick, who was a foreign service officer, sensed a difference between how nondiplomats and diplomats behaved in the room, but also how men and women did. "The Navy guy was so stern at first, I asked him if he had to rise to a certain rank before he was issued a sense of humor," she recalled in an early 2000s interview. The Sit Room is "this space with a lot of major egos coming in, and people may or may not pay attention to the fact that human beings run [it]." Glick made a point of checking in on people's well-being, an unofficially designated "Jewish Mother" to the NSC staff. She recalled once disarming a cranky Sandy Berger with a granola bar and a bottle of water she'd brought in, telling him, "I think you need this more than I do."

Glick handled Sit Room attitudes with humor and a light touch. But some others found themselves pushing back, hard, to be heard.

I asked Jane Lute whether she ever ran into implicit sexist bias in the room. "Oh my god," she replied. "You don't know a senior woman who has not." She then recounted how things had changed for women in the military over the years.

"When I went into the Army in the seventies, the unspoken rule was, *whatever you do, don't make my job harder*," she recalls. "So, don't be a ditz. Don't be coming on to anybody. And if you're gay—and there was a fair chance that you were, 'cause a lot of them were—then just be discreet about it. Don't make my job harder." In Lute's recollection, rather than lifting each other up, women mostly tried to stay out of each other's way.

"Over the course of time, what you learn is that everybody wants to be at the table, and not everybody wants to do what it takes to be at the table," she told me. "But if you've done what it takes . . . you're at the table." Lute had made it into the corridors of power, and she was determined to make the most of her time there. "I'm not apologizing to anybody. You want to know what I think? I'll tell you."

Lute recounted several instances when she had to speak forcefully to ensure male colleagues heard her. There was, she told me, "a four-year knife fight between me and [NSA director] Keith Alexander that played out in the Situation Room most weeks" while she was serving as deputy secretary of homeland security. "He said, 'The only way I can defend the country is if [the NSA is] in all the networks.' I said, 'Over my dead body. We are not deploying military soldiers to every street corner of the Internet in the United States of America.'" In Lute's recollection, no one else in the room dared talk to Alexander the way she did. "I thought, *This is bullshit. Why are we all [tiptoeing]? He's wrong here!*"

Lute was frustrated by what she called the "well-worn grooves of how we made national security decisions." This included the fact that her male colleagues often didn't listen to the women in the room. "Time and time and time again, a woman would make a really smart interjection or observation," she recalls. "And people would blow past it." Then a man would say the same thing, and everyone would praise his insights.

Once again, it was Madeleine Albright who came up with a solution. In conversations with other women, she pointed out that this was happening. Undersecretary of state for global affairs Paula Dobriansky remembers her saying, "Women, you have to stop it! You've got to have a network." Albright urged the women to speak up, right there in the room, when men took credit for their ideas.

"There were women with serious jobs at the table," recalls deputy secretary of state Wendy Sherman, who served in the Clinton, Obama and Biden administrations. "But voices were still heard differently. It was almost like we understood it amongst ourselves. And so we would try to have each other's back." Whenever a woman's suggestion was ignored and a man later given credit for it, "one of us would pipe up and say, 'Great that you underscored the point that she just made!'" Some of the men noticed and changed their habits. Many never noticed at all.

Sherman, who was a friend and close colleague of Albright, also became a mentor to young women. She spent years fighting the good fight for her female counterparts, though now, she jokes, she's "post-ambition. I'm seventy-three years old." She also feels that she's "earned the right to say what I believe. So I tend to call things out."

Many of those serving under Biden worked together in the Clinton and Obama administrations, which "means we are all much more direct with each other," Sherman told me. There's a comfort level. But also, "norms have changed," she says. "You guys have more awareness that sometimes you could be, shall I say, less than understanding of what's happening to the women around you."

IN MAY 1999 the Situation Room broke another barrier, welcoming its first African American director, Elliott Powell. A Navy captain who had commanded a minesweeper during the Gulf War, Powell was also a history buff. So he was excited to be taking command of the Sit Room—and even more thrilled when, on his first day, he found himself witnessing a call between President Clinton and British prime minister Tony Blair.

Outgoing Sit Room director Kevin Cosgriff walked Powell into the Oval Office and introduced him to the president. "We shook hands, and then Admiral Cosgriff said, 'He's going to sit in for the call, to see how things work,'" Powell recalls. "Because that's one of the things the Situation Room does, we set up the calls for heads of state." In fact, this is one of the most important tasks the Sit Room team takes on— and it's much more complicated, and more diplomatically fraught, than most outside the room realize.

"I used to joke that it was like a Bolshoi ballet choreography," Obama-era Sit Room director Larry Pfeiffer said with a laugh. Ideally, you wanted the two leaders to get on the call at the same time, but that was extremely difficult to do, as each side maneuvered to make sure their guy didn't have to wait. "Sometimes it could get prickly," Dave Radi told me, "because we always want to bring our president on last. Our president waits for nobody."

Former senior duty officer Rob Hargis makes the mundane process of connecting a call sound like an action film. "We've got headphones on, down in the Sit Room," he told me. "We've established the call: 'Hey, 10 Downing. This is Rob in the Sit Room, setting up the Clinton call with Tony Blair. How far out is Blair?' 'Blair is going to be on time. He's gonna be here in about three minutes.'...And then they'd say, 'Hey, Rob, I've got the prime minister. Blair is about thirty seconds from the phone.'" At that point, the Sit Room would transfer the call to the Oval Office, where an aide would give a second-by-second update on the president's position. *He's walking down the hall! He's getting closer! Please hold for the president!* And then the handoff, with aides on both sides crossing their fingers that the timing was perfect and the connection clear.

From the president's perspective, "I'm sure it looked like things are smooth," Hargis said with a laugh. "'Hey, I've got a two o'clock with Tony Blair, let's go!' You walk in at 1:59, he picks up the phone and says, 'Hey, Tony! How ya doing? Let's catch up!' But that takes a half hour of work. The feet under the duck were hauling duck butt, all the time."

Because the calls were time-consuming, the duty officers hoped not to have to do more than one or two a day. A busy day might see five or more. In the hours following the 2011 raid that took out al-Qaeda leader Osama bin Laden, the Sit Room had to set up *sixty-five* such calls—the most anyone ever recalls being made in a twenty-four-hour period.

No one wants to be made to wait, but of all the world leaders, Russian president Vladimir Putin hates it the most. His people would manipulate the situation, telling the Sit Room that Putin was on the line when he wasn't. "President Obama would come on and say, 'Hello, Vladimir,' and the Russians would say, 'Please hold for the Russian president,'" recalls former Sit Room duty officer Drew Roberts. "Every fucking time."

Putin "always made Obama wait, and I'm gonna tell you, time travels very differently when you're standing in the Situation Room" trying unsuccessfully to get the president connected, recalls Pfeiffer.

"There was one time we must have waited, it felt like twenty minutes. It was probably five," he went on. "And I finally looked at President Obama and said, 'Sir, if you would like, we can disconnect. I'll go downstairs and we'll get this call connected again.' And he laughed. He said, 'Nah, it's fine. Gives me time to play Words with Friends.' And he'd have his iPad up and be playing Words with Friends with God knows who. I think he actually enjoyed being put on hold by Putin, because it gave him a few minutes of time just to chill."

Occasionally, the Sit Room staff turned the tables on the Russians. A duty officer who could do a passable impression of the president would get on the line and imitate his "hello." The U.S. side would then hear a click, followed by Putin's voice. "And then you heard a Sit Room duty officer break in and go, 'President Putin, please hold for the president of the United States.' Then boom, you have the U.S. president come on," says Hargis. Mission accomplished, though Hargis always felt a little bad about the ruse. "You had to think, *Oh, I bet someone is on their way to Siberia right now. I got someone in trouble.*"

Prank calls to the Sit Room are not unheard of. When in doubt, duty officers occasionally give little pop quizzes to callers who claim to be heads of state (or calling on behalf of one). Usually, these questions will root out impostors, but every once in a while, the person turns out to be who they say they are. Once, during the Reagan administration, someone called claiming to be Prince Charles. People thought it was a crank call, but then David Sedney quizzed the man on British history. He answered everything correctly—and it turned out that it was indeed Charles. Yet even when the caller is who he or she claims to be, the Sit Room never connects the person to the president. Instead, they report it to the national security adviser, who sets up a return call for later.

Even for scheduled calls, it can be difficult to confirm who's on the other end of the line. In March 2012, Saudi Arabian crown prince Nayef bin Abdulaziz flew to Ohio for medical treatment at the Cleveland Clinic. President Obama wanted to offer his well-wishes, so the Sit Room tried to arrange a call between the Oval and the clinic. But the receptionist there didn't believe it. "They said, 'Sure, fella!' and hung up," recalls Drew Roberts. "We called five more times with various 'No, wait! I'm serious!' ploys and were hung up on five more times." Finally, he says, the Sit Room staff stole a plot point from a scene in the movie *The American President*: "The sixth time we called back, we told them to call the number we provided, which was the White House switchboard, and ask for the Situation Room." They did, and the president finally got to wish the Saudi prince well.

Clinton had an excellent relationship with Tony Blair, and he was obviously comfortable speaking his mind. But when Clinton first came to office, Conservative party leader John Major was the prime minister—and relations between those two were decidedly chillier. Toward the end of the 1992 presidential campaign, Major had approved a search for damaging information about candidate Clinton, in hopes of helping George H. W. Bush win reelection. Upon taking office in 1993, the new president was still salty about it.

Jim Reed, who was the Sit Room director at that time, remembers how the first scheduled call between the two leaders unfolded.

"We set up the phone call," he told me, "and I think we were on the phone with John Major for perhaps forty-five minutes. It was a very long time, and we're sitting there making small talk with [him]" while

Clinton kept him waiting. This was obviously a power play—but the new president wasn't content simply with keeping his counterpart waiting. "[Major] finally realized Clinton wasn't going to take his call. And he said, 'This is ridiculous!' and slammed down the phone."

I asked Reed if the Sit Room staff knew in advance that Clinton had no intention of taking the call. "No, he didn't tell us that this was his way of punking John Major," Reed said with a laugh. "When we finally called back up to the Oval Office to let him know that Major had hung up the phone, I think Clinton had already departed for the Army-Navy golf course...You know, for a man who's a brand-new president, I thought it was a pretty good way of sending a message to a foreign leader: *Don't mess with me.*"

The vast majority of head-of-state calls are conducted over nonsecure telephone lines.

Perhaps the strangest occurred when the Sit Room had to find a Turkish interpreter with the requisite security clearance on extremely short notice. President Obama needed to speak with Turkish prime minister Recep Tayyip Erdogan, but the only available interpreter was driving down I-95 from New Jersey to D.C. She agreed to interpret while driving, and with all parties alerted to the unusual circumstance, the call went forward.

"About halfway through the call, she interrupted the conversation, saying she needed a three-minute break, which annoyed both President Obama and Prime Minister Erdogan," Drew Roberts remembers. She told them she was about to drive through a tunnel near Baltimore and would lose cell service there, but that once through, she'd pull over and call them back. "No more than two minutes after she did this, we hear a knock on her window, and it's the state police going, 'Ma'am, are you okay? Do you need assistance?' And she's going, 'No, no! I'm fine! I'm just trying to finish a phone call!'"

————◄o►————

To this day, none of the calls between heads of state are recorded. Instead, three Sit Room staffers listen in on headsets, typing furiously as the two parties talk. When the call is finished, they compare notes and try to compile as accurate a document as possible. This is called the memcon—the memorandum of conversation. And creating it is a stressful, thankless job.

"Our best friends during this time were the talking points outline provided for us in advance by the White House staff and the word 'inaudible' to fill in conversation gaps we missed," says Drew Roberts. Trying to create an accurate record of two people speaking in real time is incredibly difficult. "Now throw in interpreters, broken English, and multiple other people on the call speaking when we cannot see them," he says, and it's nearly impossible to create a document that's 100 percent accurate.

"Erdogan talked so fast, and he talked in broken English," recalls Roberts. "He would say something, and if you paused to say, 'What was that word? I don't know what he meant by that,' you're two sentences gone. He's just plowed on...We always said, 'Just hire stenographers, for God's sake!' But they never would." Anyone listening in to the president's calls had to be an intelligence professional with a security clearance.

"The reason we had two intelligence analysts during the day was to cover the extra workload of typing out what we were hearing on presidential phone calls," Rob Hargis told me. Everyone would do their best to capture the conversation, and at the end, "we would look at each other and go, 'Okay. One of us now has to produce the memcon.'" Nobody wanted to do it, so the group would do a round of rock-paper-scissors. "Everybody would print out what they had typed in a Word document to the best of their ability, and give them all to the poor SOB" who lost the game. That person would have to painstakingly piece together the full conversation into a memcon.

"It wasn't an exact conversation," says Hargis. "It wasn't a legal transcript." So, why not just record the phone calls, in order to have the exact words?

"I was told that 'gentlemen don't record other gentlemen's conversations,'" Tony Campanella says. "I didn't believe it. I believe it was the plausible deniability." In Campanella's view, the president might prefer to have a little wiggle room. "Maybe they wanted the human error in there so the president could turn around and say, 'No, that's not what I said. Somebody in the Sit Room misunderstood.'" This would come into play in the infamous call between President Trump and Ukrainian president Volodymyr Zelensky that led to his first impeachment.

Phone calls weren't the only way the president could communicate with other global leaders. There were also dedicated video connections—created, not surprisingly, by the ever-present Gary Bresnahan. He told me about the impetus for setting them up, during George H. W. Bush's administration.

"Bush 41 was in the lower conference room, and he was talking to the Iraqi prime minister," Bresnahan told me. "It was scheduled for a certain time, say two o'clock. And the president went down there, and half an hour later they came out. They never did the call." Assistant secretary of defense Steve Hadley walked out of the Sit Room, his face stony, and said, "Gary, it didn't happen. You need to fix this." Hadley wasn't happy, but he was professional about it. Then, Condoleezza Rice emerged, giving Bresnahan a death stare. "Steve Hadley yells like a mouse," Bresnahan told me. "Condi Rice yells with her eyes."

As it turned out, the problem wasn't technological—it was a security issue, with the Iraqi prime minister unable to get to the designated phone in time for the call. "When does security become a comm guy's problem?" Bresnahan asks. The answer is, when the president demands an untraceable way to communicate with someone. Which is how, two days later, Bresnahan found himself on a plane to Iraq, tasked with setting up a secure video for the Iraqi prime minister on his own turf.

Once Bresnahan set up that first dedicated connection, others followed. "There's twenty-five of them now out there," he told me, "to talk to adversaries as well as our friends. And I've done every one of 'em."

For decades, Bresnahan kept the Situation Room on the cutting edge of audio and visual technology. But in other respects, the Sit Room tended to lag behind the times. During Clinton's second term, articles from the *Washington Post* and *New York Times* were still circulated by making photocopies of the physical newspapers and faxing them. Then duty officers started noticing that the papers' websites were posting all the news online. Around 1998—nine years after the invention of the World Wide Web, four years after the Yahoo! search engine went online and two years after the "dancing baby" became the first viral video—senior director Kevin Cosgriff finally had an "Internet terminal" installed in the Situation Room. It was well and truly overdue.

"Even in '97, they didn't have any kind of automated message handling system," Tony Campanella recalls. "So we would just be reviewing feeds of message traffic that came either out of CIA, the State Department, DOD, NSA...and we would have distribution groups that would send out those messages." Much of the duty officers' time was spent compiling mundane message traffic, a time-consuming job that didn't take advantage of their skill sets. So when Kevin Cosgriff asked his staff how they would modernize the Sit Room, Campanella was ready with an answer.

"One of the things I was an advocate for was doing some kind of push system, instead of *us* being the push system," he told me, referring to the kinds of alerts we all get every day now on our phones. The technology existed for NSC members to develop a profile of subjects they were interested in, then have that intelligence automatically sent to them. And yet, "It was still GS-11 Tony Campanella reading the message traffic and going, 'Ehhh, I guess [a higher-up] needs to see this,'" he said. "It was a little bit backwards."

Tony Lake was also dismayed by the Sit Room's lack of capabilities. In his book 6 *Nightmares: The Real Threats to American Security*, he opined that this was emblematic of bigger problems facing the nation: "One day in 1996 the President's national security team (I was his national security adviser) met for a discussion of chemical and biological terrorism. I found the low-tech setting symbolic of our position in addressing such new threats to our nation's security."

When considering what the Sit Room does on a 24/7 basis, however, it's understandable why change is slow to come. The staff must fulfill its core function of funneling information to the president. They cannot miss a beat. Even upgrades to equipment have to be done in a way that minimizes disruption, as Elliott Powell described to me. "When we were changing networks, going from copper to fiber optic, that train had to continue on regardless," he said. The team built a whole backup network, to make absolutely sure there was no gap in service. "It's the old saying," Powell laughed. "How do you eat an eight-hundred-pound gorilla? One bite at a time."

◄○►

OF ALL THE incredible technological feats Gary Bresnahan pulled off, one request caught him completely off guard.

It came in the summer of 1998. "Sandy Berger calls me and says,

'Gary, Charles Ruff is going to call you.'" Ruff, who was then serving as White House counsel, was representing the president in the investigation over the Clintons' long-ago real estate deal known as Whitewater. In the course of the investigation, independent counsel Kenneth Starr's team had uncovered his relationship with twenty-two-year-old White House intern Monica Lewinsky, a revelation that sent a seismic jolt through Washington, D.C., and beyond.

In late July, Lewinsky received immunity in exchange for testifying to a grand jury about the relationship. She directly contradicted statements Clinton had earlier made under oath, confirming that they had been intimately involved. Now in legal peril, he agreed to give taped testimony to the grand jury. Which is why Sandy Berger was calling Gary Bresnahan.

Berger told him, "When Chuck Ruff calls, he's gonna say that the president wants you to be his videographer for the Whitewater thing," Bresnahan recalls. "I said, 'Why me? I'm not a videographer. I can spell the word "videographer," but that's about it. You need a professional.' He said, 'No, they want you because they can trust you.'"

"Clinton wanted it to be secure," Richard Clarke told me. "He didn't want to have the deposition in the lawyer's office. He wanted to have the deposition with him in the White House. He wanted it to be highly secure, point to point. And no unauthorized recording." He chose the Map Room—the former billiard room where, more than four decades earlier, FDR had set up his Sit Room–style war headquarters—to make the videos.

"All these press people were [assuming], 'Oh, we'll be able to get this link and hear everything they say in the Map Room,'" Bresnahan recalls. "I so badly wanted to tell somebody, 'They're not gonna get this,' because we used one of our NSA encryptions." He was taking no chances. The president wanted his testimony to be secure, so

Bresnahan would make absolutely sure that it was. "We wired that place," he said.

Bresnahan told me about one of the practice sessions, in which the president's lawyers peppered him with questions about the Whitewater deal. "They were drilling him," Bresnahan recalls, and then they "took a break. And he's in a corner of that room . . . and he turns to me, which, I'm ten feet from him, and he goes, 'How do you think I'm doing?' I said, 'You're doing great, sir!' You know—how do I know?"

By this point in his career, Bresnahan had been present for dozens of extraordinary situations and great historical moments. He masterminded the communications between President Carter and the Desert One rescue mission. He was at the hospital when President Reagan underwent surgery following the assassination attempt. He traveled to Iran in 1986 on the secret "cake and Bible" mission, when national security adviser Robert McFarlane gave a Bible inscribed by Reagan to the Iranian leadership. He snuck into Beijing following the Tiananmen Square massacre. Later, he would set up the communications between President Obama and the team that took out Osama bin Laden. He would be present in the Sit Room complex when bin Laden was killed, and he was also there on September 11, 2001. Bresnahan is the most important White House figure you never heard of, the guy jerry-rigging technology for every turn of history throughout seven presidential administrations.

And when I asked him what his most incredible memory of all those times was, he said, "Doing all the stuff for Clinton during his time from Whitewater on to the impeachment stuff. That was quite exciting for me, as a technical guy, being totally involved with that." He remembers thinking, *I can't believe I'm in the Map Room with the president of the United States [testifying] in a session of court.*

"It was amazing," he said.

———◄○►———

AS THE TWENTIETH century drew to a close, Americans were on edge. In August 1998, simultaneous terrorist bombings of U.S. embassies in Tanzania and Kenya killed more than two hundred people. Four months later, President Clinton was impeached for lying under oath and obstruction of justice in the Lewinsky affair—at that time only the second president in history, after Andrew Johnson, to have been impeached. In 1999, two students at Columbine High School in Colorado murdered twelve of their classmates and a teacher, horrifying the nation. And in October of that year, EgyptAir Flight 990 plummeted into the ocean off the coast of Nantucket, killing everyone aboard, in a crash that was later deemed intentional.

Adding to the feelings of dread and uncertainty was the looming threat of the Y2K bug. For decades, the code underlying computer programs had been written using only the last two digits of the year. With the year 2000 coming, many feared that these programs would confuse "00" with the year 1900, causing them to crash. Some predicted worldwide outages of banks, stock markets, airline systems—anything that relied on computers. The worst doomsayers warned that these disruptions would provoke an apocalyptic societal meltdown.

In the months leading up to December 31, 1999, businesses, NGOs and governmental agencies spent hundreds of millions of dollars to update code in hopes of averting catastrophe. Coders developed and disseminated patches, without any real idea if they would work—or even if they were truly needed. Radio provocateurs like Glenn Beck and Alex Jones revved up their listeners, who rushed to buy software-fixing kits along with doomsday prep staples such as freeze-dried foods, guns and gold bars.

Richard Clarke was "the lead White House person for Y2K," Gary

Bresnahan told me. A room at the General Services Administration served as Y2K headquarters, and in the months leading up to New Year's Eve, Clarke, Bresnahan and others had multiple meetings to prepare for every possible outcome. In the Sit Room, director Elliott Powell recalls, "We did look at what we would do for backup, and how quickly it would take to put up—I don't want to say a 'shadow network,' but another network to run in parallel.

"We had those computers set up just in case, because if worse came to worst, we're expected to continue to keep going," Powell told me. "Everybody was prepping for the worst and hoping for the best."

"Talk about crisis, I don't think I slept for the three days leading up to it," deputy national security adviser Jim Steinberg told me—but not because he was worried about a possible computer meltdown.

"I had no idea about Y2K," he told me, "but we had actual knowledge of planned terrorist attacks." On December 14, U.S. border guards at Port Angeles, Washington, had detained an Algerian man named Ahmed Ressam, who turned out to have more than a hundred pounds of urea sulfate in the trunk of his car. Ressam, who had trained under al-Qaeda in Afghanistan, revealed that his mission was to blow up Los Angeles International Airport on New Year's Eve.

"So, a known plot had been thwarted. But the thing about terrorism is," Steinberg says, "it's not the plots that you discover that you worry about. It's the plots you haven't discovered." In the last two weeks of December, there were meetings every day, because the chatter—meaning intercepted communications among potential terrorists—was constant. "If you ever saw *Spinal Tap*," he said, referencing the classic film *This Is Spinal Tap*, "we were at eleven on terrorism. We were at ten on Y2K."

When December 31 finally arrived, Steinberg was at home. "I was so sure that something would happen, that the terrorists...would get through," he told me. "The whole thing was terrifying—the combination of Y2K and a terrorist attack." All day and into the night, Steinberg waited for the dreaded phone call. "It's just, 'Is the phone gonna ring? Is the phone gonna ring?'"

Elliott Powell was in the Situation Room on December 31. "The funniest thing about that was, of course, Australia gets the New Year first" because of time zone differences, he recalls. "So, you're in the Sit Room, and the president's there and the vice president's there [by phone] and all the other principals from the other places are there, and it's like, *Okay, here we go now*." One million revelers in Sydney rang in the New Year with hugs, drinks and a huge show of fireworks over the harbor. And the lights stayed on, and the ATMs kept dispensing cash. All was well. It was 10:01 a.m. in Washington, D.C.

"The moment the clock struck midnight [in Australia], I know I breathed a sigh of relief, and I think everybody on the other end did as well," Powell recalls. "I think we all just wished each other Happy New Year, and *Hey, here we go—on to the new millennium!*" By the time midnight was striking in Europe, hours later, "it was just me and the other guy in the Situation Room for England," Powell says. The Y2K crisis had ended with not so much as a whimper. But the threat of terrorism was still real, as the United States had yet to ring in the New Year.

Elliott Powell remained in the Situation Room until midnight East Coast time, popping open a bottle of champagne. Jim Steinberg stayed on high alert at home for another three hours, until midnight Pacific time. At that point, he too finally breathed a sigh of relief: There hadn't been a massive terrorist attack on American soil. Everything was going to be fine.

Or so we all thought.

Chapter 9

"THIS IS WHERE WE FIGHT FROM"

———⟡———

O N THE MORNING of September 11, 2001, Situation Room senior duty officer Ed Padinske had an important mission: He and his wife, Heidi, were taking their daughter to her first day of preschool in Fairfax, Virginia.

At the school, Padinske gamely folded his six-foot-one frame into a kindergarten-sized colored plastic chair for the orientation. "I'm just sitting there trying to get comfortable," he told me, "and then one of the teacher's aides came in and tapped me on the shoulder and said, 'I think you may need to call work.'" The aide, who knew that Padinske worked at the White House, had heard something about a plane hitting the World Trade Center.

Padinske jumped up from the tiny chair and was heading toward the parking lot when his pager went off. This was a signal from fellow senior duty officer Rob Hargis that he and others should be "ready to surge into the Situation Room," Padinske recalls, "or in the case of circumstances that may involve a threat to the White House, a COOP—a continuity of operations plan, where there's alternate locations for the Situation Room." He got in his car, turned on the radio, and called the Sit Room from his cell phone. A watch officer told him that *two* planes had now struck the towers, in what was clearly a terrorist attack.

That was all Padinske needed to hear. He raced back into the school, grabbed his wife and daughter, and said, "We have to go." He flew down the Fairfax County Parkway at "about a hundred miles an hour, pulled in, dropped them off, changed into something resembling professional attire"—in this case, his U.S. Navy uniform—"and started making my way up to I-95," he says. At 9:37 a.m., as Padinske was racing toward Washington, American Airlines Flight 77 made its fatal, spiraling descent and smashed into the Pentagon.

He called the Sit Room again, getting Hargis on the line. "I don't remember the exact words, but the basis of it was, 'There are planes missing,'" he recalls. Hargis instructed him not to come to the White House, in case a hijacked plane was headed there. "We may need you to establish us elsewhere," Hargis told him—a strikingly clinical way of implying that the Sit Room, and everyone in it, might not survive the morning.

For the next half hour or so, Padinske drove around slowly, "far enough away from the White House as necessary," he says. Washington, D.C., had shut down, with police and National Guard rushing to set up checkpoints. Just after ten a.m., when United Flight 93 went down near Shanksville, Pennsylvania, Padinske made a decision: He was going to the Situation Room. He approached a checkpoint, held up his West Wing badge, pointed at the Ellipse and said, "I need to go there."

Padinske raced to the White House, which had been evacuated at 9:45 a.m. (The Capitol would receive the order within the next half hour.) But down in the Sit Room, a stalwart group of duty officers and other staff refused to leave. In fact, many of those who, like Padinske, weren't even on duty that morning had insisted on coming in.

Bob Schubert, a Marine officer who was off that day, saw the news and made the snap decision to head to the Sit Room. Knowing that the city was on lockdown, he decided against taking his car, instead hopping on his bicycle and pedaling furiously toward the White House. When D.C. cops stopped him near the Washington Monument, he flashed his badge and got a police escort to the White House, riding his bike behind the car.

"I got a call from West Gate Secret Service," recalls Hargis, "and they said, 'Rob, there's a Bob Schubert here. Will you authorize him to come in?' I said, 'Yep, send him in.' Bob looked at the Secret Service officer and said, 'Hey, if I leave my bike here, will you make sure no one takes it?'"

Like the firefighters in New York who rushed toward the burning towers, Sit Room staffers raced toward the White House. But the more people showed up, the more concerned Hargis got about two possible complications. "One, no one's going to be around to relieve us when we come off duty," Hargis told me. "And two, if we get hit, there's no one to reconstitute the Sit Room somewhere else."

Three minutes after the White House got the evacuation order, "one of the Secret Service officers came around, hit the phone"—the security videophone outside the Sit Room door—"and said, 'We're evacuating. You guys need to go.' And we said, 'Okay,' and went back to work," Hargis recalls. No one had any intention of leaving.

A few minutes later, NSC executive secretary Steve Biegun, who happened to be in New York that morning, called the Sit Room. "Hey, we just heard the White House evacuated," he said. "Why are you guys still there? The White House could be a target."

"We can't evacuate," Hargis told him. "If we leave, the president will have massively degraded communications." For all the planning that went into the White House's sophisticated communications networks, the terror attacks created a problem no one had foreseen.

"Here's the little-known issue that we had that day," Hargis told me. "Presidential communications were set up to support the president wherever he was, and the Sit Room was the node for that... [so] if the president is on Air Force One, we could get to it through UHF radios and phones." Similarly, if the president was in the Presidential Emergency Operations Center (PEOC), the bunker-like shelter underneath the East Wing that serves as an emergency headquarters, "we could get to him through all the lines we had set up inside the eighteen acres" of the White House complex, said Hargis.

"You know what they didn't have? They didn't have good comms links between the shelter and the aircraft," Hargis told me. "Because why would the president ever need to call himself?" No one had imagined the scenario that arose on 9/11, with President Bush on Air Force One and many of his closest advisers in the PEOC: Vice President Cheney, national security adviser Condoleezza Rice, counselor Karen Hughes and many others. If the Sit Room shut down, there would be no direct line between them.

But Steve Biegun wouldn't give up. He called the Sit Room several times, each time insisting that people leave. Finally, a frustrated Hargis spelled it out for him. "I said, 'Here's the deal. I'm going to let everybody know we need to evacuate.' And I turned and I said, 'Okay, we're being ordered to evacuate!' There was a two- or three-second pause. People kind of looked around, looked at me, and then went right back to work. And I said, 'Steve, I've ordered everyone to evacuate. We can talk about this when you get back.'"

Around the time Ed Padinske arrived at the Sit Room, senior

director for defense policy Frank Miller also walked in. He too urged the staff to leave, believing that at any moment a hijacked jet could turn the White House into flaming rubble. But still everyone refused. "I'm a Navy guy, so these are general quarters stations," Padinske recalls, using the term for battle stations on a ship at sea. "This is where we fight from. And the president and Dr. Rice and the entire NSC needs us here. So we'll take the risk."

Finally realizing that none of the twenty-odd people in the complex were budging, Miller changed tack. "Great," he said. "Give me your names and Social Security numbers, because we want to know what bodies to look for." He handed Hargis a pad and pen, and one by one, every person there jotted down their vital information.

To Padinske, this was "jaw-dropping." Not Hargis. "It wasn't a big dramatic moment," he recalls. "It was really understated." No one panicked in the Situation Room. Miller gave the handwritten list to a Navy enlistee who was working as a Sit Room communications assistant, with instructions to type it up and send it via secure fax to watch centers, including the CIA and Air Force One. This became known as the "dead list"—the official record of who would have perished in the Sit Room if the White House had been destroyed.

It wasn't only the Situation Room staffers who stayed. Two women from the chief of staff's office asked permission to remain in the complex when the rest of the White House evacuated. And the U.S. Navy detailees to the White House mess, which was adjacent to the Sit Room, also refused to leave. "There's a senior chief in there that I had befriended just because I was a Navy guy in the Sit Room," recalls Ed Padinske. "He would always make me great Tex-Mex fries and other things. So I went to him and said, 'Hey, Senior Chief, the West Wing is evacuated. You guys are free to go.'

"And he said, 'Sir, what are *you* doing?' I said, 'Well, we're staying here.'

"He said, 'You guys are gonna need to eat. What do you want?' And he just started making food for us and sending it in."

———◄○►———

THE DIRECTOR OF the Situation Room, U.S. Navy captain Deborah Loewer, wasn't in the complex on the morning of September 11. She was in Sarasota, Florida, with President Bush.

Anytime the president traveled, he was accompanied by one of three NSC reps—either the executive secretary, the deputy executive secretary, or the Sit Room director. It was just a coincidence—"purely dumb luck, a one in three chance," as Rob Hargis put it—that Loewer was with him that day. The president was scheduled to visit a local elementary school, where he would read to a classroom of second graders.

"I had just finished briefing the president with [CIA analyst] Mike Morell at the hotel," Loewer told me. "And we jumped into the motorcade. We were en route to Emma E. Booker Elementary School when, at 8:48 a.m., my cell phone rang." It was Hargis, calling from the Sit Room.

"Deb," he said, "we have this just in, saw it on a news feed. At 8:46 an aircraft impacted the World Trade Center."

"OK," Loewer replied. "Tell me what you've got." She wasn't particularly bothered, she told me, "because we get these kinds of reports all the time, that an airplane hit a big building." Hargis said he didn't know much yet about the pilot, the aircraft, the weather or other details. "I'm going, 'So what?'" she recalls. But as she thought about it, she realized that there would be press at the elementary school, and they might ask President Bush about the crash. So, when the motorcade arrived, "I jumped out of the control vehicle and ran up to the [presidential] limo." She told chief of staff Andrew Card and the president what she knew, and the group headed into the school.

White House technicians had set up a communications room in the school, and Loewer now made her way to it. "Have you checked all the secure comms?" she asked. Assured that the technicians had everything in order, she said, "Can you guys go find a TV?"

"They looked at me like I was crazy," she recalls. But she said it again. "Find me a TV." It was now 9:00 a.m. The president walked through the comms room to get to the classroom, and Loewer poked her head in after him, to see what the setup was in there. She still didn't know whether this plane crash was anything more than an accident, but she wanted to be prepared.

"And then I looked up, and there was a TV," she recalls. "I said, 'Okay, plug it in and turn on CNN.'" Using one of the secure phones, she then called Rob Hargis in the Situation Room. "And Rob gives me the report that turns my stomach. He says, 'Deborah, the weather is clear. It was a jetliner. The pilot had no issues. The plane flew straight into the tower.'

"I think my heart stopped," Loewer says. She had begun taking notes: *This feels really bad.* She stayed on the line with Hargis, who was also watching CNN in the Sit Room, as the two of them tried to sort out what was happening.

Rob Hargis describes what happened next. "We've got a big plasma screen up, and we were looking, and I had Captain Loewer on the phone." Hargis watched as CNN showed footage of a plane streaking toward the tower. "Hang on a second," he told Loewer. "There's a replay." But then he noticed the word "LIVE" in the corner of the screen. "And in the course of one and a half seconds, I realized that the first building is on fire, and I'm watching a second plane come across the screen." The jet sliced into the South Tower and exploded in a gargantuan fireball.

"What the—" Loewer uttered.

"Ma'am, a second aircraft has hit the second tower," Hargis said. "We are under attack."

"It was an 'oh my god' moment," Loewer recalls. "I said, 'Rob, I gotta go.' He said, 'Deb, I gotta go.' We both slammed the phone down because we both knew what we had to do."

Loewer knew there were two cardinal rules to traveling with President Bush: He always had to be on time, and he was never to be interrupted. But this wasn't like any other time. So she walked up to the Secret Service agent guarding the classroom door. "He gave me the *no, you are not gonna interrupt the president* look. And I just pointed to the TV, and I said, 'Look at that. I'm going in.' And he said, 'Yes, ma'am.' And he opened the door.

"The president saw me walk in," she recalls. "It was maybe fifteen feet from where he was sitting to where the door was. And so he knew something was up." Loewer had traveled many times with Bush, "so he knew I wasn't gonna come in just because I was being a nosy-nose. That's not gonna happen. I found Andy [Card], and I whispered to him what had happened. I said, 'A second aircraft has impacted into a second World Trade Center tower. The nation is under attack.'

"It didn't even strike me what I had just said. I mean, it was automatic in my brain: *This is what's happening,*" Loewer told me. "I said that to Andy. And Andy looked up at me, and I said it again." It was as if Card had to hear it twice to fully comprehend what she was telling him. And then he walked to the president, leaned down and whispered into his ear.

The images of Card whispering to the president became famous, as did the words he said: "A second plane hit the second tower. America is under attack." What most people don't realize, though, is that those words originated in the Situation Room, coming from Rob Hargis, through Deb Loewer, to Andy Card, to the president.

AT THE TIME the second plane hit, national security adviser Condi Rice was in the Situation Room complex. She was doing her normal rounds, asking NSC staff for updates from around the globe, when an aide handed her a note. She too understood instantly that the United States was under attack.

"There was a back room off the Situation Room where all the comms were," she recalls. "I went back there to try to call Colin [Powell], who was in Peru. I tried to call [CIA director] George Tenet. He'd already gone to a bunker. And then I tried to call Don Rumsfeld, and his phone was just ringing and ringing." At around 9:40 a.m., she happened to glance behind her at one of the TVs and saw that a plane had now hit the Pentagon. Was Rumsfeld alive? Or was he in the inferno now consuming one side of the Pentagon? Rice hardly had time to think before Secret Service agents suddenly appeared at her side, jostling her roughly out of the room.

"I was physically taken—almost levitated," she told me. "They're lifting and pushing at the same time. It's incredibly disorienting." The agents were tasked with getting Rice to the PEOC bunker as quickly as possible, but she stopped them. "There's a phone outside the Situation Room," she recalls. "I said, 'No, no, no! I gotta call the president.' So I called him from just outside the Situation Room and told him he couldn't come back, that we were under attack."

The world outside descended into chaos, but the Sit Room staff stayed at their posts, methodically managing the incoming. "We rolled right into coordination," Rob Hargis told me. "Instantly, it's *We're under attack. What do we need to do? Who do we need to call from the White House?*...There was zero panic. There was zero *I gotta call [my] family.*" When he could steal a moment, Hargis would call spouses of those in the room, to let them know that everyone was safe but they would probably be late coming home.

I asked Hargis what kind of training helped Sit Room staff act so coolly under pressure. "A lot of the drills I would run with my team were specifically to build that muscle memory," he told me. "Think of professional athletes. They get hit, or they get hurt, and they still cross the finish line, because they can disconnect emotion and doubt with 'This is the job I'm here for.'" Referring to the more mundane task of typing up memcons, he added wryly, "You brought me over so I could type with two fingers when I'm listening to the president talk. But *this* is what I'm not supposed to fail at."

Deputy national security adviser Steve Hadley recalls several disparate groups working in the Sit Room complex as events unfolded. "Dick Clarke had his counterterrorism working group in a back room," he told me. "And in the main [conference] room, I had assembled the NSC staff to handle all the various aspects of how to respond. We got word that another plane was headed toward Washington and that they were evacuating the White House and the Old Executive Office Building." But just as the duty officers had done, the NSC staff also elected to stay. "We all thought, *No, the president needs us to stay and keep doing what we're doing.*"

About five minutes later, Condi Rice called Hadley and told him to come immediately to the PEOC, before the door was shut and the room secured.

"I can't go," Hadley told her. "We just decided that we're all going to take the risk of staying here…I can't leave and go to the safety of the bunker—that's not the leadership we want to show the troops."

"I don't care," Rice responded. "I need you down here." Reluctantly, Hadley left his Sit Room post and hustled over to the East Wing.

Drew Roberts described the PEOC bunker as being like an underground submarine. "It always smelled funny down there. And my Navy friends said it smelled like the inside of a boat, because it's metal all the way around." Once the room was sealed, no one else would be allowed in.

Hadley got there in time, and he found that the conference-room-sized space was already crammed with people. In addition to Cheney, Rice and Hughes, many top figures would take refuge in the PEOC that day, including adviser Mary Matalin, deputy chief of staff Josh Bolten, transportation secretary Norman Mineta, First Lady Laura Bush and Second Lady Lynne Cheney, along with Secret Service agents and a handful of other staffers. Laura Bush memorably described walking "along old tile floors with pipes hanging from the ceiling and all kinds of mechanical equipment" to get to the bunker.

"A bunch of people showed up," Josh Bolten told me. "And at some point, whoever was in charge of the watch there comes over to me and says, 'Uh, sir, there are too many people in this room. We're going to run out of oxygen.' He said, 'It's not configured to provide adequate oxygen for this many people.' And I could actually feel it."

Safely underground, the PEOC bunker was the only place in the White House that might survive the impact of a jetliner. If a hijacked plane really was heading for the complex, then sending someone out of the PEOC was like issuing a death sentence. "Someone has to take the responsibility," recalls Bolten. "The watch officer can't do that. And you probably shouldn't be asking the vice president. And so I had to pick."

How do you tell someone they have to leave the safe space in the middle of a catastrophe? "Very gently," Bolten told me.

Lack of sufficient oxygen wasn't the only problem in the PEOC that day. "One thing that 9/11 revealed was that we didn't actually have good comms in the Situation Room," Rice told me. "When we got to the PEOC, we realized that we couldn't simultaneously have televisions on and talk to the Situation Room. One or the other would cut out. [And] we just had terrible communications with Air Force One."

With all the information that came out in the weeks and months following 9/11, it's easy to forget how chaotic and confusing that day actually was. Rumors flew about how many planes were still unaccounted for and where they might be heading. Reports came out that the State Department had been bombed. As Rob Hargis was working in the Sit Room, he received a call asking whether the EEOB was on fire. He asked a duty officer named John Sherman to check, and Sherman rose from his desk, walked to a bank of windows along one side of the complex, looked out and said, "Well, if it is, it's not bad."

Everyone was desperate for information, and the technical breakdowns created immense frustration up and down the chain of command. "The VP was *pissed*," Bolten recalls. "And I rarely saw him actually visibly angry. I recall him slamming the phone down once and cursing." In the midst of an attack on American soil, the president and vice president kept getting cut off when they tried to talk. "I don't know whether that was at the bunker end or at the Air Force One end," says Bolten, "but it was a high degree of frustration."

I asked Gary Bresnahan about the communications problems on 9/11. "Everybody was sort of bitching and complaining that they couldn't do anything," he recalls. "But I always defended by saying, 'Well, the man got through.' They were able to do what they needed." Yet he acknowledged that the complaints about 9/11 were the catalyst for major Sit Room renovations. "You know, as the provider, you hear that," he told me. But that doesn't salve his irritation about the complaints.

"The president [said] how everything sucked and didn't work well, and it actually worked," Bresnahan says. "It did work. He was just frustrated because he wasn't here."

On that point, at least, everyone agrees: President Bush desperately wanted to be in Washington, D.C.

EARLY IN THE morning of September 11—before al-Qaeda launched its attacks—Secret Service agents had told Deb Loewer that they had a credible threat of harm against the president. So, by the time two planes had crashed into the World Trade Center, the president's team was on high alert. Was he the next target? No one knew for sure, and the information flooding in from all sides was more confusing than clarifying.

"The best filter in the world is the White House Situation Room," Loewer told me. "But there were a whole lot of other entities—Secret Service, state and local police, a whole gang of different sources coming into the traveling party when we were down there in Sarasota." One source reported that unknown people were standing at the end of the runway where Air Force One was scheduled to take off. "And so there's an assumption," Loewer recalls, "that these suspicious people could possibly have MANPADS"—hand-held surface-to-air missiles capable of shooting down the president's jet.

This led to the most extraordinary moment of Deb Loewer's professional life. She had boarded Air Force One with the rest of the group, and while people buckled into their seats, she stood by the president at his traveling desk to brief him. At the time, she didn't know about the potential threat at the end of the runway. But the pilot, Colonel Mark Tillman, knew. And he made the decision to get the plane as high into the air as possible, as quickly as he could.

"The door closes at the front of the aircraft, and the plane starts to move all of a sudden," Loewer recalls. "I mean, the engines scream, and you feel everything on the plane shaking. The president looked at me, and I looked at him, and I knew there was no way I was gonna get back to the staff area and get buckled up before that plane took off," she says. And then the jet shot into the sky on a hockey-stick trajectory. As Bush adviser Karl Rove would later say, the captain "stood that thing on its tail—nose up, tail down, like we were on a roller coaster."

Loewer hit the floor, attempting to brace herself with "one foot on his desk, my back against a bookcase," she recalls. As Air Force One shot skyward, she went weightless. "The president of the United States put his hand in front of me," she recalls. "I literally came off the floor, and he held on to me." Like a parent protecting a child when a car makes a sudden stop, Bush kept his arm across Loewer, saving her from being thrown about the cabin and seriously injured. "That was the moment that bonded George W. Bush and Deborah Loewer for life," she told me.

Within minutes, the plane was at 30,000 feet, well on its way to an extremely high cruising altitude of 45,000 feet. Loewer recovered and went to her seat. If she was shaken, she didn't show it. Because now it was time to focus on the job at hand: making sure the president could communicate with whomever he wanted.

"I was the connection to the White House, and all the communication to the WHSR, to the PEOC, to everything," Loewer told me. "I went up to the comm deck and basically commandeered it in the name of the National Security Council of the White House." She knew that others on the plane would want to use the comms channels, and she intended to shut that down. "One of the military guys wants to call and check on X, and somebody else wants to check on Y," she recalls. "But at that point the communication circuits were strictly going to be used for the president of the United States."

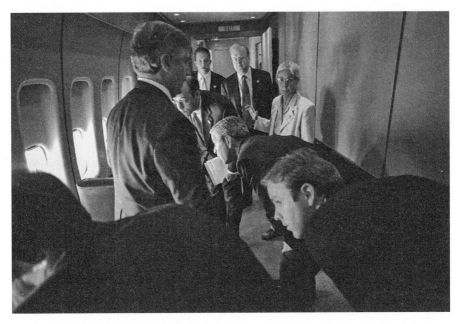

Sit Room director Deb Loewer was traveling with President Bush on 9/11. Seen here on Air Force One. | *Photo by Eric Draper, courtesy of the George W. Bush Presidential Library*

Like Bresnahan, Loewer recalls the communications working well enough that day. "The president had no problem communicating," she told me. "From Air Force One, the president of the United States was in communication with the vice president or whoever else he wanted to speak with. That was not an issue." One of the first connections she made was to Vice President Cheney and Secretary Rice in the PEOC. "They had an extensive conversation, of which the prelude was that the Pentagon was hit at 9:37," she recalls. "We were just finding that out when we were up at altitude." This new piece of information, plus uncertainty about how many planes were still unaccounted for, would be the deciding factor in keeping President Bush out of Washington, D.C., for most of the day.

"Andy Card and the military aide and I got together and discussed where we would go," recalls Loewer. "And my recommendation was Offutt Air Force Base in Nebraska." Alternatively, "There was also a discussion of keeping the plane in the sky for a long time, and we could do that," because Air Force One has a midair refueling capability. The jet circled for about twenty-five minutes while these discussions continued. Finally, President Bush decided he wanted to land at Barksdale Air Force Base in northwest Louisiana, so he could make a statement.

On the ground at Barksdale, Loewer recognized an officer named Curtis Bedke, whom she knew from her days working at the Pentagon. "I always carried three-by-five cards for the president," she recalls, "for passing little notes. So I pulled out one of my three-by-five cards and I said, 'Curt, would you please call my mom and dad and tell them that you saw me and that I'm okay?' Because if I had some emotion, it was like, *What the hell's going on? Where are we gonna be in the next two hours?*" Bedke told her he'd be glad to call her parents.

That was the only personal moment Loewer allowed herself. Then it was back to work.

———◆◇◆———

MEANWHILE IN THE Sit Room, the duty officers were busy with—among many other tasks—fielding incoming calls from other governments and leaders. "We probably received somewhere around fifty head-of-state phone calls," recalls Ed Padinske. Normally, when the phone rang it would be a staffer on the other end, asking to connect their leader with the U.S. president. But 9/11 was anything but normal.

"On about half of the calls I fielded, it was the actual head of state calling," Padinske told me. He was surprised to find himself "talking to them like they're human beings, and they're passing along sympathies, and 'Anything my country can do to support you, just ask. What do you guys need right now?' And I'm like, 'Well, I'm just a lieutenant in the Situation Room, but let me get back to you.'"

Rob Hargis remembers one surprising call in particular. "Phone rings. I can see it's 10 Downing Street, and we assume it's the Brits reaching out to offer assistance, to offer condolences," he says. "We'd had a ton of calls coming in that day, but we weren't putting any of them through to the president. We were putting most of them, if any, through to Dr. Rice," who was still down in the PEOC.

"I picked it up and said, 'This is Rob.' He said, 'Rob, it's Nick at 10 Downing.' I said, 'Does the prime minister want to speak with the president? We're not putting those calls through.' And he said, 'No. We're sitting here at 10 Downing and watching this go on. And we just wanted to call you guys and tell you we're with you.'"

The most remarkable conversation, however, took place between Condi Rice and Vladimir Putin. Ensconced in the PEOC, Rice realized it would be a good idea to call the Russians. "People talk about the 'spiral of alerts,'" she told me. "Our forces go up, theirs go up"—an escalation in threat preparation that unintentionally creates a volatile situation. Rice wanted to head this off.

She expected to speak to an aide, but Putin himself got on the phone. He told Rice that he'd been trying to reach President Bush, and she replied that he was being moved to a safe location. "And then I said,

'Mr. President, our forces are going up on alert.' He said, 'I know. I'm bringing ours down and canceling our [military] exercises,'" she told me. Unlike the day of the Reagan assassination attempt, when the Soviets took advantage of the chaos to move their submarines closer to U.S. shores, the Russians were purposefully backing off. "They knew what was going on, and he wanted to reassure us that they were not going to go up," Rice said.

Putin's response was so measured, calm and helpful that Rice—an expert on Russia who speaks the language fluently—was struck by a comforting thought: *The Cold War really is over.* She couldn't have imagined then that two decades later, the United States and Russia would come full circle, adversaries once again.

———◀○▶———

AFTER A SECOND detour to Offutt AFB in Nebraska, Air Force One at last brought President Bush back to Andrews Air Force Base in Maryland. At 6:54 p.m., the president arrived at the White House—and Deb Loewer went straight down to the Situation Room. When she saw how many people were there, she was proud of her team.

Loewer didn't know until that moment that they had all been ordered to leave after the second plane hit the towers. "Just as the firefighters stayed, so did my people stay," she told me, growing emotional. "They kept talking to me and they kept sending me information...I had been speaking with my deputy and he told me they were all there, and he never gave a hint to me that they had been told to evacuate multiple times."

In fact, even though everyone in the Sit Room had been working in the most stressful environment imaginable for ten hours or more, Loewer had trouble persuading them to go home. "I had to force them to leave that night, because we're a 24/7 operation, and I needed fresh eyes," she recalls. "Because this was going to be a long fight."

Gary Bresnahan was among those reluctant to leave. He hadn't been in the Sit Room when the attacks started—he'd been at home, mowing his lawn. But he got to the White House midmorning, not long after the "dead list" had been compiled. "So my name wasn't on it," he told me. "I would have been the unknown soldier, I guess."

Yet even though Bresnahan wasn't present from the beginning, he would end up staying far longer than anyone else. Three days, to be exact.

"I slept in one of the conference rooms in the back, on the floor," he told me. "Richard [Clarke] wanted me to go home, but it was the wrong thing to do...I was in charge of all the technical stuff. If it didn't work, I'm responsible." Besides, he adds nonchalantly, "I had slept there before."

Deb Loewer finally made it to her apartment just after midnight. She had been running on pure adrenaline since 8:48 a.m., sifting through conflicting information, assessing threats, and managing communications for the president of the United States during the greatest homeland crisis since Pearl Harbor. Her mission that day "wasn't just to keep the president informed," she told me. "It was to protect the president, protect the presidency...We had evolved from 'this is an attack on the government' to maintaining the presidency of the United States. It was that serious as we worked through the day."

But now that she was home, Loewer could allow herself to contemplate what had happened—which led to what she called the most "heartbreaking moment of the day."

"I had gotten a ride home from the White House to my apartment in Crystal City, [Virginia]," she told me. "I'm on the ninth floor. I have a view of the Pentagon. And I went out on my balcony...and I was downwind of the Pentagon." She could see the orange glow of the fires there, and she smelled the acrid tang of smoke, burning metal and charred rubble. At that moment, she was "finally able to acknowledge that people who I knew, who worked in the Navy Command Center and the Army Command Center, had died." She thought also about those who had died in the Twin Towers and in Shanksville. "It was a very difficult few minutes in my life," she said.

Loewer wasn't the only Sit Room staffer who had worked in the section of the Pentagon that was destroyed. Ed Padinske had left his position as an intelligence officer there just four months earlier. "The team I had left at the Pentagon in April of 2001 were all killed on 9/11," Padinske told me, "including my best friend and the guy I turned over [my position] to." In the weeks to come, he would attend eight funerals of his Pentagon colleagues.

That morning, as Padinske had raced down the Fairfax County Parkway with his wife and young daughter in the car, his wife had turned to him and asked, "Who did this?" Without hesitating, he had told her, "This has all the earmarks of al-Qaeda."

Until the attacks of 9/11, most Americans weren't familiar with the Osama bin Laden–led terrorist group, but Padinske knew there were few organizations in the world that could have pulled off attacks on this scale. He couldn't help but think, *Did we miss something?*

"There's a truism in the military side of the intelligence community," he says. "There's no such thing as an intelligence success. There are only operational successes and intelligence failures." Padinske tells this to new recruits, urging them not to obsess about events that have just happened, but to focus on the threats that are still out there. Learn from the past, but be ready for the future.

So, in the weeks and months to come, Ed Padinske tried not to dwell on what al-Qaeda had done to his country, his colleagues and his friends. And he would absolutely be ready when, nearly a decade down the road, he found himself in the most unexpected position of encountering Osama bin Laden once again.

———◦———

IN THE EARLY morning hours of September 12, while Deb Loewer stood on her balcony watching the Pentagon fires burn, Richard Clarke left the Situation Room to go home for a shower and a change of clothes. He returned about an hour later, having brought with him something that almost nobody else was allowed to bring into the White House: a .357 Magnum. Over the next few days, he would preside over meetings in the Sit Room with the gun stuck in his belt.

"I know it sounds odd," he told me. "There was a time before 9/11—in fact, during the Clinton administration—when there was intelligence that bin Laden had put a contract out on me." He didn't take the threat seriously at the time, but Clinton did. He told the Secret Service to provide full protection for Clarke. "And I didn't want that," Clarke says. "It attracts too much attention. So I worked out a deal with the Secret Service that we could do something less." Their solution was to issue Clarke a sidearm, "which, you know, was a terrible idea, because I'm a terrible shot. And I don't like guns. But that was the way I got out of having full protection."

Clarke was one of only a handful of people with a red dot on his White House badge indicating that he could be armed. He decided to bring the gun into the Situation Room in the days following 9/11 because "at the time, none of us would have been surprised if al-Qaeda people had come over the wall."

As the sun rose on September 12, everything felt different. When Deb Loewer returned to the Sit Room after just a few hours of sleep, she was struck by the change. "The level of intensity that was there on the morning of the twelfth wasn't there when we left on the tenth," she told me. In anticipation of a morning meeting of the National Security Council, Loewer arrived at six a.m. to prepare with her team.

"We went into the conference room, took cleaning gear in," she recalls. "We had towels, rags…we cleaned every inch of the table and chairs. We checked the coffee, we checked everything." This wasn't simply to provide a nice clean environment for the meeting. "I'm thinking biological germ warfare," she told me. At that point, no one knew whether the hijacked planes were al-Qaeda's only prong of attack. Richard Clarke was packing heat against possible intruders, and Deb Loewer was packing disinfectant against possible bioweapons. In those unsettled days of September 2001, Vice President Cheney was sent to Camp David, the White House was on edge, and letters containing anthrax spores were mailed to senators and media outlets, ultimately killing five people.

The NSC met every day, in either the Situation Room or the Oval Office. So every morning, for weeks on end, Loewer and her team sanitized the Sit Room.

"There are probably people not as paranoid as I am. But I'm going to make sure that we are going to take care of the boss," she says. "We're at war. That was the president's feeling. He believed that and told us that, multiple times."

The Bush administration had failed to heed intelligence warnings in the months before 9/11. In the days following the attacks, George W. Bush's presidency was transformed. In a short speech at the White House on the night of September 11, he declared, "The search is underway for those who are behind these evil acts. I've directed the full resources of our intelligence and law enforcement communities to find those responsible and to bring them to justice. We will make no distinction between the terrorists who committed these acts and those who harbor them." By the next day, the administration had taken a deliberate tack, branding the terrorist attacks "acts of war," the first step in building support for sending troops to Central Asia and the Middle East. In a series of meetings that week, some of them in the Sit Room, the administration launched itself on a war footing. Congress authorized the president to use all "necessary and appropriate force" against those responsible for the attacks.

Much has been written about the wars in Iraq and Afghanistan, in far greater detail than is possible to get into here. Less than a month after the 9/11 attacks, U.S. troops invaded Afghanistan, a country that was known to harbor active al-Qaeda cells. In March 2003, in a far more controversial decision, the president ordered troops into Iraq. On ABC, I had several contentious interviews with secretary of defense Donald Rumsfeld about the situation in Iraq. In one, he claimed the war would cost less than $50 billion. In another, he said the administration knew where Saddam Hussein was hiding weapons of mass destruction, jabbing his finger for emphasis. Dick Cheney declared that U.S. forces would be "greeted as liberators." In fact, the war in Iraq would drag on for more than a decade, ultimately costing nearly $2 trillion. No significant WMD were ever found. And our two-decade involvement in Afghanistan would become the most protracted war in U.S. history—longer than World Wars I and II and Vietnam combined.

The attacks created other fundamental changes in American life: We now live in a post-9/11 world, where terrorist threats are forefront in our minds. From TSA checks to "see something, say something" announcements on subway cars, to the presence of heavily armed officers in public places, "homeland security" became a major part of our war footing, too.

Six days a week, President Bush received a "threat matrix" briefing from the CIA. "Between 9/11 and mid-2003, the CIA reported to me on an average of 400 specific threats each month," he wrote in his memoir. "For months after 9/11, I would wake up in the middle of the night worried about what I had read."

"There are just so many poignant moments about what the country was going through," Condi Rice told me. She recalled a particularly unsettling episode in mid-October, when she was with President Bush, Colin Powell and Andy Card in Shanghai for the Asia-Pacific Economic Cooperation summit. The traveling team had set up a temporary sensitive compartmented information facility, or SCIF—essentially a Sit Room on the road—and the group squeezed into it to speak with Vice President Cheney, who was in New York, by video.

"The vice president came on the screen and said that the White House detectors had detected botulinum toxin," Rice told me, "and we all—those of us who were exposed—were going to die." Samples of the suspicious substance had been sent to the Centers for Disease Control for testing on laboratory mice, and when Rice called her deputy national security adviser Steve Hadley, he gave her some colorful context. "If the mice are feet-up, we're toast," he said. "If the mice are feet-down, we're fine." They would know in twenty-four excruciating hours.

When Hadley called the following day, he told her "the mice are feet-down"—a message she relayed verbatim to the president, who was meeting with representatives from China. "I'm sure the Chinese, who probably got a translation, thought it was some sort of code," she says. It was a rare lighthearted moment in a time of unrelenting stress.

I asked Rice how difficult it was to discern between real threats and false ones. It had to have been exhausting to react to every single warning or potential terror act that came down the pike.

"The problem was that having missed 9/11, you didn't stop to ask whether it was real," she replied. Because the consequences of missing something that big again were too terrible to contemplate.

—◄○►—

FIVE YEARS AFTER the 9/11 attacks, the Situation Room finally got a desperately needed renovation. While the communications failures of that day were the catalyst, President Bush had made it clear from the very beginning of his first term that he wanted upgrades to the complex.

In March 2001, Bush had gone to Camp David for the weekend. Normally, he'd travel there by helicopter, but because of a snowstorm, he went by motorcade instead. Deputy chief of staff Joe Hagin was in a different car than the president, and when they all arrived back at the White House at the end of the weekend, he noticed to his dismay that Bush was waiting for him. "Instead of bolting up the sidewalk, he stopped, turned around and crossed his arms, which I knew was not a good sign," Hagin recalls. "And he pointed at the mil aide and me. And so we went up to the Oval Office with him.

"He said, 'Look, two and a half hours in the car on Friday, driving to Camp David, two hours on Sunday driving back...and I couldn't make a damn telephone call. Not once.'" The president had tried every phone in the limo: a normal cell phone, a secure phone, and finally "the red doomsday phone system," Hagin says. "He said, 'I tried 'em all, and none of them worked.' And he was pissed off. He said, 'What would happen if we had a major emergency? You gotta do something about this.'"

Hagin directed the White House Communications Agency to prepare an end-to-end review of presidential communications—voice, data and video links, both secure and nonsecure. This was a detailed survey, so it took a few months to finish. "The preliminary report was delivered to my desk on September 10," Hagin told me. "So it was sitting on my desk on 9/11."

Two weeks after the attacks, President Bush again summoned Hagin to the Oval Office, where he gave him a two-word order: "Fix it." Now that the events of 9/11 had made the comms failures glaringly obvious, funding for a major overhaul would be easy to get.

Though a full Sit Room renovation wouldn't happen until 2006, Hagin immediately got to work on a communications upgrade. Two years later, in August 2003, the new capabilities got their first real test: President Bush was visiting a military base in California when a huge power outage left much of the northeastern United States, from New York City to the Great Lakes, without electricity.

"We told him we had the new system in place, and that it was fully functional," Hagin recalls. "He was skeptical." At the base, Hagin arranged for a secure video connection with the Sit Room, "and it worked like a charm," he recalls. "And I got into the limo with him, and we went to a hotel. We had secure comms the whole way, from the base to the hotel. We got him up into the suite. We had another secure video capability up there. It never blinked."

The final test, however, would come aboard Air Force One. "We had put a big new screen in the conference room of Air Force One, and we started rolling down the runway," Hagin says. "I held my breath, as everything usually falls apart when the plane takes off. And there wasn't even a line across the screen. It was a steady signal the entire time. And that's when I knew we had fixed the problem."

Hagin was relieved. The technology "performed flawlessly," he told me. "That communications capability was a key component to the new Sit Room," which was then still in the planning stages.

Gary Bresnahan, whom Hagin calls "the godfather" of the renovation, had plenty of ideas about how to improve the Sit Room. From upgrading communications technology, to rolling out secure video teleconferencing, to installing sensors that could detect when a cell phone was brought into the room, Bresnahan had big plans. "He thought a lot of this stuff up," Hagin told me. "He worked with the designers and executed all of it. He was a national treasure that nobody had ever heard of."

But before Bresnahan could get into the room to create his dream setup, Hagin discovered that the entire complex would have to be gutted, "down to the point where we found the old columns," he told me. "The West Wing used to have an atrium from the basement all the way to the roof...and there were Roman[-style] columns around it. When we opened the walls, we found some of the columns were still there, from when it was all open to the sky." Finding these architectural remnants was "amazing," Hagin says, but something else the contractors found was troubling.

"They came to see me one day," Hagin recalls, "and said, 'It turns out the electrical switch for the West Wing was installed in 1932...and the whole place could burn to the ground on any day.' And when they got into the walls, they found all these old-fashioned cloth-covered wire cables that were frayed, and it was just a disaster." At that point, a decision was made to take out all the wiring and start from scratch. "The West Wing was a firetrap," Hagin says. "There were miles of old wires in the walls, some of which were still hot...It's a miracle there hadn't been a terrible fire."

Gutting the entire complex had a secondary benefit, according to Doug Lute. "It got rid of the old musty, moldy smells," he told me. While the Sit Room isn't technically belowground, it's still in the "basement" of the White House, and the main conference room had no windows to the outside world. Since its creation, says Lute, it's been "the same air being circulated. And don't forget, those forty years had smoke...and lots of ghosts coming through."

Better-smelling air was just a side bonus. Hagin's main goal, he told me, was "to move presidential support into the twenty-first century, because the basic design of the complex hadn't changed since the Kennedy days." This meant upgrading the technology, of course. But it also meant expanding and streamlining the layout.

The renovation created "dramatic increases in the communications capabilities out of the Sit Room," John Bolton told me. "And also having more conference rooms there." Before, "there were a lot of secretarial desks, and the watch was spread out all over the place. And the Sit Room as such was just one conference room." The new complex would be much larger, including a dedicated comms section, a watch area for duty officers, and four conference rooms of varying sizes.

Hagin had a specific reason for insisting on the variety of sizes. "There are times when the president doesn't want a full room," he told me, "and White House rule number one is, if there is an empty seat, it will be filled." Everyone wants to be in the room if the president is there. "So I pushed really hard to have the small and medium rooms, because we didn't want thirty people, or however many fit in the big room."

The layout was also carefully planned. "The duty officers who used to sit facing the walls were put in theater-style seating," says Hagin. "They were on two different levels looking at a common set of big screens. And then of course they had their own screens." Alongside that watch space was a medium-sized conference room with panels that would slide open, enabling the duty officers in the two rooms to make eye contact.

"The idea with the connectivity is, when the shit's really hitting the fan, you having eye contact with the guy who's talking directly to the [CIA] or to the National Military Command Center is very valuable," says Hagin. "You can just talk. And there had never been anything set up like that." Further, it allowed the higher-level staff people, such as the deputy national security adviser and the homeland security adviser, to hear in real time what the duty officers were hearing, and to bounce information off each other.

Listening to Hagin describe these upgrades makes one wonder: How on earth did the Sit Room function without them for so long? It seems like a pretty basic notion to have rooms where people can make eye contact and communicate while a crisis is unfolding. Why was Hagin having to reinvent the wheel? The answer is, he wasn't. "We looked at a lot of operation centers as we were trying to figure out what we wanted to do," he told me. The upgraded Sit Room was ultimately modeled on a system at the Pentagon, in which each service branch has its own "pod," with all of them tied together through a common operating procedure.

Tom Bossert, who served as deputy homeland security adviser in the Bush 43 White House, told me the technological improvements were legion: Five SVTS rooms instead of two, with improved capabilities that enabled Bush to have regular video calls with foreign leaders. A secure video connection to Air Force One. Enormous flat-screen TVs. Digitally encrypted fax machines. Windows with privacy glass that could be turned from clear to opaque in seconds. Secure Voice over Internet Protocol (VoIP) telephone lines, rather than the analog phones that "sound like you're screaming into a tin can," as he put it.

"We moved into the modern Internet world," Bossert continued. "We created a standard that was cutting edge...and the secretaries would come to these meetings and say, 'Hey, this is really cool. I want this. These are fancy phones that work!'" For the first time, the Situation Room began to resemble—at least a little bit—the futuristic set-ups in Hollywood productions.

The renovation took a little less than five months, with all the work undertaken by contractors with top secret security clearances. I asked Joe Hagin if he knew how much it cost, and he told me he had no idea. This was the kind of project where money was no object—and in the years just after 9/11, the upgrade had support on both sides of the aisle.

IN THE FINAL year of his presidency, Bush pulled Josh Bolten aside and said, "This transition has to be top-notch. This is the first presidential transition in modern history where the country is under threat." The specter of terrorism had continued to hover over the White House in the years since 9/11, and Bush's words were prescient.

In the weeks following Barack Obama's election in November 2008, U.S. intelligence picked up chatter about a possible attack by Somali terrorists at the upcoming inauguration. This was a "credible threat of an attack on the inaugural crowd," Bolten recalls. And it led to remarkable scenes of cooperation between the outgoing and incoming administrations—all the more notable since they were of different political parties.

Bolten invited incoming Obama chief of staff Rahm Emanuel to the Situation Room in December, to brief him on the Somali plot. This was the first of several such meetings during the transition. "I wouldn't call it weekly, but it was frequent," Emanuel told me. "A hundred percent we thought [the terror threat] was real. Real enough that we had a draft of a speech and a plan of moving everybody out to secure locations."

Emanuel brought in adviser David Axelrod to draft an alternate inaugural address for the incoming president in case a terror attack did occur; he turned to Axelrod because Obama's speechwriters didn't have the necessary security clearances to learn about the plot. On Inauguration Day, just before Obama walked down to the podium to take the oath, Emanuel would hand him that speech—just in case.

Incoming deputy national security adviser Tom Donilon was in constant touch with Steve Hadley and Josh Bolten during the transition. Together, they formulated an unprecedented plan. "The idea was to have the outgoing principals and the incoming principals meet in the same Room, to go over some specific issues that were pending at the time," Donilon told me. This was absolutely unheard of—a level of bipartisan cooperation that showed how seriously both administrations were taking the threat. The teams sat facing each other across the big conference room table, "going through some of what the outgoing folks thought were the most important issues facing the new national security team."

On the morning of Inauguration Day, President and Mrs. Bush hosted a coffee for the Obamas and their family. Bolten and Emanuel were both in attendance, but after a few sips of coffee, the two men departed for the Situation Room to get an update on the terror threat. There, they found security advisers from both administrations working together, with Bush's secretary of homeland security Michael Chertoff and Obama's incoming secretary of homeland security Janet Napolitano on the secure video.

Kevin Dunay had been working as Sit Room director since November 2007. He was one of very few people in the West Wing who would retain their jobs in the new administration, so unlike others, he was prepared for a full day's work. "I was never asked to stay," he told me. "But I was never told to leave. That's how they operated." Contrast this with the senior Bush official who came in to help on Inauguration Day, then bolted at 12:05. "He rolled out of the West Wing with his gym shorts and ran," Dunay recalls with a laugh.

As the noontime swearing-in drew near, "a lot of the national security or senior staff of the Obama administration actually came into the Sit Room to watch the inauguration," Dunay told me. He was nervous, as "that's the weakest part of a transition, when people are coming and going. Do they have the right comms? What happens at 12:05 if something [goes wrong]? I had to have backup plans and backup plans for that."

Fortunately, the inauguration went off without a hitch. Obama was sworn in, and the Bush staffers filed out of the Sit Room while the Obama people got to work. "We were in implementation mode," Dunay says. Did it feel strange to suddenly be working with a new team, serving a new president from a different political party?

"My job is to make everybody successful," Dunay told me. "I'm agnostic as to what their politics are. They're all human, and they don't want to screw up in front of their new bosses. So my job was to make sure I could set them up for success." And then he summed up his job—and the job of everyone in the Sit Room—perfectly in four words: "I support the presidency."

Chapter 10

THE PACER

———◆◆———

VALERIE JARRETT HAD heard enough.

The White House senior adviser came up in the world of bare-knuckle Chicago politics, where she mentored a young lawyer named Michelle Obama, becoming close to both her and her husband, Barack. She was more like a family member than a staffer, and the strength of that bond was the source of Jarrett's power. When it came to defending the personal interests of the First Couple, she was fierce. And that was on display at one particular Situation Room meeting early in Obama's second term.

Larry Pfeiffer, who served as Sit Room senior director from September 2012 to September 2013, was in the meeting that day. As he recalls, the discussion was going down a familiar road. The topic: renovating the West Wing of the White House. The reason: national security. "I don't have all the details," Pfeiffer told me, "but if someone were to blow up a large enough bomb out on Seventeenth Street, apparently the West Wing would just be pulverized. It would just collapse. It was a poorly constructed building back in Teddy Roosevelt's era. And it's never been reinforced, I guess, since then. So it is a security concern, and remains one to this day."

Plans for a major renovation had been in the works for decades, ever since George H. W. Bush's presidency. "The Bush people had scheduled it, expecting to be in office for their second term," Richard Clarke, who served with me in the Clinton administration, noted. "And so everything was cranking along. No one told anybody in our administration. I think I found out from Gary [Bresnahan], and went to Tony [Lake] and said, 'Do you know that they're going to close the West Wing?' And he said, 'You're out of your mind.'"

The simple truth is that no president, having finally made it to the Oval Office, wants to be turned out of it—even temporarily. So each successive administration just kicked the can a little farther down the road, from Bush 41 to Clinton, to Bush 43, and finally to Obama. "The White House Military Office was desperately trying to convince the Obama White House to move out of the West Wing," recalls Pfeiffer. "They wanted to gut the West Wing completely—take it all the way to the girders and rebuild it because of counterterrorism."

In preparation, Gary Bresnahan actually built an entirely new West Wing complex in the Eisenhower Executive Office Building across the alley from the White House. It included a nearly identical replica of the Oval Office. "We were within days of being ready to go," Bresnahan told me. "We had the whole West Wing set up. It was going to face West Exec in the EEOB on the first and second floors. And the third floor would have been the Sit Room."

Then came this pivotal meeting in the actual Situation Room. With everything set up, the president just had to agree to vacate the West Wing for the expected renovation period of two years. "I'd sat through a series of these meetings," recalls Pfeiffer, "and finally, [Valerie Jarrett] just went 'Okay, you know what? Enough. We are *not* moving the first Black president of the United States out of the Oval Office. It ain't happening.'"

For her part, Jarrett claims she demurred primarily because the administration had already endured a disruptive two-year renovation of the North Lawn. "In my opinion, we'd done our fair share, and now it's up to the next president to do the next leg of it," she told me. In addition, she felt that a recent renovation of the EEOB, which included adding blast-resistant windows and doors, would help to protect the nearby West Wing—thereby making the overhaul less urgent.

Jarrett neither confirmed nor denied Pfeiffer's account, but deputy national security adviser for strategic communications Ben Rhodes told me that "everybody used that line. Like, 'They're not gonna make the first Black president move.'" In fact, Rhodes said with a laugh, senior adviser Danielle Gray even joked dismissively that the temporary EEOB quarters would be "like *Sanford and Son*—a bunch of junk in the West Exec."

So it's no surprise that President Obama never budged from the West Wing during the entire eight years of his presidency. Which is fortunate, because it enabled White House photographer Pete Souza to capture the most iconic picture ever taken in the Situation Room complex: the image of President Obama, surrounded by advisers and military brass, watching the raid unfold in Abbottabad, Pakistan, which would end in the death of Osama bin Laden.

━━━━◄◦►━━━━

BIN LADEN, THE bearded, fanatical, Saudi-born leader of al-Qaeda, had been hiding from U.S. forces for years. In the late 1980s, he had established training camps for jihadist fighters, who then launched terror attacks worldwide. In 1993, al-Qaeda's operatives struck on U.S. soil, detonating a bomb in a parking garage underneath the World Trade Center. Five years later, his terrorists bombed U.S. embassies in Kenya and Tanzania. That landed bin Laden on the FBI's Ten Most Wanted list. Two years later, al-Qaeda attacked the U.S.S. *Cole* off the coast of Yemen, killing seventeen Navy sailors. And then came the horrifying attacks of September 11, 2001.

Six days after the attacks, President George W. Bush vowed to find bin Laden. "I want justice," he declared at the Pentagon. "There's an old poster out West, I recall, that says, 'Wanted: Dead or Alive.'" Military officials thought they had a bead on him late in 2001, when they attacked Tora Bora. But the trail went cold, and in the seven remaining years of his presidency, Bush could not fulfill his vow. When Barack Obama was running for president, he staked out his hawkish credentials by making the capture or killing of bin Laden the core of his foreign policy argument.

Early in his first term, Obama stepped up the search. On May 26, 2009, he ended a meeting in the Situation Room by pointing at CIA director Leon Panetta, National Counterterrorism Center (NCTC) head Mike Leiter, deputy national security adviser Tom Donilon and chief of staff Rahm Emanuel: "You, you, you and you—come upstairs." The men left the Sit Room and headed up the back stairs to the Oval Office, where Obama gave them a directive. "I want to make the hunt for bin Laden a top priority," he told them. "I want a report on my desk every thirty days describing our progress."

I asked Mike Leiter about that meeting. "Rahm was eloquent, and no cursing, as you can imagine," he said with a laugh. "Rahm was like, '*Go fucking find him! Fucking find him!*' And my favorite line during one of those meetings came from the CIA director of the counterterrorism center, Mike [D'Andrea], who was quite a character. We finished the meeting—and [D'Andrea] never made a joke with me about anything, except this time he's like, 'Mike, would you please tell these guys: You know why it's so hard to find him? Because *he's hiding.*'"

At Obama's direction, the manhunt intensified. "There were hundreds of analysts at NSA and NGA, CIA and NCTC and the FBI who were poring through everything," Leiter recalls. And all of that information would flow into the Sit Room, where the staff would sift through for nuggets to pass along to the president. "Running down all the areas of false hope, that was a value," Leiter says. "Trying all the things that didn't work, that was a value... You don't get there magically by one person saying, 'I'm convinced he's *there!*' Because that's not how the world operates. And it's not how you narrow the options."

Panetta took personal charge, tasking a CIA team to report to him every week. "They would come in and I'd tell them, 'Give me five new ideas about looking for bin Laden.'" As Leiter recalls it, no idea was too small or out-there to run down. "[If] you went in and told Bush, 'We think we saw where bin Laden farted seven years ago'—oh my god! Everyone was gonna focus on that for the next two years. Everybody wanted this to happen. Everybody wanted to find him. No matter how crazy the report was, it got run down."

The big break came when the CIA turned its focus to a man whom they believed to be a courier for bin Laden. "At some point, to be relevant at all, he has to be communicating," Leiter recalls thinking. And if the courier was in fact bin Laden's conduit to the outside world, then it made sense that he would be coming and going from wherever the al-Qaeda leader was located.

The CIA began tracking the courier's white SUV. In the summer of 2010, it hit the jackpot. Satellite images showed the vehicle arriving at a large compound in Abbottabad, Pakistan, a city of about a quarter million people just north of the capital, Islamabad. It was "three times the size of the other compounds in the area," Panetta told me. "It had eighteen-foot walls on one side, twelve-foot walls on another side. It had an eight-foot wall on the third floor, which was a little strange. And we were able to identify a family living on the third floor that never came out, because we checked the clotheslines and figured out how many members of the family were there." When the CIA began doing 24/7 surveillance on the compound, it discovered that "somebody would come out and walk in circles in the yard."

This man, dubbed "The Pacer," was suspected to be bin Laden, though there was no way to know for sure. Efforts to obtain DNA from the site had proven inconclusive.

"I remember asking the CIA team, 'For goodness sakes, give me a tele-scope or a camera to see if we can get a facial ID,'" Panetta recalls. "And they said, 'We just have a hard time doing it because we've got walls, we've got barriers. We just can't get a good picture.' And I remember saying to them, 'You know, I've seen movies where the CIA can do this, god damn it!'" Panetta laughs. "We couldn't actually get a firm ID. We pulled together other intelligence…but it was at that point that the president was very concerned that it might leak, and that we would lose the possi-bility of getting bin Laden."

With so many people working the problem, the worry about leaks was ever-present. This led to extraordinary measures in the Sit Room.

"I'll tell you that in my two years there, there's a lot that happens in the White House that's secretive," U.S. Navy admiral Kyle Cozad, who was director of operations for the Situation Room, told me. "This was by far the most secretive event that I was part of."

"Three or four months prior to the actual raid," Cozad recalls, "John Brennan, who at the time was the deputy national security adviser for counterterrorism and homeland security, came into my office and said that he had a very sensitive meeting with the president later that day...and he said, 'I need a couple of things to happen.'"

"'The first one,' he said, 'I've got some briefers that are coming over from CIA that have something that they're gonna bring in, if you could make sure they get through Secret Service,'" Cozad says. "They always entered the west door of the West Wing, the visitors' entrance, and then the back door to the large Situation Room—the conference room—was right there. So he said, 'I need help getting them through Secret Service. But then we need to do some things that we don't typically do.'"

The large conference room, Cozad explained, "holds probably up to forty people, with people on back benches. And there are cameras in each room, and then there's also audio in each room. And John Brennan said, 'I want you to make sure that we've got the cameras secured and that there's no audio that comes out of the conference room during this meeting.'"

I asked whether Brennan had ever made such a request before. "Never," said Cozad. "Absolutely not...We want to make sure, as a Situation Room staff, we know who's in there—who's come, who's gone...So this was the first time in my ten and a half months that we'd ever received a request like that."

There were other indications that these proceedings were exceptionally secret. Usually, Sit Room meetings were listed according to topic and attendees, but "Mr. Brennan asked us to just put 'Sensitive Meeting' up there. We don't need to share attendance for the meeting," Cozad recalls. "So it really was an anomaly."

Ben Rhodes noticed the change right away. "There started to be these meetings in early 2011 that were not listed on the Sit Room schedule," he told me. I asked if he poked around to try to find out what was happening. "It's a dry hole," he said. "So, like, I'm already embarrassed and resentful that I wasn't invited to the meeting, and asking would only compound that embarrassment...If you don't get invited to someone's birthday party, you kind of don't want to call the other friend and be like, 'Did you get invited?'"

Meanwhile, what was the item Cozad helped the CIA briefers bring in? "They had a large...it looked like a big plywood folding box that— you know, when I was a kid, I would open it up and it looked like some sort of small-gauge railroad track that I could play with," says Cozad. This was no model train, of course, but it was a model: a detailed scale rendering of the buildings under surveillance. "In retrospect, I can say it was the Abbottabad compound. It wasn't labeled, we couldn't tell anything other than, 'Hey, there's a place here, and they want to make sure they can talk in specifics about this location.'"

This model of Osama bin Laden's Abbottabad compound was so secret, director Kyle Cozad personally walked its CIA handlers into the Sit Room. Cozad would not find out what it was until after the raid. | *Angela Weiss / Getty Images*

After escorting the CIA briefers and their model into the Sit Room, Cozad turned to walk out. Brennan told him not to interrupt the meeting, but that if it was absolutely necessary to pass along a message or pull someone out for a phone call, only Cozad himself or the Sit Room senior director, John Buchanan, who was detailed from the CIA, could do it.

Nick Rasmussen, the NSC's senior director for counterterrorism, told me that as soon as there was a degree of confidence the man at the compound was bin Laden, they directed the CIA to work with the military on options. Vice Admiral William McRaven, who was commander of the Joint Special Operations Command at Fort Bragg, "was brought into the conversation with CIA to begin to develop different contingency plans and options." At this point, the Situation Room became a hive of activity, setting up the most perilous decision of Obama's presidency.

"As you enter 2011," Rasmussen told me, "it sets off this entire string, or set, of seventeen or eighteen National Security Council meetings of various levels. All at the level of either deputies, which would be chaired by Denis McDonough and John Brennan; principals, which were chaired by Tom Donilon; or the NSC, chaired, of course, by the president himself." Things were happening, he says, "at a pretty high tempo... All of these meetings are in the White House Situation Room, but under extraordinary secrecy."

ON MARCH 14, President Obama met with his NSC team in the Situation Room. He wanted the options for taking out The Pacer.

McRaven had devised three possible operations, according to Panetta. "One was to take a B-1 bomber and just blow the hell out of the place. And you know, that had a certain attraction, but the problem was, we'd never know if it was bin Laden. And besides that, it would have taken a lot of firepower and probably destroyed some nearby villages."

The second option was more targeted: "A drone strike against the guy who was walking in circles," Panetta says. This, too, was problematic. "Having worked with drone strikes, they don't always hit the target, number one. Number two, again, we wouldn't know if it was bin Laden. So we settled on a third approach, which was to use two teams of SEALs on helicopters going in, rappelling down to the compound and conducting a commando operation.

McRaven flashed slides on the Sit Room projector as he walked the president through his plan. "We had a small, maybe five- or six-man planning team by March 14," McRaven told me. "I had already developed the plan well before that, which was pretty simple: We'll fly, we'll get to the compound, we'll get the bad guy, we'll come back." These types of operations happened several times a night in Iraq, and by this time in his career, McRaven had been involved in "ten thousand missions," he said. "I had either commanded them, I had overseen them, or I had reviewed the concept of operations." And this one, he felt, "wasn't a tactically difficult plan."

Then came the next question: Should the Pakistani government get a heads-up? "We'd had a lot of instances where we would share information on targets with the Pakistanis, and those targets would disappear," Panetta recalls. "And so the president said, 'You know, I don't think we can trust the Pakistanis on this.'" This decision added a new level of complexity, as the helicopters would have to travel 150 miles into Pakistani territory, complete the mission, and get out again before their military got wind of what was happening and possibly responded.

I asked McRaven what the president seemed most concerned about.

"Well, we talked about a lot of things," he told me. "I mean, the president was very involved in the planning process. He wanted to understand about our helicopters and their capability. He wanted to understand how many guys we were going to have on target because we were limited based on helicopters. He didn't get into the 'who on the ground is gonna go left and who on the ground is gonna go right'…But in the Situation Room, I gave the president the overview of exactly how we were going to take the compound down.

"We were worried about a lot of things. Was the compound booby-trapped? There was no way to determine, and we had been in Iraq and Afghanistan a number of times when my SEALs went on target and the target was booby-trapped," says McRaven. "And the guy either cranked off a suicide vest or he had a command-detonated device and the whole house blew up…I mean, bin Laden, we knew he'd been there potentially five years. Surely he had a bugout plan."

McRaven exuded a calm confidence that was fueled by more than just his decades of experience. His level of preparation was off the charts. "I had made a decision matrix," he told me. "I sat down with the guys and said, 'What I *don't* want to do is have to make a decision in the heat of the moment. So we are gonna plan out all the potential options. So, if we launch and we cross the border and the Pakistanis pick us up and we're compromised, do we keep going? Yes or no?' These were binary decisions."

Yet with all of the planning, all the decision frameworks and matrices and diagrams, nothing on paper came into the Situation Room. Nick Rasmussen, who served as staff support to Tom Donilon and John Brennan during these sessions, described to me how different they were from other Sit Room meetings he'd taken part in.

"The White House has a pretty structured paperwork process that documents everything," Rasmussen said. "There are agendas, meeting notes and read-ahead materials that are always sent around with high-level principal meetings. In this case, we chose to forgo all of that and basically operate with no notes, no paper being sent around in advance."

This is unusual to the point of being bizarre. Imagine being called to a meeting with the president, in the White House Situation Room, to discuss a top secret mission that could radically alter the global dynamic—and having to come in blind because secrecy precludes producing a paper trail. "They were being asked to show up and just participate, with no preparation, no advance," Rasmussen says.

Not only that, but the principals were then forbidden from discussing anything they heard in the Sit Room with their teams, colleagues or spouses. "Secretary [of State Hillary] Clinton could not go back from these meetings to the State Department and download anything to anybody so that she could have help in thinking through whatever pieces of this were important to her," Rasmussen says. "Every person who was involved in these meetings was a by-name invite with no substitutes permitted...[and] we weren't allowing any video conference participation."

At least one person in the room was acutely aware of the impact paperless meetings might have on history. As Rasmussen recalls, "Literally, one of the first things Tom Donilon did after the raid was successfully carried out was tell us, 'Quickly, write everything down from all of those meetings, as much as you can remember.' Because...in the aftermath, we do want to have a historical record as much as possible."

PRESIDENT OBAMA WOULD chair five NSC meetings in the Situation Room prior to the raid on May 1. And as these and other high-level

Sit Room staffers called President George H.W. Bush "the government's desk officer for China," as he knew the country intimately from his time as a diplomat there. Shown here with Barbara Bush at Tiananmen Square in 1974. *George H.W. Bush Presidential Library and Museum*

National security adviser Brent Scowcroft with Bush 41 at the Bush compound in Kennebunkport, Maine. Republicans and Democrats agree, Scowcroft was the best ever to hold the position. *George H.W. Bush Presidential Library and Museum*

Sit Room senior duty officer Dave Radi marveled at how friendly the Bushes were with staffers. At an NSC picnic, Radi's young son makes a grab for the president's beer. *Courtesy Dave Radi*

Gary Bresnahan, shown here at the ribbon-cutting following the 2006 Situation Room renovation, was the most important guy you never heard of: the MacGyver of the Sit Room over seven administrations. (L–R: Phil Lago, Dick Cheney, Gary Bresnahan, President Bush, Martin Gross, Jeff Foltz) *Photo by Eric Draper, courtesy of the George W. Bush Presidential Library*

President Clinton told me we needed to "bust our rear to get a settlement" in Bosnia. "Explore all alternatives, roll every die." I'm pictured here in the Oval Office with him, Vice President Gore and Leon Panetta. *David Hume Kennerly / Getty Images*

Secretary of state Madeleine Albright became known as a vocal advocate for women in the Sit Room, often interjecting when a man took credit for an idea originally put forth by a woman. (L–R: Madeleine Albright, Hillary Clinton) *Diana Walker from* HILLARY, The Photographs of Diana Walker.

A nondescript room at Fort Myer military base became a de facto Situation Room when President Clinton met there with top aides following a memorial service for three U.S. diplomats killed in Bosnia. *Courtesy William J. Clinton Presidential Library*

Elliott Powell, the first African-American Sit Room director, was on duty New Year's Eve of 1999, when threats of Y2K disruptions and terrorism hung over the room. Shown here with press secretary Joe Lockhart and President Clinton on Marine One. *Courtesy William J. Clinton Presidential Library*

To Elliott Powell—Thanks for your good work, good nature, and good spirit in the cab games
Bill Clinton

The photo inscription President Clinton wrote to Powell. *Courtesy Elliott Powell*

Senior duty officer Rob Hargis was one of the many Sit Room staffers who refused to evacuate the White House on September 11, 2001. He's shown here in the Sit Room on November 12, 2001, after an American Airlines flight crashed in Belle Harbor, New York. (L–R : [Unidentified], Ari Fleischer, Admiral Charles Abbott, Rob Hargis, Joshua Bolten) *Courtesy Robert Hargis*

So many people crowded into the Presidential Emergency Operations Center on 9/11, the oxygen in the room became dangerously low. *Courtesy Archival Operations Division, NARA*

Senior duty officer Ed Padinske, shown here receiving a promotion from Condi Rice, rushed to the Sit Room on the morning of 9/11. Nearly a decade later, his path would cross with Osama bin Laden once again. *Courtesy Robert Hargis*

Robert Gates, who served as secretary of defense and director of Central Intelligence, spent time in the Sit Room under seven presidents. Shown here with Leon Panetta, a veteran of the Obama and Clinton administrations. *Brendan Smialowski / Getty Images*

Perhaps the most famous photo ever taken in the Situation Room complex, this scene of President Obama and his team watching the bin Laden raid unfold actually took place in a small side room, rather than the main conference room. *Courtesy Barack Obama Presidential Library*

A study in power: President Obama meets with former national security advisers in the Situation Room. (Clockwise around table: President Obama, Brent Scowcroft, Bud McFarlane, Colin Powell, Dennis Ross, Sandy Berger, Frank Carlucci, Zbigniew Brzezinski) *Courtesy Barack Obama Presidential Library*

For the first months of Coronavirus Task Force meetings in the Situation Room, participants remained unmasked. (L–R : Tony Fauci, Deb Birx, Russell Vought, Vice President Pence, Kellyanne Conway) *Official White House photo by D. Myles Cullen*

President Trump and his team posed in the Sit Room during the military operation that killed terrorist Abu Bakr al-Baghdadi. (L–R : Robert O'Brien, Vice President Pence, President Trump, Mark Esper, General Mark Milley) *Official White House photo by Shealah Craighead*

The Secure Video Teleconference System makes it possible for U.S. presidents to have face-to-face virtual meetings with their counterparts abroad. Here, President Biden talks with Russian president Vladimir Putin in the Sit Room. *Official White House Photo by Adam Schultz*

The newly renovated Watch Center. The Situation Room finally looks like it does in the movies. *White House Photographers Office*

meetings played out, some participants took note of a particular advantage the teams had.

"I think one thing that made a difference was that this did not happen in the first year of the Obama administration," Rasmussen told me. "This happened in 2011, the third year of the Obama administration. So, counterterrorism had been pretty high on the agenda for the president and his cabinet during that period." In fact, the president had a standing weekly meeting, called "Terror Tuesdays" by some, in which a couple dozen officials would gather in the Sit Room to talk about developments in the war on terror.

"McRaven, for example—even though he was a three-star admiral, he was a known commodity in the Situation Room," Rasmussen recalls, "because he had been in the Situation Room for dozens of meetings on other topics at other times during the first three years. So, Secretary Clinton or Secretary Gates would not have been wondering, 'Who's this McRaven, the guy who's telling us this is gonna work out?'"

Contrast this with Desert One. President Carter had not met the mission's commander, Charlie Beckwith, until eight days before the mission launched. Obama and McRaven knew each other well, and the teams involved in planning the operation had been working closely together for three years. It was like a football team playing together an entire season, then rolling into the Super Bowl at peak performance. There was a shared language, a familiarity and trust that helped the process run smoothly, and the experience of being in the Sit Room helped strengthen the decision-making muscle. "You weren't just winging it based on emotion or exigencies of the moment," says Rasmussen.

Mike Leiter echoed this view. "This wasn't a group of ten, twelve, fifteen people who were getting together for the first time about bin Laden…We all knew each other very, very well. Many of us had worked together for ten years, and all of us had worked together for at least two years. And I think that was a secret sauce."

Clearly, the planning and preparation of the bin Laden raid was superior to that of Desert One. And two of the men involved knew that better than anyone—because they'd been involved in both. One was Bob Gates, who was now the secretary of defense. The other was the ever-present tech wizard Gary Bresnahan.

I asked Bresnahan when he learned about the upcoming bin Laden raid. "Two weeks out," he told me. "Because I had to set up some things." The "things" to which he refers are the audiovisual links between the Situation Room and the field. "You've seen the famous [photo]," he says, meaning Pete Souza's iconic image of Obama and his advisers in the Sit Room watching the raid unfold. "You could see that the group of people in that room…I mean, they were glued to the TV. They were getting those live shots. And I had to make those connections, which we never had before"—because normally they would be routed through the Pentagon, not directly to the White House.

I asked how he got those connections set up. "Well, some of it's still classified, so I'll have to leave it," he said. Then he added with a chuckle, "I told my [girlfriend]—she thought I was having an affair for the last two weeks, because I hadn't come home until like one or two in the morning every day. [But] I was spending all the time with a bunch of guys in the Situation Room."

"It reminded me of an episode of *MacGyver*," Kyle Cozad told me. "'How are we going to pull this off?' And so that team came in, and we had to connect this site with that site. And within about a day, we were successfully connected on a secure network downrange. And you know, we weren't sure exactly where 'downrange' was, but [USAF general] Brad Webb was driving the computer that allowed that to happen."

Cozad and the other Sit Room staff didn't know precisely where the mission was taking place, but as preparation continued, he began to get an idea. "You can start to stitch together different bits of classified intelligence...You could piece those together to say, 'Hey, this is starting to sound like a cogent story.'"

◄o►

DESERT ONE HAUNTED defense secretary Bob Gates. At the time, he had been an aide to then–CIA head Stan Turner.

"It really affected my position for a long time," Gates told me. "I had two concerns. First of all, I basically favored using a drone and killing [bin Laden], because my worry with a boots-on-the-ground attack was that whether it was successful or not, the Pakistanis would be so outraged that they would cut off our only supply line to Afghanistan, and we would lose the war overnight." This, he told me, was his primary concern.

Then there were the helicopters that would ferry the Navy SEALs in and out of Pakistan. "All I could think about as we were planning and thinking about the bin Laden raid was those helicopters going down, and the [1980] disaster in the desert, because it started with a helicopter crash." Gates told me that "the one actual contribution I made for the planning in the bin Laden raid was, I told them, 'Take a couple of extra helicopters.'" Much has been written about the raid, and other accounts don't specify Gates's comments as the primary motivator in adding helicopters. But Michèle Flournoy, who served as Gates's top policy adviser on this mission, told me, "I think McRaven, hearing his concerns, went back to the plan and said, 'Hey, we could position some backup helicopters here without being seen.'"

The Desert One fiasco also loomed large for Admiral McRaven. He had studied the failed mission, and in his opinion, it had two fatal

249

flaws. The first was lack of communication—the result of a desire to make sure the Iranians didn't pick up any radio chatter. "When the C-130s went through the dust storm, they didn't communicate back to the helicopters because they were concerned that the Iranians would pick up communications," McRaven told me. "What I told my guys was, 'You will communicate with me and the others every chance you can do it. Do not worry—let *me* worry—about the Pakistanis picking up the communications.'"

The second flaw was the lack of a full-dress rehearsal. The Desert One teams had done partial rehearsals, working out the various parts of the mission, but never a full-scale, start-to-finish run-through. McRaven was determined to rehearse the entire mission—not once, not twice, but multiple times.

"I had written a thesis in the Naval Postgraduate School about a number of missions," he told me. "And the full-dress rehearsal was something that, every time that people failed to conduct a part of a mission in the rehearsal, invariably that failed on the actual mission."

McRaven stood ready to prepare the SEAL team. He just needed the go-ahead from the commander in chief, which came on March 29. During an NSC meeting in the Situation Room, President Obama asked him a simple question. "Well, Bill," he said, "can you do this?" McRaven told him he needed to do full-dress rehearsals to find out, and asked for three weeks to prepare. Obama told him to go ahead.

The clock was now ticking. Throughout the month of April, McRaven prepped his SEALs, building a full-scale replica of the Abbottabad compound and running through the entire mission multiple times. He wanted to launch the raid on a moonless night, to give the incoming helicopters maximum cover of darkness. And unlike the Desert One raid three decades earlier, he would have much better data on weather and conditions. As Gary Sick recalled, in 1980 many weather stations in Iran weren't functioning, and satellite images didn't pick up the enormous dust clouds that slowed the mission and ultimately brought down one of the helicopters.

"It's a different world," Sick said, comparing the raid preparation in 1980 versus 2011. "The extraordinary degree of professionalism that we have now to conduct operations like this simply didn't exist, and has been born of that experience."

The next moonless night in Pakistan would occur on Saturday, April 30. As the month of April drew near its end, the SEALs were ready, but President Obama hadn't made his final decision about whether to undertake the raid. So on Thursday, April 28, the NSC gathered in the Situation Room to thoroughly hash out the riskiest decision of Obama's presidency: To go, or not to go.

—————◄○►—————

PRESIDENT OBAMA OPENED the discussion with an important clarification. "He mentions at the start of the meeting that he wants to hear everybody's advice and perspective, but he won't, in that meeting, himself actually render a decision," Nick Rasmussen recalls. "And so that, in some ways, changes the character of the meeting a little bit, as no one's trying to align to what they think he thinks."

The SEAL team had already deployed to Afghanistan. They were ready. The lunar position and weather conditions were perfect. The only sticking point was the question that no one could definitely answer: Was The Pacer bin Laden? If not, it was possible that the U.S. government would be staging a hazardous night raid, putting in danger the lives of not only our SEALs, but of Pakistani bystanders, even running the risk of inciting a war with Pakistan, over a random individual.

The NCTC's Mike Leiter prepared a final "red team" report,

assessing the CIA's intelligence about The Pacer's identity. But even with the best analysts working the case, Leiter announced to the room that there was only a 40 to 60 percent certainty that the man was in fact bin Laden. The CIA's estimate was higher, at 60 to 80 percent certainty, so the red team's final estimate was disappointingly low.

Admiral McRaven, who was already in Afghanistan, joined the meeting via secure video. Upon hearing Leiter's red team report, his heart sank. "When he said 40 percent, I remember thinking to myself, *Man, this mission's over,*" he told me. "Who in the world would launch a bunch of SEALs to fly 152 miles into Pakistan to take down a compound when the chance it's bin Laden is only 40 percent?"

With all the numbers being floated, President Obama summed it up with a hint of frustration. "Ultimately, this is a fifty-fifty call," he said. Not a great percentage upon which to stake your entire presidency.

Then, the president polled the principals. "He went around the room, around the rectangular table in the Situation Room, and asked each of the principals at the table—to include Vice President Biden, Secretary Gates, Secretary Clinton, [director of national intelligence James] Clapper, Brennan, Panetta—all what their view was on whether to proceed with one of the options," Rasmussen recalls. "Either with the raid that was authorized or the standoff raid."

As President Obama recounted in his memoir *A Promised Land,* "Leon [Panetta], John Brennan and [JCS chair] Mike Mullen favored the raid. Hillary said that for her, it was a 51–49 call, carefully ticking through the risks of a raid." Rasmussen painted the scene: "She did very much 'on the one hand, on the other hand, on the other *other* hand, on the other *other other* hand'—and I don't blame her for that…She was clearly working out in her own mind the inherent contradictions of having a 40 percent and a 70 percent level of probability." Then, she came down on the side of the raid. As Panetta recalls, "Hillary said,

'Obviously it'd be great to have more intelligence, but I think we're at the point where we've got to make a decision.' And her recommendation was to go."

Vice President Biden "had concerns about the risks that were involved," Panetta told me, "and [he] thought that we should get more intelligence as to whether or not bin Laden was there." So many things could go wrong: The raid could be targeting an innocent family. A firefight could erupt. SEALs could be injured or killed in the operation. Pakistani military or police forces, if alerted while the raid was in progress, could retaliate. Relations between Pakistan and the United States could be severely damaged.

Some participants recall Biden as being a hard no, while others suggest that he was trying to raise multiple options to give President Obama cover. Obama himself seems to have taken it the latter way, writing in *A Promised Land* that "I appreciated Joe's willingness to buck the prevailing mood and ask tough questions, often in the interest of giving me the space I needed for my own internal deliberations."

Bob Gates was a hard no. He had already expressed his concerns in earlier meetings, never hesitating to invoke Desert One. In late March, when plans for the helicopter raid began to gel, Gates brought it up by remarking dryly, "They said that was a pretty good idea, too." In an April 19 Sit Room meeting, sensing the growing wave of enthusiasm for the mission, Gates had taken a step back, suggesting to the president that his input might be too colored by the 1980 disaster. "I told him in front of the rest of the team that perhaps in this case my experience was doing him a disservice because it made me too cautious," Gates wrote in his memoir *Duty*. "He forcefully disagreed, saying my concerns were exactly what he needed to take into account as he weighed the decision."

Now, in this final April 28 decision meeting, Gates argued for the drone strike, the safer option in terms of putting American lives at risk. As Ben Rhodes described the moment to me, "Gates presents very well. He's kind of monotone, no extra words, analytical. So he's laying this all out, and he didn't linger on it, just referenced it…He's going through the different scenarios of what could happen. And one was like, 'We could lose a helicopter.'

"It wasn't a long discussion of Desert One, but it was like—you felt this ghost come in the room with him saying 'I was here for that'…We all knew the political import of what [Gates] had said," Rhodes recalls. Even though the Sit Room is mostly apolitical, it was Rhodes's job to think through the consequences of a failed mission. "As soon as he said that, I knew—oh god, not only would that happen, it would surely be in the paper that the secretary of defense had warned you that this could happen and you still did it, and then it happened."

Rhodes had believed all along that President Obama would authorize the raid. But in this moment, he thought the president might waver. "You're like, 'Shit, man, the secretary of defense is not for this!' Like, that's a big deal…that's a hard thing to navigate."

Panetta also believed that Gates's hesitancy made a strong impression on Obama. "He thought Gates was a straight shooter, respected his thinking, and if anything, he thought Gates was a little hawkish," Panetta told me. "So when Gates says, 'You know, I'm not so sure here,' I think that was probably the voice that affected Obama on the other side."

Panetta himself was all-in. "The president turned to me," he recalls. "I said, 'You know, Mr. President, when I was in Congress, I had an old formula I used when I faced a tough decision, which was to pretend I was talking to an average citizen in my district and telling them what was involved in that issue and what would they do?' And I said, 'If I told the average citizen in my district that we had the best information on the location of bin Laden since Tora Bora, I think that citizen would say, "We have to go." And that's what I'm recommending to you.'"

When the principals had finished giving their opinions, President Obama took an unusual step. "After working his way around the room, he then did something that I had never seen in the Situation Room before," Nick Rasmussen told me. He turned to the people ringing the wall—the advisers and aides who normally sat silent except when whispering in their principals' ears—and asked them what they thought. "You know, you're used to being there, taking notes and trying not to create any kind of disruption, and all of a sudden the president's working his way around asking each of us what we think."

"He clearly wanted to hear every opinion in that room," Rasmussen says. "So I found that really quite extraordinary."

What do you do when the president of the United States unexpectedly asks your opinion on a decision of historic importance? "I spoke very, very briefly," Rasmussen told me. "I can't remember my exact words, but I spoke in favor of the assault option because I had high confidence that bin Laden was there." With a chuckle, Rasmussen added, "It wasn't exactly a profile in courage for me to do that because John Brennan, my direct boss, had spoken with that same view ahead of me in the meeting. So you're never in a terrible spot when you align yourself with your boss's point of view . . . I tried to be as concise as possible about why I thought the case had been made and why I thought that the decision was worth taking the risks."

This is the Situation Room at its best: a place of sober discussion, informed thinking, apolitical attitudes and an absence of grandstanding. The men and women in the room that day understood their roles and appreciated the gravity of what they were being asked to decide.

The give-and-take in the room was genuine, and the scale of it—specifically, the inclusion of the non-principals—unprecedented.

As the president went around the room, the last person to speak was, by chance of seating arrangement, the man who'd presented the red team's 60-40 percent figure, Mike Leiter.

For a long time, Leiter was skeptical that The Pacer was bin Laden. "I just thought that as the CIA presented the evidence initially, they never looked at the alternatives," he told me. "It was, 'It is him because there's a guy who walks around alone and that means it's him.'" I asked Leiter how much his skepticism was informed by the WMD fiasco during Bush 43. "Oh, a lot," he said. "I mean, a lot...I just felt like, having interviewed the case officers who interviewed Curveball"—the code name for the primary Iraqi source on WMD, who turned out to be making up his information—"for the mobile biological weapons lab, no one really pressed it hard, and in part people didn't press it hard because they all wanted to think there were WMD there. And I knew everyone wanted to think—*I* wanted to think that bin Laden was there."

Yet while the specter of the WMD fiasco loomed large for Leiter, Desert One did not. "That one was easier to overcome," he told me, "because first of all, you can't understate the degree of confidence people had with Bill McRaven...He's like, 'We've done this mission 12,265 times in the last ten years. The only difference is we move it from here to here to here.' The bigger problem was if you went and [bin Laden] wasn't there."

Leiter had never offered an opinion on whether to launch the raid; he didn't see that as his job. "I played my cards about what I thought very, very close to the vest," he told me. "Until the end, when I was asked by Obama."

His message to the president was simple and direct. "Even if we take the lowest likelihood...that's 38 percent higher than we've been for ten years. So we have to do something…We can't let this opportunity slip away."

The president thanked the group and promised a decision by morning.

Bob Gates headed back to the Pentagon. His under secretaries of defense who were read into the mission, Michèle Flournoy and Mike Vickers, knew that he had recommended the use of the drone. "We were like, 'This is the wrong option,'" she told me. "This thing's experimental. It has a real chance of failure. We won't get the SSE [sensitive site exploitation], the intel, all this other stuff. And so together we marched up to the front office, unannounced, and asked if we can get fifteen minutes of his time unscheduled.

"He sort of, grumbling, lets us in and we sat down with him and walked him through again why the raid was the better option." Flournoy told him, "'Here are the twenty-six or thirty-two or fifty-eight things that we've done to buy down the risk and address all of the concerns you have.' And at the end of the conversation, to his credit—Gates listens, you know—he called the White House, called Tom Donilon and said, 'I've changed my mind. I want to change my recommendation to the president. I'm supportive of the raid.'"

It's unbelievably rare for a principal to express an opinion in the Sit Room, then call the president hours later to retract it. Flournoy went on, "I don't mean to sound self-aggrandizing. But I mean, I think Mike and I were his closest advisers on these things, and both of us together saying, 'Boss, we think you're wrong and this is why' and really walking him through" was the catalyst for Gates to change his mind.

Then Flournoy said something that floored me. "George," she said, "you have a footnote in here. You won't remember this, but back in the Clinton administration, you were working for President Clinton and I was working on this very controversial Somalia-lessons-learned report that would be telling people some very ugly facts and lessons. And I remember talking to you and saying, 'I'm really worried that people are just not gonna want to hear this and I'm going to get fired.'

"And you said to me, 'Michèle, you know, civil servants are trying to protect their careers. Military, they're thinking about their next [posting]. The job of a political appointee is to tell the boss what they *need* to hear, not what they *want* to hear.' And I remember thinking of that when we approached Gates." It was, she said, her "truth to power" moment. She knew Gates wasn't going to like what she and Vickers were telling him. "[But] you told me, 'Look, I get yelled at by the president of the United States every day. That's my job. And so you can risk getting yelled at by people. It's OK.'"

It would never have occurred to me that a conversation I had in the White House almost two decades earlier might have influenced the bin Laden raid. But this is the beauty and the benefit of having dedicated public servants working across multiple administrations. Men and women like Bob Gates and Michèle Flournoy carry their knowledge forward through the years, bringing their own special set of experiences to bear on current situations. That continuity is often the key to effective decision-making.

On the morning of Friday, April 29, President Obama made his decision. "It's about eight o'clock. I see the email, 'Let's meet in the Diplomatic Room,'" recalls Tom Donilon. He, John Brennan and Denis McDonough headed to the room, on the ground floor of the White House.

"It's the room that leads right out to the South Lawn...it's a beautiful view," Donilon says. "You look out the back door and you see the helicopter, you see the Washington Monument in back of it." Marine One was there because President Obama was scheduled to fly to Alabama that day to view storm damage. "He's in a windbreaker...and he gathered us around. We didn't sit down. He came in and said, 'I've decided we're going to do the raid. Send him the orders.' And that was it. That was the whole conversation."

The raid was a go. It would launch the following day—Saturday, April 30. The date of the WHCD, the White House Correspondents' Dinner.

MY WIFE, ALI, and I attended the WHCD that evening, where we found ourselves seated at a table with Tom Donilon and Obama's chief of staff Bill Daley. Donilon popped up and down from the table like a jack-in-the-box all night, while Daley kept checking his phone. This would have been impolite at any dinner, but it was especially strange at the WHCD, where people tend to let loose, have a few drinks and put the office away for a night.

Modern Family actor Eric Stonestreet was also seated at our table, and he could not stop talking about the fact that his planned tour of the White House had been canceled. As I watched Bill Daley sweat and punch at his phone, and listened to Stonestreet moan about the closure of the White House, it seemed obvious that something was up.

"Have you guys got something big going on over there?" I finally asked Daley. He stared at me for the briefest of moments, then mumbled, "No, no, there's just a plumbing problem at the White House."

This seemed unlikely, but it was clear I wasn't going to get any more information. My wife gently needled Daley for continuing to poke at his phone, but he kept on doing it throughout the dinner. I just turned my attention to the other activity of the evening, listening to President Obama eviscerate Donald Trump in his speech, and watching Trump scowl from his seat.

As the world would later learn, the raid on Abbottabad had been pushed to the next day, Sunday, May 1. Now in Afghanistan with his team, Admiral McRaven had determined that fog in the low-lying valleys made it unsafe for the helicopters to fly into Pakistan, so he rolled the mission for twenty-four hours. Daley and Donilon knew the raid was planned for the next day, but they—and President Obama and Ben Rhodes and the other handful of people present who were read into the mission—had to pretend all night that this was just like any other WHCD. That's tough enough, but put yourself in Mike Leiter's shoes. He was actually getting married that night and had to postpone his honeymoon but couldn't tell his wife why. "She swears that she knew," he told me. "But I did not tell her."

———◄○►———

BEN RHODES COULDN'T tell his brother, who was the president of CBS News and bunking with him for the WHCD that weekend. On Sunday morning, Rhodes was too keyed-up to sleep in. "I remember coming to work early that Sunday and going in the Situation Room and realizing we had nothing to do," he told me. "[CIA deputy director] Michael Morell gave the exact same presentation at least once a day of the latest intelligence case, and 'We saw them burn their trash' and this and that—but there was no new information."

The mission was scheduled to launch between 2:00 and 2:30 p.m. East Coast time. While Rhodes was camped out in the Sit Room, NSC staffers began arriving at the White House in a staggered schedule, so as not to arouse any attention. President Obama went to Joint

Base Andrews for his usual round of golf (though he cut it from eighteen holes to nine), while one of the Sit Room watch officers went to Costco and loaded up on sandwiches and chips for the long day ahead. As Cozad recalls, "It was as casual as could be...an otherwise quiet day in the West Wing of the White House."

The principals began arriving around eleven a.m., and at noon, they convened for a final review. Just after two p.m., President Obama walked into the Situation Room. It was go time.

Everyone in the room knew it would take the helicopters more than an hour to reach the compound in Abbottabad. So, how do you spend the most stressful ninety minutes of your life, when there's absolutely nothing you can do about the events to come? President Obama went upstairs to play Spades with several aides and photographer Pete Souza. The rest of the group stayed in the Sit Room complex, "making small talk," as NSC adviser Matt Spence told reporter Garrett Graff. "It had this feeling of a wedding—the ceremony had happened, and everyone's waiting for the bride and groom to get back for the reception."

"It was weird," Ben Rhodes told me. "It felt like nine hours. We were just sitting in this room with literally nothing to do...[and] we all just started to tell our stories of where we were on 9/11, which I thought was quite poignant."

Ben went first. "I told this story of, like, 'The reason I'm in this room is because I was working a city council campaign and getting a master's in fiction writing and I witnessed the 9/11 attacks,'" he recalls. Rhodes had watched in person as the towers collapsed that day, and it was the reason he'd decided to enter government service. "I was like, 'I'm here in this room because of 9/11, and now I'm here waiting to see if we're going to kill Osama bin Laden.' And I was kind of overwhelmed by it."

Once Rhodes told his story, others began sharing theirs. Letitia

Long, now the director of the National Geospatial Intelligence Agency, had been at the Pentagon. Denis McDonough was at the Capitol, which he fled along with others in a chaotic evacuation. CIA spokesperson George Little recalled losing a family member in the Twin Towers that day. And "Brennan's story was [that] he'd spent the better part of the last fifteen years trying to kill bin Laden," recalls Rhodes, dating back to his time as CIA station chief in Saudi Arabia years before 9/11.

Everyone's lives had been profoundly altered by the terror attacks of Osama bin Laden. And now, in an extraordinary scene, they all huddled together in the White House Situation Room, sharing their personal stories, as they waited to see whether McRaven's teams could finally bring the man to justice—dead or alive.

"It was the most painful limbo," Rhodes told me. "It was white-knuckle, like nobody's business. Because you know, the helicopters could crash at any moment, or the Pakistani radar...there's a world in which they scramble jets. Like, there was shit that could have gone wrong." For McRaven and his SEALs, the raid itself was routine. But the real fear was that they might be discovered by the Pakistanis before getting safely out of the country.

To the shock and horror of the assembled group, shit did go wrong almost as soon as the teams arrived in Abbottabad. One of the helicopters went down in the compound—and most of the principals were watching it happen in real time, in the small conference room where Pete Souza captured that indelible photo.

THE TICKTOCK OF the bin Laden raid has been told in multiple books and articles, in much greater detail than is possible to include here. But as I researched the Situation Room's role in the events, one question kept coming up: Why was everyone crammed into that tiny room, rather than in the larger main conference room where the NSC usually gathered?

The answer lies—as so many answers do—with Gary Bresnahan.

Bresnahan had set up an audiovisual link between the Situation Room complex and the teams in the field. In the large conference room, a video feed connected Leon Panetta at CIA headquarters in Langley and the NSC team in the White House. In the small conference room, General Brad Webb, in his blue Air Force uniform with a chest full of military ribbons denoting service and awards, had not only a direct link with McRaven, but also live feed from Abbottabad, taken by a Sentinel drone with night-vision capabilities flying high above the compound. As McRaven told me, "Brad's in that little room. He's video teleconferencing with me. He's chatting with me and is also seeing what I'm seeing."

The original plan was for President Obama and the other principals to receive updates from Panetta, who was in constant contact with McRaven. Gary Bresnahan was in the smaller room, "talking to McRaven all the time. Then Mullen would come in every once in a while, get a two-minute brief," and then go back into the larger room to relay the information. Once people started realizing there was a live feed from Pakistan in the smaller room, however, they started drifting over to watch for themselves. Vice President Biden went, and then Bob Gates.

At that point, Bresnahan told me, Tom Donilon asked him to switch that video feed from the smaller room to the main conference room. "I told him I couldn't do it," Bresnahan recalls. He could have tried, but he was afraid. "It was like a white lie...I just didn't want to take the chance that when I did move it, something failed." Bresnahan has mixed feelings now about declining Donilon's request. "I wished I hadn't," he told me, because "it would have been a bigger room. But on the other hand, I'm glad I did, because I think [Souza's photo] became more iconic."

The president remained in the larger room, continuing to get updates from Mullen, but eventually he asked, "Where are you getting this information?" Mullen informed him that there was a video feed from the compound in the room next door, and the president got up and walked briskly to the smaller room to watch the live feed himself. And that, as Mike Leiter put it, "is how you end up with this rather clown-car-like image of everyone trying to cram into the small room—because no one can quite figure out how to move the video over to the big room."

In Jalalabad, McRaven was aware that the entire NSC was now watching the raid take place in real time. "We're about two minutes out from hitting the target, and I get this chat from Brad Webb," McRaven told me. "He says, 'Sir, the vice president just walked into the room'...And the next thing I hear is, 'Sir, the president just walked into the room...They're all in the room.'" That, as he recalls, "is right about the time that the helicopter goes down."

As planned, two helicopters had approached the compound. But one of them experienced a "vortex ring state," an airflow problem caused by the unexpectedly warm temperatures and high compound walls, inhibiting its ability to hover. The helicopter's tail clipped a wall, and it went down hard inside the compound, ending up propped against a wall at a 45-degree angle.

"When that helicopter went down at the bin Laden raid," Bob Gates told me, "I thought I was gonna have an aneurysm...My god, not again. And it literally was almost thirty years to the day." It was actually thirty-one years—yet even with that length of time, the memories still felt searingly fresh.

Watching the helicopter go down on the live feed, the group in the small room froze. This was a disaster in the making—the event they had all feared, the ghost of Desert One descending. And then, Admiral McRaven's calm, steady voice came over the feed. "As you can see, the helicopter is down," he said, as if narrating a nature documentary. "We're going to Plan B," he said—"just like calling a cab, just as calm and cool as he could be," as James Clapper told Garrett Graff. Remember McRaven's decision matrix? He had gamed out every possible scenario, including this one.

As Michèle Flournoy told me, "We planned for that. We had two helicopters sitting inside Pakistan behind a land feature that would protect them from detection by radar. But they were literally sitting there, rotors whirring, waiting to be called in, just in case." Lessons had been learned, and the past would not repeat itself.

It's difficult to pinpoint exactly what was happening in the moment Pete Souza snapped his now-famous photo. Souza told me he was squeezed tightly "in the corner of the room, and I couldn't move, literally, because there was somebody right in front of me. Somebody right to my right, somebody right to my left, and my ass was against a laser printer in the corner." He estimates that he shot "about a hundred pictures in those forty minutes," but as soon as he saw that one, "I knew that was the picture." He has tried to figure out what was happening in that moment, and as best he can tell by looking at the time stamps, it was toward the end of the raid.

"My conjecture is, they know they have bin Laden, but they don't know they have everybody out safe yet," he told me.

I asked Souza what it felt like in the room during that time. "In every other situation in the Situation Room—any of those rooms—it was always dialogue back and forth," he told me. "People making their presentations to the president, him listening, him responding, him asking questions. And for these forty minutes in that little conference room, it was not much chatter at all."

According to various reports, there was initially some confusion as to when exactly bin Laden was killed. The SEAL team communicated the word "Geronimo," which was the code word indicating that bin Laden had been found (a choice that was later, understandably, decried by Native Americans). But the message didn't include information on whether he'd been killed or merely captured. McRaven quickly asked for clarification, and the message came back: "Geronimo EKIA"—enemy killed in action. Absolute confirmation of his identity would come later, through DNA matching with other members of the bin Laden family. But for Obama, this was enough. "We got him," he said.

The president would repeat those words when he walked out of the small conference room. Gary Bresnahan had been squeezed out of the small space when so many principals crowded in, so he was standing just outside the door when the action went down. He didn't mind being outside, he told me, because "we're supposed to be behind the scenes anyway." Besides that, his positioning came with an unexpected bonus. "I was the first one to get a fist bump as [Obama] walked out the door," he recalls. "He said, 'We got him.' I said, 'Yes we did, sir.'"

◄O►

MEANWHILE, IF THE Sit Room had been quiet during the raid itself, the chatter began in earnest after the SEALs made it safely back to Jalalabad. At that point, the Situation Room staff had to quickly set up calls with U.S. political leaders, international heads of state—anyone who needed to hear the news from President Obama himself rather than from CNN or other sources, since word was certain to get out quickly.

Former Sit Room duty officer Drew Roberts told me that "a good day was one or two calls, a bad day was five or more," since the calls required not only preparation but fast, accurate, in-the-moment transcription after the fact. Roberts wasn't in the Sit Room on the day of the bin Laden raid, as he had rotated out a month and a half earlier. But he was told that the staff had to make sixty-five calls—an unheard-of number, especially since they had to be done so quickly.

"These poor folks from the day shift stayed," he told me, "because they knew what was coming for the night shift. It took about fourteen of 'em to recap all those phone calls for the national record...All of them have to be typed and checked and redone and sent out." Mike Mullen made the three a.m. call (Pakistan time) to army general Ashfaq Parvez Kayani to let the Pakistanis know the raid had happened.

Well before the president announced at 11:35 p.m. East Coast time that bin Laden was dead, rumors were flying that something big had happened in Pakistan. In fact, they had started while the raid was in progress, when an Abbottabad resident named Sohaib Athar tweeted, "Helicopter hovering above Abbottabad at 1AM (is a rare event)."

I had suspected the night before that something was brewing, but dropped the subject when Bill Daley told me it was nothing. Now, on the evening of May 1, White House press secretary Jay Carney woke me up. "Hey, George," he said. "You should get to work." I wouldn't normally have been on camera that Sunday night, but Jay's heads-up sent me straight to the studio.

At around the same time, Gary Bresnahan, exhausted from two solid weeks of stress leading up to the raid, went home to his girlfriend. Late that night, "she's half-asleep in bed, and I said, 'Good night for America!' And then I go to sleep," he told me. "About two or three hours later it came out, and she wakes me up, and she's like, 'Good night for America, my ass!'" At least now she knew he hadn't been cheating on her for the past two weeks after all.

Bob Gates left government service less than two months after the bin Laden raid. He had served our nation through five decades, ever since being recruited by the CIA as an Indiana University student in 1966. Johnson, Nixon, Ford, Carter, Reagan, Bush, Clinton, Bush, Obama. Nine presidents. Dozens of cabinet officials. Wars. Accidents. Triumphs and defeats. Hundreds if not thousands of meetings in the Situation Room, bearing the burden of those decisions. Toward the end, he seemed to grow weary of the process.

"At the end of the day . . . it's the same eight people dealing with every issue that ends up in the Situation Room," he told me. "The president and vice president, secretary of state, secretary of defense, national security adviser, head of CIA and the chairman of the Joint Chiefs of Staff. The process is tense, with egos and institutional rivalries at play for the highest stakes. It's often tedious, grinding through detail after detail. But the pressure is always there.

"Presidents never get to make easy decisions," he went on. "If any problem is easy to solve, somebody at a lower level will solve it and take credit for it . . . and so almost every decision the president makes is selecting the least bad option."

Having recounted the processes followed for the bin Laden raid, my conclusion is: Whatever you think about Barack Obama, it's difficult to dispute that he did the job the right way. On the big questions, he was methodical and he was prepared. And with regard to the Situation Room, he utilized it in the most efficient, productive way possible. He respected history, he took all viewpoints into account, and he acted decisively.

But let's give the last word to Gates. "I was very proud," he wrote in *Duty*, "to work for a president who had made one of the most courageous decisions I had ever witnessed in the White House."

———◄○►———

Osama bin Laden's body was flown to the U.S.S. *Carl Vinson*, a *Nimitz*-class aircraft carrier in the northern Arabian Sea. The body was wrapped in a white shroud and placed on a large plank for burial at sea within twenty-four hours of his death, per Muslim religious tradition. No more than ten people were present on deck for the brief religious rites that preceded the burial. But standing nearby was a man who, more than most, had reason to find closure in bin Laden's death and final sendoff.

Remember Ed Padinske? The former Sit Room senior duty officer had courageously rushed to the White House on the morning of September 11, 2001, insisting on staying the whole day even though he wasn't scheduled to be there. He had lost multiple friends and colleagues in the Pentagon, attending eight funerals in the two weeks following the attacks. And now, by a stroke of pure chance, he happened to be serving on the *Carl Vinson* when it received Osama bin Laden's body. "It was kind of a bookend to a mission set, handed to me in life," Padinske told me.

As the carrier's senior intelligence officer, he had been alerted that bin Laden's body was coming to the ship. "I couldn't even tell my deputy what was going on," Padinske recalls. But "at one point, one of my warrant officers who was standing watch poked his head in the door and said, 'Hey, sir, I just want to let you know that CNN is reporting that we killed bin Laden.' And I put my operational security face on and said, 'Matt, I've heard that a dozen times. Great. I'll be right with you.'"

Whatever emotions Padinske felt, he tamped them down in the interest of completing the task at hand. "The small group of senior leaders on the ship were focused on the mission, and not really dwelling on what it might mean for the nation," he told me. "It's like, we just don't want to mess this up, and we want to show the nation and the Navy and the U.S. military how we do things on 'America's favorite carrier,' as they call themselves."

Padinske couldn't tell me the operational details, but he said that the ship went on lockdown. "There were no people permitted in passageways and doing normal business," he told me, "except for certain designated people, and I happened to be one of those. It was amazing to see how quiet the ship got. As you're walking down the passageway, you could hear TVs tuned in to CNN and other news channels, and a certain amount of excitement and hope that it was all true... but there are people knowing that yeah, this has been planned for a long time." He didn't show any emotion at all until his deputy figured out what was happening, and then "we just kind of high-fived each other," he told me.

When the burial took place, Padinske "was not a pallbearer, but close by," he says. In his typically understated way, he reveals only that there was "certainly some closure, and it was certainly an honor to be even a collateral witness to it."

But in correspondence with his friend and mentor Lieutenant Commander Mary Sobray, Padinske revealed his deeper feelings about watching bin Laden's body slide into the sea. Sobray had helped Padinske and others pull through the horrifically sad days after the entire Chief of Naval Operations Intelligence Plot team, CNO-IP for short, had perished at the Pentagon. Now, following the burial at sea, Padinske sent her an email saying simply, "Don't worry, Mary. The CNO-IP was there—in spirit and in person."

Chapter 11

POSTCARDS FROM
THE EDGE

———— ◆ ————

"YOU'RE FIRED!"

That signature line from Donald Trump's reality show, *The Apprentice*, was also the singular innovation his administration brought to the Situation Room. On December 12, 2017, chief of staff John Kelly summoned top Trump aide Omarosa Manigault Newman there to inform her that her services were no longer needed in the White House. We know exactly what he said, because breaking all norms and security rules, Omarosa carried a concealed recorder into the Sit Room.

"It's come to my attention over the last few months that there have been some pretty, in my opinion, significant integrity issues related to you," Kelly told her. "We're not suggesting any legal action here...If we make this a friendly departure...you can look at your time here in the White House as a year of service to the nation. You can go on without any type of difficulty in the future relative to your reputation."

Omarosa, who served as an aide in the Clinton administration before becoming a reality TV fixture in three seasons of *The Apprentice*, later said she interpreted Kelly's words as a threat. She continued surreptitiously recording as a human resources aide named Irene Porada entered, handed her a bottle of water and said, "I know this is a bad day." The two women negotiated the terms of Omarosa's departure. And then Porada noted that in two decades of serving in the White House, this was the first time she'd ever been in the Situation Room.

In Omarosa's telling, she wasn't allowed to leave the Sit Room for two hours, despite asking multiple times. "I asked repeatedly—on the recording you can hear me saying, 'Am I allowed to leave?'" Omarosa told me. "And three times they said no. When I asked if I could get my inhaler, because I'm asthmatic, they said I could not leave to get my inhaler." She says she was locked in, effectively held prisoner.

Sit Room senior director Geoff Fowler was on duty earlier that day, though he'd left the White House by the time Kelly and Omarosa met. He told me he knew about the meeting, but not what the topic would be—and he takes issue with Omarosa's claim that she was locked into the room. "I laughed," he says, "because it only locks on the inside. It's like being in a bathroom, it locks from the inside to keep other people from coming in . . . People tell stories, but that just wasn't true."

When it came to the Trump administration, it was often difficult to know what was true and what was not. As Omarosa put it in an NBC interview: "This is a White House where everybody lies. The president lies to the American people. [White House press secretary] Sarah Huckabee stands in front of the country and lies every single day." The only reason we know for sure what was said in the Sit Room that day is because Omarosa recorded it. But how did she manage *that*, in what's supposed to be one of the most secure rooms in the world?

"My understanding is that she had one of these fake pen recording devices," former Sit Room director Larry Pfeiffer told me. "The Secret

Service has capabilities throughout the White House that can pick up on electronic emissions." Meaning, if somebody brings a cell phone— or any other device that transmits signals, such as an Apple Watch, iPad or Kindle—into the Sit Room, sensors will pick it up. But it's still possible to sneak in a small, unconnected device.

There are signs outside the Sit Room complex reminding people not to bring in electronic devices. The receptionist also reminds people verbally, and there's a lockbox outside the room where people are supposed to park their devices. But there's no magnetometer, and "nobody's being frisked as they come in the door," Pfeiffer says. "It's an honor system…Most of the people coming in and out of there tend to be very high-level, very important people. Certain assumptions get made that they're going to do the right thing."

Occasionally, people simply forget. In those instances, the sensors pick up the device, and a Sit Room staffer will come in to retrieve it. Sometimes, incredibly, people still try to sneak in their phones. Before the installation of the sensors, "We had instances where, because of the cameras we have inside the different conference rooms, we could see somebody with their hands under the table, looking down," Pfeiffer recalls. "We'd bring a note in to Tom Donilon saying, 'Somebody's got an active phone in here.' And that's shameful on those people, for feeling like they were either too busy or too important to park their phones like everybody else."

"Security is sort of like an onion," Fowler told me, with layers of protection, from physical security to background investigations. But "the thing that is most critical of all is trust," he says. "The worst thing you can have is an insider who breaks trust. It breaks faith."

Faith and trust were apparently in short supply in this White House, because people in Trump's world—such as his fixer Michael Cohen and Omarosa—were taping each other all the time. Trump habitually taped phone calls before he came to the White House. Whenever I spoke with someone close to him, I assumed I was being taped.

Amusingly, while in the Sit Room that day, Omarosa actually asked whether *she* was being taped. She declared that she hadn't consented to being recorded—even as she was clandestinely recording the meeting herself. It was a moment of comedic moxie in a uniquely bizarre situation.

The Omarosa incident is almost certainly the only time the Sit Room was used to fire a staffer. It's certainly the only time such a firing was recorded. And it reveals a larger truth about the Trump presidency: Almost nothing about it was normal. This book examines crisis management in the modern presidency. During the Trump administration, the president was the crisis to be managed.

It took a toll on those who had to do it. Trump tore through and wore out his national security team: Four secretaries of defense. Four directors of national intelligence. Four White House chiefs of staff and five secretaries of homeland security. The most damning judgments of his competence and character come from those he appointed to these most sensitive positions. His first secretary of state, Rex Tillerson, famously told colleagues that Trump was a "moron." James Mattis, the former Marine Corps general who served as Trump's first secretary of defense, described him as a threat to the Constitution "who does not try to unite the American people—does not even pretend to try." Fellow Marine general and White House chief of staff John Kelly called Trump "the most flawed person I have ever met in my life."

Here, then, are tales of the Sit Room from those who served President Trump—their manic confessions and moments of absurdity. Their postcards from the edge.

◄○►

"He was the least disciplined, least organized human I ever met in my life," homeland security adviser Tom Bossert told me. No matter how hard his top aides and cabinet members tried, "None of them stopped him from constantly undermining us and making decisions outside the process."

"Anybody with any sense—somebody like Mattis or Tillerson—they immediately shunned and stayed away from Trump," Bossert recalls. "I mean, you couldn't get Mattis into the White House. His view was, *That's a madman in a circular room screaming. And the less time I spend in there, the more time I can just go about my business.*" In fact, Tillerson and Mattis began meeting regularly outside the White House in order to circumvent the president.

National Counterterrorism Center head Nick Rasmussen served for two years under Obama, followed by a year under Trump. The difference, he told me, was profound. "The tempo of the White House Situation Room meetings went way, way down in the Trump administration," he recalls. "In the Obama years, I would have been to the White House three, four, five times a week" for meetings at all levels. "In the Trump administration, it could be weeks and weeks without any involvement or meetings."

"I don't think we got Trump into the Situation Room, in my year and a half there, more than four times," Bossert told me. "He didn't like that room. He didn't like the idea that he had to go to it. He wanted everybody to come to him." Bossert tried to tailor the Sit Room processes to fit Trump's unique style. During the transition, he sat down with senior officers to refine their training manuals, "and I began an effort to try to shape them, because Obama consumed information differently than I knew Trump would." Ultimately, it's up to the incoming president to make clear how he'd like to receive his information, "but Trump wasn't going to pay attention to that kind of detail."

Trump rarely sought out information from the Sit Room. He didn't request reports, and he never called down with questions. I asked Bossert whether it was fair to say that for Trump, Fox News Channel was as much a conduit of information as the Sit Room. "I don't even think that's in question," he replied. "I think that's 100 percent accurate." Then he told me something I'd never heard before.

"For a while, he didn't want to see what the news channels were saying. He wanted to see what the chyrons were reading," Bossert says. Chyrons, of course, are the news briefs crawling across the bottom of the TV screen. "He wanted the chyrons captured and printed…And so the Sit Room would do that. They would produce for him books of chyron prints"—surely one of the most prosaic tasks ever required of the highly trained intelligence officers serving in the White House.

Nick Rasmussen remembers an exchange in the first week of Trump's presidency that neatly summed up how different this administration would be.

"I remember going to a meeting on Yemen with [deputy national security adviser K. T. McFarland]," he says. "And someone asked at one point, 'What's going to happen next?'" The group discussed possible scenarios, including what the president might do. "And she said, 'You guys, you're all invested in this process. But this is *your* process, not *his* process.'" McFarland then explained that Trump preferred to make decisions by gathering his family and trusted advisers—which could, and often did, include political strategists and hangers-on—in a closed setting.

Trump's penchant for inviting random people into sensitive meetings led to some uncomfortable moments. Those who didn't have clearances, but were reluctant to defy the president, would find themselves facing irritated intelligence officers. Classified briefings became fraught, with no one in the room comfortable except for Trump, who seemed happy to have his posse with him.

Anytime a president is in the Sit Room, people are going to try to worm their way in. "There's always subordinate interest," says Bossert. "They want to get into the room and hear what's said." During the Trump administration, so many people wanted to join Sit Room meetings that an overflow room was created. People would sit in another part of the complex and watch on a screen—another Trump-era innovation, uniquely suited to a man who became a household name through his appearances on the nation's TV screens.

After Bossert had left the White House, he received a call one day from President Trump. Bossert was in South Korea at the time, and both he and the president were using cell phones. "I said, 'Sir, don't even begin this conversation,'" Bossert recalls. "I'm in a foreign country where I'm connected to their network. There's a hundred-percent chance your phone's being listened to, and a 90 percent chance mine's being listened to in this country. Us together on this phone call, it's a hundred thousand percent guaranteed that they're listening." The math is questionable, but Bossert's point was made.

Trump replied, "Okay, Tom. You tell them I'm sick and tired of them!" And then he went on with the conversation, completely ignoring the warning. "You know, he just wouldn't listen," Bossert says, a sense of wonderment still in his voice.

And as much as Trump complained about leaks, he also used that phone to become, essentially, leaker in chief.

"I caught him doing it," Bossert told me. "I was walking out of the room, and he picks up the phone before I'm out of earshot and starts talking to a reporter about what just happened. And I turned around and pointed right at him. 'Who in the hell are you talking to?'" The president essentially shrugged, seemingly unbothered at being caught.

"He does it, so he assumed everybody was that way," Bossert says. "His paranoia was in part because he assumes everyone else acts like he acts."

John Bolton, who served in high-level positions under presidents Reagan, Bush 41, Bush 43 and Trump, is as methodical and rigorous as they come. So President Trump's capriciousness drove him particularly crazy. I asked him how different Situation Room meetings were under Trump than under the other presidents. "They were a disaster," he told me. "He had no idea what the issues were. He never learned anything." Bolton believes that Trump felt "out of his element. He was surrounded by people, every one of whom knew a lot more than he did. And so he liked to retreat to the Oval Office."

Bolton contrasted Trump with George W. Bush, under whom he served as U.S. ambassador to the United Nations. Bush 43 "was not a foreign policy hand like his father had been," Bolton says. "He knew he had a lot to learn and he learned it. Trump had a lot to learn and he didn't bother." Bolton had assumed that Trump would grow into the role of president. "I just felt that as with every one of his predecessors, the gravity of the issues he had to deal with, the level of responsibility, would impose discipline...but it didn't take long to figure out that wasn't going to happen."

Trump's attitude about foreign policy particularly rankled. "He came in thinking that his personal relationship with foreign leaders would define the quality of bilateral relations," recalls Bolton. "He's still saying it today. 'I had a good relationship with Putin...friends with Xi, or had a bromance with Kim Jong Un' or whatever." While personal relationships undoubtedly matter in international affairs, "they don't override national interest," says Bolton. "Not for the likes of Putin and Xi and Kim and the rest of them. But he never understood that."

The worst episode for Bolton—the moment that nearly led him to resign as national security adviser—came in June 2019, when Trump unilaterally called off a planned strike on Iran just before the missiles were set to launch.

Iranian forces had destroyed a $130 million U.S. Global Hawk surveillance drone in the Strait of Hormuz, an act of aggression that led to a push for a retaliatory strike. "We had a Brent Scowcroft–style meeting of the NSC," Bolton told me. "I mean, I couldn't have scripted it better. We went through everything—all the considerations, the options, the whole thing." During an afternoon meeting in the Situation Room on June 20, which included congressional leaders from both parties, plans were finalized to launch the strike.

After the meeting ended, Bolton went home to shower and change clothes, anticipating a long night to come at the White House. He was stuck in traffic on the George Washington Memorial Parkway, talking on the phone with Mike Pompeo, when the Sit Room broke in with a call. The president wanted to have a conference call with Bolton, Pompeo, [acting secretary of defense Patrick] Shanahan and [JCS chairman General Joseph] Dunford, the duty officer said. When all were on the line, Trump announced to the group's dismay that he was calling off the strikes.

What had happened? Why was Trump suddenly throwing the carefully considered, agreed-upon plan out the window? "Because one of the White House lawyers had come running in and said he had heard that maybe 150 Iranians would get killed," Bolton says. "And Trump got spooked and called it off. Literally, his planes had already been dispatched, and they were all called back."

In his memoir, Bolton wrote that "in my government experience, this was the most irrational thing I ever witnessed any president do." It was a classic example of Trump's acting on the advice of whoever was the last person in his ear. The lawyer's warning that air strikes were out of proportion to the Iranians' offense "was utterly inaccurate, unfiltered, and unconsidered," as Bolton wrote, "but just the kind of 'fact' that inflamed Trump's attention."

COVID-19 BROUGHT ITS own unique chaos to the Situation Room. Mike Stiegler, the duty officer who served during the January 6 insurrection, recalls that the pandemic upended protocols in the White House.

"At one point, in the early onset of Covid, we had certain people who were 'designated survivors,'" he told me. These people, including Stiegler, were directed to go nowhere other than work or home, to minimize the chance of getting infected. He received instructions to limit his movements and have a go-bag in his car, in case the White House had to be shut down.

"If somebody on the Sit Room floor gets Covid at the time, the whole team would have to be wiped out until quarantine's over," Stiegler says. "And then they'd have to clean the Sit Room and sanitize it and all that. And during that process, we would have to go to an alternate location." The staff ran drills, practicing what to do in the event someone brought the virus into the White House.

During the early months of the pandemic, the directives to remain isolated made for a lonely existence. "We would have group chats, where they would check in daily and just kind of make sure we were okay down there," Stiegler told me. "Because for a while, we were completely on our own. The government basically shut down during Covid…so if something happened, we were on our own for a little bit."

The safety protocols were complicated by the president's attitude. "The Sit Room was a no-fail mission. We had to wear our face masks 24/7," Stiegler says. "But if you were to leave the Situation Room, they want you to take it off, because they don't want the optics of fear." Donald Trump famously hated masks, believing they projected weakness. "We were allowed to wear them to the bathroom, but not off the compound," says Stiegler. "And it just started taking a psychological toll on a lot of us. We were raising concerns, and sometimes we'd snap at each other. It just created a lot of unnecessary friction."

Stiegler's frustrations finally boiled over one day outside the White House. The senior director had instructed staff not to wear masks when entering the compound, even when having their temperature checked at the health screening point. This made no sense; if someone did have the virus, standing close to the screener carried the risk of spreading it. "At that point I was a little more flippant than I needed to be," Stiegler recalls. "I asked him, 'What's going to happen if I walk in with a face mask and just disregard [the rule]?' And he said I would be removed from my position." Wearing a mask anywhere outside the Sit Room itself was cause for dismissal.

An irritated Stiegler called his wife on the way home later that day. "I don't think I'm going to be working here in a week," he said. "I'm not going to take that risk anymore." As it happened, he had the next three days off. By the time he returned to the White House, the mask policy had been changed, so he stayed.

————◄○►————

It wasn't just Sit Room staffers who were dismayed at the lack of masking in the Trump White House. Coronavirus response coordinator Deborah Birx, a physician and immunologist who had spent decades working in global health, took it upon herself to educate people working in the West Wing.

"A lot of them had comorbidities, so I was worried about them all the time. We had people with sickle cell trait, we had people with diabetes. We had a full spectrum of ages," Birx told me. "I'm running around trying to make sure that they're all taking Covid really seriously, because the White House was probably the worst masking situation." In the spring of 2020, no one wore masks in the Situation Room. It wasn't until Vice President Pence's spokesperson, Katie Miller, tested positive on May 8 that some people—but not all—began taking masking seriously.

"All of a sudden you find out that Katie was infected," recalls Tony Fauci, director of the National Institute of Allergy and Infectious Diseases and a member of the Coronavirus Task Force. "It was like, *Whoa, what do we do now? Do we wear masks or not?* It was a tough situation, because Trump didn't like masks at all." Fauci started wearing a mask in the Sit Room—"not all the time, but more often than not," he told me. "It was very spotty. It was not like uniformly everybody wearing a mask."

It's shocking to think about now, but the Coronavirus Task Force met in the Situation Room every single day, crowded around the table in the main conference room, breathing each other's exhalations in a windowless room, often without masks. "It was the most intense Situation Room experience I had," says Fauci. During the anthrax scare in the Bush 43 years, "weeks would go by, maybe months, before you went in," he told me. "With Obama, it was a bit more frequent, because they liked to use the Situation Room, particularly when we were talking about Ebola and Zika" viruses. During Covid, "we had one literally every day for months, until [Trump] decided that he didn't want to have anything to do with Covid anymore."

Did Trump attend those early meetings? "I would say, maybe 10 percent or less of the time," Fauci says. "Once every three weeks or so, he would come in, and it was mostly just to show his face." Deb Birx recalls the same: "I think he was in the Situation Room probably four times."

She then described an incident that "illustrates in one episode what was wrong with this White House."

The Task Force was in the Sit Room, being briefed by the Department of Homeland Security's acting head of science, William Bryan. A new DHS study had shown that natural disinfectants such as bleach, alcohol and sunlight could kill the coronavirus on surfaces. Birx was particularly encouraged by the news about sunlight, as she was eager to persuade mayors and governors to reopen playgrounds, which had been shut down in the early days of the pandemic.

Usually, after Sit Room meetings ended, Vice President Pence and his chief of staff, Marc Short, would go to the Oval to brief Trump on what had been discussed. The president would then address reporters in the Press Briefing Room. Fauci often joined the group in the Oval, but "that day, for one reason or another, I didn't go up to brief him," he told me. "I just had a bad feeling about going up."

Unbeknownst to either Fauci or Deb Birx, Bill Bryan—who had neither a scientific nor a medical background—had gone up to the Oval to brief Trump himself. "And in typical fashion," Fauci says, "when the president hears something, he completely takes it out of context and [gets] enthusiastic about something you shouldn't be getting enthusiastic about."

After the Sit Room meeting broke up, Birx had headed to the press room for the briefing. But minutes ticked by, and Trump didn't come.

"Finally, [Bryan] and the president walk down the hallway and we go into the briefing. So, I have no idea what they've been doing" in the interim, Birx recalls. In the briefing, Bryan presented the data about sunlight and bleach. "I'm like, *Great. Now people understand that sunlight is effective.*"

But then, Trump pushed it further. "Supposing we hit the body with a tremendous—whether it's ultraviolet or just very powerful light," he theorized. "Supposing you brought the light inside the body, which you can do either through the skin or in some other way." The president was excited now. "I see the disinfectant where it knocks it out in a minute—one minute! And is there a way we can do something like that by injection inside, or almost a cleaning?" Birx was horrified—this wasn't what the Task Force had discussed in the Sit Room. Where was this nonsense coming from?

Later, in the Q&A period, Trump said, "There's been a rumor, a very nice rumor that you go outside in the sun, or you have heat, and it does have an effect on other viruses." He then turned to look at Birx. "Deborah, have you ever heard of that? The heat and light—relative to certain viruses, yes, but relative to this virus?" Was the president really suggesting, without any medical evidence, that sunlight could kill the virus in people's bodies?

Birx looked as though she wanted to melt into her chair. She mumbled, "Not as a treatment. I mean, certainly fever—is a good thing when you have a fever, it helps your body respond. But I've not seen heat or light as a—"

"I think that's a great thing to look at. Okay?" Trump interjected, clearly eager to cut off an opinion counter to his own.

It was a profoundly uncomfortable moment, and Deb Birx was later pilloried for not objecting more strongly to Trump's dangerous musings. But Fauci defends her. "She didn't realize that [Bryan] had gotten the ear of the president," he told me, calling the whole scenario "really unfortunate for Deb."

Yet while Birx didn't publicly confront the president in the briefing room, she did so immediately after, in the West Wing.

"When I left the press briefing, I went screaming up first to [Pence adviser] Olivia Troye, and was like *four-letter-word, four-letter-word, four-letter-word,*" Birx told me. "And then I found Jared [Kushner] and said, 'You go to the president right now and you make sure he knows that this is bullshit.' And he did." The following day, Trump backtracked, telling a group of journalists that "I was asking the question sarcastically to reporters just like you, just to see what would happen."

Even now, years later, Birx still can't believe that this was how the White House functioned.

"This was about playground equipment," she says. The talking points coming out of the Sit Room had been clear. "No one else knew that he was talking therapeutics. There was nothing, I can promise you, in the Task Force meeting" about that.

WHITE HOUSE PROTOCOLS have been honed over decades. Every rule is in place for a reason, whether for security, or recordkeeping, or to keep checks and balances on the executive branch. But Donald Trump is a man who bristles at rules. He wanted to do things his own way, and he had no patience for the conventions and behavioral codes expected of a president.

"He hated the idea that people were listening to his telephone calls," John Bolton told me. "And you know, I listened to almost every one if I was in Washington." Mike Pompeo, James Mattis and defense secretary Mark Esper also often listened in, and of course the Sit Room duty officers were on the line, taking contemporaneous notes. "He couldn't stand that," says Bolton. "He just thought the Situation Room was the source of many of his problems. And it just drove him crazy…It fed the conspiracy that the whole deep state was watching everything that he did."

On July 25, 2019, the NSC's director for European affairs, Alexander Vindman, was listening to a call between Trump and Ukrainian president Volodymyr Zelensky. During the call, Trump threatened to withhold aid to Ukraine unless Zelensky provided damaging information on Hunter Biden, the son of Vice President Joe Biden. "I would like you to do us a favor, though…" the president infamously said. "There's a lot of talk about Biden's son, that Biden stopped the prosecution, and a lot of people want to find out about that…"

Three weeks later, Vindman filed a whistleblower complaint, alleging that President Trump was "using the power of his office to solicit interference from a foreign country in the 2020 U.S. election." This complaint led to congressional investigations, culminating in the first of Donald Trump's two impeachments.

I asked Vindman about his time at the NSC, and more specifically about his experiences in the Situation Room. Even before he came to work for the Trump administration, he had an experience in the complex that foretold the chaos that was to come.

"Donald Trump was highly unpredictable. And so I did my exhaustive due diligence to find out what I'd be walking into," Vindman told me. He asked one of his military mentors to connect him with people serving in the White House, to find out what it was like to work under Trump. One person he spoke with was NSC deputy chief of staff Colonel James Gallivan, who invited him into the Sit Room complex to discuss the matter.

Gallivan brought him into the same small room where President Obama and his team had watched the bin Laden raid unfold. "It was just the two of us," Vindman recalls. "[He told] me that he'd been to combat three times, and that I was about to enter the most dangerous environment that he'd experienced thus far." This was a sobering and shockingly honest comment, and it gave Vindman pause. But because he, along with NSC senior director for Russia and Europe Fiona Hill, was an architect of the administration's Russia strategy, he believed he was the right man for the position. "I thought it was my duty" to serve, he told me.

Vindman's first day at the NSC was July 16, 2018—the day President Trump, at a Helsinki summit with Vladimir Putin, infamously sided with the Russian president over his own intelligence services. Referring to foreign interference in the 2016 election, Trump announced, "They said they think it's Russia. I have President Putin, he just said it's not Russia...I don't see any reason why it would be." As if that wasn't enough, he then declared that "President Putin was extremely strong and powerful in his denial today."

I was in Helsinki covering that summit, and Trump's words stunned me. Anchoring a special report right after the press conference, I said, "All of you who are watching today will be able to tell your friends, family, your children, your grandchildren, you were watching a moment of history. It may not be for the right reasons." I couldn't imagine how the intelligence officials must have felt, hearing their president call them into question while praising an adversary.

"This was literally my first day on the job," Vindman told me. "You have to do all the bureaucratic processing, you're in briefings, getting your IDs. So half the morning was that normal first day on the job. But then once I came in to listen to the press conference, the rest of the day was basically putting out fires, trying to craft a way to claw back some of the damage." The NSC press person was getting bombarded with calls, as reporters tried to ascertain whether there were different talking points coming out from the White House as opposed to the president's statement.

Given the dichotomy, I asked Vindman whether he felt like he was working for President Trump or the National Security Council. "The National Security Council. Absolutely," he replied. "We were ahead of the rest of the government in crafting a Russia policy...I was going in implementing this strategy that I had a great hand in shaping." So, how did that carefully crafted strategy line up with President Trump's remarks? "It was at odds, because the strategy itself was principled. It was based on the notion of countering Russian malign influence and increasing military aggressiveness."

Vindman now found himself a combatant in a two-front war, against Putin and against his own president. "I was unique in the fact that my obligations to the Constitution were at odds with my commander in chief," Vindman says now. "That's kind of a surreal place to be."

So, why had Trump signed off on the strategy if he clearly had no intention of following it? "The president was generally disinterested in national security," Vindman recalls. "He couldn't have cared less about Ukraine for most of my stint in the White House, because to him it was irrelevant until it became relevant for leverage in the 2020 election. That's when he took an interest in it.

"Basically, he'd parachute in to policy every now and then and throw a hand grenade," he says. "And we would have to pick up the pieces afterwards."

IN THE DAYS leading up to the infamous Trump-Zelensky call, Vindman drafted talking points for President Trump, along with an action plan for nurturing the bilateral relationship and helping Zelensky, a political novice who'd taken office just two months before. It included nearly $400 million in security aid for Ukraine that had been authorized by Congress and announced by the Defense and State Departments.

But when Vindman convened a meeting in the Sit Room complex on July 18, 2019, he discovered the president wasn't on board. Representatives from State, Defense, Treasury, the intelligence community and teams on the ground in Ukraine and Russia were all present, many of them by video. One by one, Vindman asked them to state their opinions about the plan.

Every person in the meeting "confirmed the same kind of principal position, in support of a deeper relationship with Ukraine," recalls Vindman. "And then OMB [the Office of Management and Budget] said, 'We can't support this position because of what we're getting from the president's chief of staff and the president.'" It was a junior OMB staffer who had been tasked with bringing this message to the meeting. No further explanation was given.

It all became clear a week later with that Trump phone call to Zelensky. The president wasn't going to release the funds until he got his "favor" from Zelensky—an act of extortion unparalleled in the history of American presidents. Less than five months later, Trump was impeached for the first time.

I asked Vindman whether Trump's behavior made him angry or merely befuddled. "Operationally frustrated, sometimes," he replied. "It's sixteen-hour days on the NSC, [including] many hours just trying to fix something that shouldn't have been broken in the first place: Get people on the record, write background papers, try to persuade the policy-making community of why we should be doing this." This is a tremendous amount of work—all of it brought down by a president who was less interested in shoring up U.S. security than in finding dirt on his political enemies.

Vindman's pique was not simply because President Trump was

wasting people's time. He draws a direct line from the Trump-Zelensky call to Putin's invasion of Ukraine in February 2022, and the profound global instability that has followed.

"We find ourselves on the edges of a hot war with Russia," he told me, "with the prospects of spillover into a military confrontation. Very low probability, but quite real—more so than at any point in recent history . . . and we find ourselves here in large part because of the Ukraine scandal. Because that is what, in my mind, planted the seeds for Vladimir Putin that U.S. support for Ukraine was not ironclad."

That said, Vindman believes that ultimately the Sit Room worked as intended. "I did my job," he says. "I tried to fix things within my purview. And other folks went to report to the inspector general . . . and exposed the wrongdoing.

"It's the beauty of our system where we have these longstanding institutions as guardrails, and the pieces fit neatly together to check the most egregious kinds of behavior," he concludes. "Which is what happened in this case."

———◆◇◆———

ELIZABETH NEUMANN IS a lifelong Republican and a committed Christian. She served as a homeland security adviser in the George W. Bush White House after a stint in the Office of Faith-Based and Community Initiatives. In 2016, she "very reluctantly" voted for Donald Trump, reasoning that his promise to appoint pro-life judges outweighed questions about his competence and character. She hoped he would learn on the job, that the presidency would change Trump more than Trump would change the presidency.

Still, the first time Neumann was asked to serve in the administration, she said no. The second time she was asked, she again declined.

The third time, there was a moment that made Neumann believe her country needed her.

"It was two days before the inauguration," she told me. "A friend called and said, 'Stuff is going on that we can't talk about on this line. We don't know who we can trust. John Kelly is safe... Will you come work with us?'" Neumann realized that the person was referring to the investigations into Russian influence in Donald Trump's circle. "The impression was not just, 'We're surrounded by people from New York who've never done government and don't know what they're doing,'" she recalls. "It was more than that. It was, 'We don't know who we can trust that is loyal to the United States.'" This was the persuasive factor. "If we're talking about [the security of] our country, I'm happy to serve."

Her reasoning is a textbook example of the classic "dirty hands" temptation in politics—the belief that if you're willing to smudge your soul a bit by sidling up to the dark side of power, you can stop bad things from happening and maybe even do some good.

Having experienced Bush 43's comparatively well-run White House, Neumann was quickly taken aback by Trump's methods.

"One of my memories early on of 'We're not in Kansas anymore' was a phone call that we had with him to prepare for some event," she recalls. "He dials in to tell us what he's thinking and starts giving us instructions. Someone said, 'I have to call our advance guy. Bring him in so he can hear the president's instructions on what he wants the stage to look like, and the backdrop, and what he wants the various [TV] shots to look like.'

"Meanwhile, the *substance*, which was what we were supposed to be talking about—he couldn't care less. I remember us putting it on mute, because he was on speaker," she goes on. "And those of us who were newer started going, 'Oh my gosh, what is happening?' They were like, 'Oh, this is normal.'"

The Trump administration "lacked a gravitas or seriousness," she says. "I remember sitting in the room during these conversations and having to mask incredulousness about the nature of the conversations that were occurring." One of those conversations was about Puerto Rico—and Greenland.

As Peter Baker and Susan Glasser memorably reported in their chronicle of the Trump White House, *The Divider*, Trump had a "fixation" with buying Greenland after it was suggested by one of his New York billionaire friends, Ronald Lauder. Neumann first heard about this in a 2017 Situation Room meeting dealing with disaster relief for Puerto Rico. Hurricane Maria had wrecked the island, killing thousands of people and causing billions of dollars in damage. The entire electric grid was destroyed. But the discussion about how to respond was quickly sidetracked when one participant offered Trump's take on the situation: "When I have bad debt, I just get rid of bad debt. Can we trade Puerto Rico for Greenland?"

Neumann was dumbfounded. "The juxtaposition between walking into these rooms where serious decisions are made, and people's lives are at risk...and then you walk in and they're like, 'So should we swap it with Greenland? I've really been wanting to buy Greenland.' And you're just like, 'What? It's not debt. It's a [territory] with people who are U.S. citizens. You can't just give them away because they had a bad hurricane.'"

Trump often responded in unusual ways to crises. He also started them. In August 2017, he tweeted: "Military solutions are now fully in place, locked and loaded, should North Korea act unwisely. Hopefully Kim Jong Un will find another path!" Neumann recalls that Kelly and her direct boss, DHS secretary Kirstjen Nielsen, were with Trump at his Bedminster golf property when this was happening. "And I was getting texts from Kirstjen, going 'We've literally had to take the phone away because he's going to launch World War III here,'" she told me.

"In a normal situation, if you want to consider military action or threats—even diplomatic threats—you would go to your Situation Room," says Neumann. "You would consult with your experts, your National Security Council, your cabinet members. And then you would do something. But no, no. *We'll just hang out at Bedminster in August and start tweeting. And that's how we make our foreign policy decisions.*"

Neumann fought many battles inside the White House. Early on, over the Muslim travel ban. Later, over the president's reluctance to confront the domestic terror threat posed by white supremacists. She estimates that about 80 percent of the DHS secretary's time was spent trying to stop bad Trump ideas, and she's grateful that John Kelly and his successors stopped so many of them.

But she ultimately came to agree with the conclusion expressed by fellow Trump administration veteran Sarah Isgur, who wrote in the *Washington Post* that those "Trump skeptics who joined the administration thinking they could temper his worst instincts" did a disservice to the country. This hit home for Neumann. "Not that our intent was bad," she told me, "but that we actually did such a good job until the very end that the American public didn't see how bad it was."

Those who went in to be guardrails unwittingly became enablers— and for Neumann, the personal toll was heavy.

"It took me a full year, and some therapy, to be able to fully process how messed up these three years were," she told me. "Because when you're in the middle of it, you keep having these moments of 'This is weird. This is wrong.' But then everybody acts like it's normal. And so it creates that gaslighting effect of 'Oh, maybe it's just me.'" Then she would remember her time in the Bush White House. "No, no, wait a second. I've done this before... This is not what the norm is."

BY THE TIME mobs stormed the Capitol on January 6, Mike Stiegler had been serving in the Situation Room for a year and a half. It had been an exhausting time, and Stiegler was nearing the end of his emotional rope.

He'd arrived for work at the White House at 4:20 a.m. on January 6, and for the next twelve hours he endured the insanity of seeing a sitting president encourage a coup, wondering if the vice president would survive the day, and unsure whether America's 245-year-old democratic experiment was crashing to an end.

As President Trump whipped up the crowd on the ellipse on January 6, 2021, Sit Room staffers anxiously tracked the events. | *AP Photo/ Jacquelyn Martin*

"It was so surreal," he says, "in the sense that you had utter chaos happening at the Capitol, and we had just witnessed all of this craziness. And you walked out of the White House grounds and nothing was happening. It was empty. There's nobody on the streets, because all of them were blocked off at that point... It was literally a ghost town."

The handful of Sit Room staffers who'd just finished their shifts walked slowly to their cars. "We just stood there for a few minutes," Stiegler recalls. "It's like when you mix cold water with hot water, you have to take a second for it to meld together to one temperature. We had to take a minute to feel, *Okay, all right. Get in the car. Keep moving. Let's get out of here.*"

I asked Stiegler what he said to his wife when he got home. "I don't, I don't think..." he said, then had to stop. "Now you're getting me all teary." He took a breath. "I don't think we even really said anything... I still don't know how to talk about half of it." He recalls that his wife asked if he wanted to watch the news. "I said, 'No, don't turn it on. I can't right now. I can't do it.' And I had to go back the next day."

That's right: At five a.m. on January 7, Stiegler was back in the Sit Room. What was it like going back in to work?

"Peaceful chaos," he told me. "You're driving by tanks and it's utterly surreal... They had to sniff your car for bombs and look underneath, and you had to be cleared and swiped for different weapons. And then you got a sticker they would put on your windshield to say that you're cleared to drive around D.C. And you're just like, 'Dude, I'm just trying to go to work. This is unbelievable.'"

This was a dream job for Stiegler. From his earliest days as an intelligence analyst, he told me, working in the White House was on his "bucket list." He even wrote his master's thesis on the inner workings of the Situation Room. On the good days, the job lived up to the hype.

"The best part was, you have complete access to the White House," he told me, smiling at the memory. "When I was on night shifts alone, I would walk around those hallways and look at the different rooms. And sometimes in the early mornings, I would take a cup of coffee and go sit in the Rose Garden, or ask the Secret Service to open up the Oval and just stand there for a minute. I mean, it's magic. It doesn't get better than that."

In addition to those special moments, he said, "there's nothing that parallels being able to pick up the phone and call anyone and get information. The authority that the White House Situation Room carries is just incredible. You're never going to have that pull ever again."

And the worst part?

"I'll say it as politically correctly as I can," he began. "I really struggled sometimes ethically, working and witnessing some of the stuff I was witnessing and then walking outside that gate at Lafayette [Park] and wanting to be on the other side of that fence." Meaning, anywhere but working in the White House.

The Black Lives Matter protests in the summer of 2020 hit particularly hard. "I was witness to many conversations and comments about what was going on," he told me. "It was difficult to be associated with [the Trump White House] and walk out, and we would get death threats thrown at us. We would get insults. As soon as you walk outside that gate, you're associated with that administration.

"I would leave sometimes and literally be escorted by either National Guard or Secret Service to my car," he went on. "And then I would just sit in my car and either have to call a friend or just sit there for ten minutes and just decompress for a moment and kind of disassociate myself. *No, I'm serving my country. I'm serving the office of the president. Even if I don't agree with certain things.* I [tried] to disassociate that, but I wasn't always successful."

In the two weeks between January 6 and the January 20 inauguration, downtown Washington, D.C., looked like a war zone, with armed patrols, hastily erected fences, and a general air of dread hovering over the capital. "Everybody was deathly afraid of something happening," Stiegler recalls. "Even around the White House…they had charter buses literally touching, making a complete wall around." When he was scheduled to work inauguration night, Stiegler knew it would take forever to get through all the roadblocks and security, so he left home at 1:00 p.m. to make his 5:00 p.m. shift. He got there in time, thanks to a surprise assist from the Secret Service.

"I made it through some of the checkpoints and I was at the final [one]," he recalls. The Secret Service stopped him to ask where he was going. He showed his White House badge and said he was heading to the Situation Room. "They're like, 'Well, the VP [incoming vice president Kamala Harris] is about to go from the Lincoln Memorial to the White House for the first time…When the convoy goes by, just join it.'" Stiegler smiles at the memory. "If there's any footage of the VP going down Constitution to go to the White House for the first time, there'll be a blue Camry hybrid in the back of the convoy, and then me peeling off to go to work."

Stiegler parked in his usual spot, then hustled over to watch Vice President Harris's arrival. There were "bands playing and people clapping," he says. "It was just jovial. It was different." How did he feel at that point? "It was a sigh of relief. It was a feeling of, not to be cliché, but a little bit of hope. Like, we made it. Maybe this will be different."

Yet Stiegler is quick to clarify: "Not different in the sense of politically, or political priorities," he told me. "But like, maybe we can just be normal for a minute? Maybe we can just stabilize for a bit." Sit Room officers are the most rigorously apolitical people in the White House, a distinction Stiegler took seriously, no matter what his personal feelings were about the changing of administrations.

"In my role as desk officer, I was chosen that night to write President Biden's first overnight briefing," he says. "But it didn't change anything. I don't care if I'm writing for President Trump or President

Biden, I still gave it a hundred percent...It was an honor, it was great, but at that point it was pretty routine." For Stiegler and his fellow Sit Room staffers, it was back to work, as usual. "Like, okay, pause, bless the moment. Appreciate the moment," he says. "But then close that off and get back to work."

I told Stiegler that I might have been tempted to add a little hand-written note to the briefing, wishing the new president good luck.

"God, I would have loved to," he said. "But no, we are apolitical. We serve in silence."

At the end of our interview, I asked Stiegler if he felt any bitterness about the difficult experience he had in the Situation Room.

"I would probably feel bitter if I didn't have the colleagues that I had," he told me. "We just formed our own family and our own defenses. But I think, if I were to apply 'bitter' to anything, it's bitter that I didn't get the traditional experience, you know? But in the same regard, once this all settles, maybe ten years from now, I've got some hell of a story to tell my grandkids, right?"

He laughed, then added ruefully, "I wanted to be in the middle of history. Be careful what you wish for."

Chapter 12

TIGER TEAM

———◆———

I T WAS THE worst day of the Biden presidency.

Shortly after nine a.m. on Thursday, August 26, 2021, President
Joseph Biden walked into the Situation Room for a briefing on the U.S.
withdrawal from Afghanistan. As he took his chair at the head of the
table, surrounded by the top principals of his national security council,
the group received unsettling news from the Afghan capital.

"The first report we got was, there's been an explosion, some U.S.
injuries, but no reported deaths," recalls national security adviser Jake
Sullivan. A suicide bomber had detonated an explosive at Abbey Gate,
outside the Kabul airport.

Just as America's longest war was finally coming to a close, chaos had
erupted in Kabul. The previous year, President Trump had made an
agreement with the Taliban to have all U.S. forces out of Afghanistan
by May 1, 2021. President Biden extended that deadline to September, but, vowing to stick to the agreement, he rebuffed requests from
the military to leave a small contingent of troops on the ground for

security. In July, he predicted the evacuation of Kabul would not echo the humiliating American exit from Saigon in 1975, when officials had scrambled from the U.S. embassy roof onto helicopters after an ignominious defeat in the Vietnam War.

President Biden's prediction was shattered on August 15 when the Afghan president fled the country and his forces collapsed, ceding control of Kabul to the Taliban. The U.S. began scrambling to evacuate Americans and our Afghan allies. History may not have been repeating itself, but it certainly was rhyming.

Under fire, the president invited me to the White House for an exclusive interview on August 18, so he could take tough questions in a relatively controlled setting. We sat across from each other in the West Wing's Roosevelt Room, and I got right to it.

> **Stephanopoulos:** Back in July, you said a Taliban takeover
> was highly unlikely. Was the intelligence wrong, or did you
> downplay it?
>
> **Biden:** I think—there was no consensus. If you go back and look
> at the intelligence reports, they said that it's more likely to be
> sometime by the end of the year...
>
> **Stephanopoulos:** But you didn't put a timeline on it when you
> said it was highly unlikely. You just said flat-out, "It's highly
> unlikely the Taliban would take over."
>
> **Biden:** Yeah. Well, the question was whether or not it w— The
> idea that the Taliban would take over was premised on the
> notion that the—that somehow, the 300,000 troops we had
> trained and equipped was gonna just collapse, they were gonna
> give up. I don't think anybody anticipated that...
>
> ...[L]ook, George. There is no good time to leave
> Afghanistan. Fifteen years ago would've been a problem, fifteen

years from now. The basic choice is am I gonna send your sons and your daughters to war in Afghanistan in perpetuity?

Stephanopoulos: But if there's no good time, if you know you're gonna have to leave eventually, why not have—everything in place to make sure Americans could get out, to make sure our Afghan allies get out, so we don't have these chaotic scenes in Kabul?

Biden: Number one, as you know, the intelligence community did not say back in June or July that, in fact, this was gonna collapse like it did. Number one.

Stephanopoulos: They thought the Taliban would take over, but not this quickly?

Biden: But not this quickly. Not even close. We had already issued several thousand passports to the—the SIVs, the people— the—the—the translators when I came into office before we had negotiated getting out at the end of s—August.

Secondly, we were in a position where what we did was took precautions. That's why I authorized that there be 6,000 American troops to flow in to accommodate this exit, number one. And number two, provided all that aircraft in the Gulf to get people out. We pre-positioned all that, anticipated that. Now, granted, it took two days to take control of the airport. We have control of the airport now.

Stephanopoulos: Still a lotta pandemonium outside the airport.

Biden: Oh, there is. But, look, b—but no one's being killed right now, God forgive me if I'm wrong about that, but no one's being killed right now.

Eight days later, that was no longer true.

In the Situation Room meeting on August 26, Jake Sullivan, a

Yale-educated attorney with an unflappable demeanor, was keeping the meeting on track as the room absorbed news of a suicide bomber. But he also kept one eye on General Kenneth F. McKenzie Jr., commander of the U.S. Central Command, who had joined via SVTS from U.S. Central Command headquarters in Tampa, Florida. Every few minutes, someone passed the general a note. He'd mute his microphone, have a brief conversation, and then update the group gathered in the Sit Room.

"It was kind of like, based on his look, *how bad is this?*" Sullivan recalls. About thirty minutes into the meeting, the general received a note that made his face fall. "We have KIA," he told the president— killed in action. There were, in fact, many dead, including U.S. Marines. With every note the general received, and every update he conveyed to the Sit Room, the number of casualties kept rising.

"Each one was like a punch to the gut," secretary of state Antony Blinken told me. "And the weight in the room just got heavier and heavier." By the time the final numbers were known, the toll was nearly 200 dead, including thirteen U.S. servicemembers, with scores more people injured.

"Everyone has a job to do, but you could just feel that weight," Blinken says. "And of course, I think it's fair to say that no one carries that burden more than the president." Biden left the room subdued, after authorizing the military to respond as necessary.

———◄○►———

PRESIDENT BIDEN HAD been in office for just over seven months when terror exploded at Abbey Gate. But he brought years of Sit Room experience to the job, having served two terms as vice president under Barack Obama, who used the complex often.

"He spent a huge amount of time there over the years," Blinken told me. "He was in that room certainly as much as any other person, either leading meetings or being a critical part of the principal-level meetings or National Security Council meetings." Biden had his own ideas, honed through experience, of how best to use the room. But his first task was reclaiming a semblance of order and process following the chaos of the Trump administration.

"We inherited a policy process that had either been systematically broken or completely neglected," NSC spokesperson Emily Horne told me. "Foreign policy for the last four years had largely been made by tweet or other form of presidential dicta." It was, she recalls, "very important to get that rigor and that discipline back, to surface the best options for the president."

Unlike Trump, Biden is extremely comfortable in the Sit Room. Like President George H. W. Bush, he enjoys simply popping by. "Biden in the first six months came down to the Situation Room— and not for briefings, just came down to see us—ten, twenty times more than Trump did the whole time he was president," Mike Stiegler recalls. "He would just walk in the door."

He is a "frequent consumer in the Situation Room," chief of staff Ron Klain told me. "He likes to hear from people in the field directly." In the same way that President Kennedy preferred to receive raw intel rather than someone else's summary of it, President Biden "wants to hear directly from our commanders out in the field, and not just get a bunch of stuff that gets chopped up and put in a book for him," Klain says. He wants to hear all points of view, even those—in fact, especially those—at odds with his own.

While serving as vice president, Biden famously acted as devil's advocate in the Sit Room. During the final discussions of whether to launch the Abbottabad raid in 2011, he raised points in opposition to it, providing cover for President Obama to make any decision. Tony

Blinken, who was then serving as Biden's national security adviser, remembers him doing this during discussions about whether to authorize a troop surge in Afghanistan. "Vice president [Biden] was the one person who was constantly pushing and pressing every one of his colleagues on their premises and assumptions," Blinken told me. "That was done very much in complicity with President Obama, [who] could sit back and not show his hand."

Blinken calls this "one of the best processes I've ever been a part of, precisely because the whole purpose of the Situation Room is to convene a multiplicity of views, of all the different stakeholders. It's like the blind mice on the elephant, or Rashomon: depending on where you sit, you're going to have a different perspective."

I asked Jake Sullivan whether anyone plays devil's advocate for President Biden. "It's hard to generate that role at a principals table," he replied. "Either you have a principal who operates that way or you don't. And you can't generate it artificially." That said, Sullivan himself often takes on that function. "I am naturally inclined to the role of pressing on the weaknesses or blind spots in any argument," he told me. "So if it falls to anyone, it probably falls to me."

But even the most rigorous and inclusive process can't eliminate blind spots. President Biden was right to argue that there was "no good time" to exit Afghanistan, and his administration was hamstrung by the Trump administration's pledge to exit without a plan for how to do so. It's also true, however, that Biden's team shares the blame for a catastrophic withdrawal. The intelligence about the Afghan military was wrong. The military pullout was too quick, and the evacuation plans were too slow. Even the State Department's own "after action" report cited "insufficient senior-level consideration of worst-case scenarios."

Sullivan and his entire Situation Room team were determined not to let that happen twice. Weeks after the Abbey Gate disaster, the process would be tested again, this time by Vladimir Putin.

By 2021, Vladimir Putin had come a long way from being the man whose behavior convinced Condoleezza Rice just after the September 11 attacks that "the Cold War really is over." The national security officials I interviewed debate whether Putin changed or simply revealed his true character. But Rice pegs the mid-2000s, around the time Russia went to war with Georgia, as the turning point. I had the chance to interview Putin ahead of the 2014 Sochi Olympics and asked him for his message to Americans who viewed Russia as an "unfriendly adversary."[1] While he stressed that the U.S. and Russia have been allies during "sharp turns in world history, [such as] the first and second world wars," he also acknowledged present-day differences.

Those differences have obviously grown dramatically over the last decade. Just a month after my interview, Russia invaded Crimea. Then came Putin's interference to help Donald Trump win the 2016 U.S. election. Henry Kissinger told me that Putin has become a "character out of Dostoevsky"—a ruler inspired by a mystic vision of a Russian empire surrounded by enemies.

President Biden's take was less erudite and more blunt, a view hardened by years of up-close observation. When I interviewed the president in March 2021, I asked him about a private meeting he had with Putin in 2011:

> **Stephanopoulos:** You said you know he doesn't have a soul.
> **Biden:** I did say that to him, yes. And—and his response was, "We understand one another." I wasn't being a wise guy. I was alone

---

1. That was my first and likely last interview with Putin. In 2022, the Russian government sanctioned and banned me from the country after a contentious interview with foreign minister Sergey Lavrov.

with him in his office. And that—that's how it came about. It was when President Bush had said, "I looked in his eyes and saw his soul." I said, "Looked in your eyes and I don't think you have a soul." And [he] looked back and he said, "We understand each other."

Stephanopoulos: So you know Vladimir Putin. You think he's a killer?

Biden: Uh-huh. I do.

That "killer" comment sent his aides scrambling. But Biden didn't take it back. And he clearly believed that there were no limits to what Putin would do to achieve his agenda. In the fall of 2021, U.S. intelligence began picking up clues to how true that was.

"WHEN WE FIRST got the extraordinary intelligence that we had about what the Russians were actually planning," Blinken recalls, it was "not just the visible fact that they were massing troops on the border, which everyone could see, but this incredibly detailed information about what they were thinking." Blinken alerted Volodymyr Zelensky, but the Ukrainian president downplayed the warning. Russian troops had massed near the border in the spring without invading. Zelensky was reluctant to believe that Putin would actually go through with it.

It was easy to understand why. "We could all see well in advance what a huge problem [the invasion] was going to be for Russia," recalls Blinken. "It didn't really compute logically, by our frame of logic, that he would do this." And of course, the credibility of U.S. intelligence had been badly tarnished by the 2003 Iraq WMD debacle. Why should Zelensky trust it?

The Biden White House, however, believed the intel was solid. So in the fall of 2021, two members of the administration put together a plan that was hatched and executed in the Situation Room.

In late October, "a colleague and I together wrote a memo to Jake [Sullivan] saying 'The intel's coming in... We don't know if it's going to happen, but we know if it happens, the consequences would be tremendous for U.S. national security,'" NSC director of strategic planning Alex Bick told me. The memo, penned by Bick and acting senior director of strategic planning Rebecca Lissner, recommended that the administration create a formalized planning exercise. The purpose: to game out all possible scenarios and major policy questions stemming from a Russian invasion of Ukraine.

The disastrous evacuation of Afghanistan was a major driver in Bick's thinking.

There had been insufficient contingency planning for the Afghan withdrawal. The administration was extremely prepared for the expected scenario, in which the Afghan government remained in control. But it hadn't planned for a situation that required an in extremis evacuation. That failure was a powerful motivation.

Bick and Lissner's memo spurred the creation of a Tiger Team. The term, coined in the 1960s, refers to a group of experts mobilized to solve a specific problem; the most famous example is the team assembled in 1970 to bring the *Apollo 13* astronauts safely back to earth after an oxygen tank exploded on their spacecraft. In late November, Bick began assembling a Tiger Team to address the possibility of a Russian invasion of Ukraine. The goal, he says, was "to try to think through what might happen—all of the questions that we would need to answer. And then to begin to develop a playbook, kind of a 'break-glass' playbook, which could be deployed if the Russians decided to go to war."

The Tiger Team included one representative each from the departments of state, defense, homeland security and energy, the office of the director of national intelligence and USAID. This gave it a cross-section of expertise as well as a diversity of views. Each person was empowered to "be creative and speak for the agency without having to go back on a day-to-day basis to get everything blessed," says Bick. "I did a lot of work in advance to make sure either the deputy or the chief of staff within the agency was aware of and endorsed the person who was on the team."

The team initially met three times a week in the Situation Room, though that soon increased to daily. Even when not there, they stayed in constant contact. This was, Bick recalls, "outside the normal policy process, not duplicative, genuinely collaborative and genuinely creative. Those are not easy things to do in the bureaucracies."

Throughout December, the Tiger Team hashed out its detailed break-glass playbook. "Let's say they invade. What happens in the first twenty-four hours, the next twenty-four hours, the next twenty-four hours?" says Jake Sullivan. The playbook covered every topic: "on sanctions, on military assistance, on coordination with allies, on preparing for contingencies like cyberattacks or escalation of various kinds," he recalls. Chastened by the Kabul disaster, Sullivan says he zeroed in on the question "When the invasion happens, what will we wish we had done that we haven't done? Let's do it now."

"We went back and forth... trying to understand whether to plan against the most likely scenario, or plan against the worst-case scenario," Bick told me. The group decided on worst-case, he says, because "it's easier to walk in from a fully elaborated plan than it is to, on the fly, expand and deal with a much more complicated and more difficult situation than you initially anticipated."

I asked Emily Horne what those worst-case scenarios were.

"I don't want to get too specific on things that ultimately did not happen, because we feel quite fortunate that they did not happen," she told me. "It was a stressful exercise to think about…what's the messaging response in the event of something truly terrible—I should say, *more* terrible than what has already happened to Ukraine."

Horne clearly didn't want to reveal more. But I pressed her a bit, saying that if I were in her shoes, I'd have been worried about events like a decapitation strike on Kyiv of the Ukrainian leadership, an assassination attempt on Zelensky, or even a low-yield nuclear strike.

"I think you're very much in the right frame of mind," Horne replied. "Yes."

Failure was not an option. Too much was at stake: Ukrainian sovereignty. Global geopolitical stability. The threat of a ground war expanding into other parts of Europe. The possibility of nuclear conflict.

Given these stakes, and the complications of planning for multiple scenarios, President Biden laid down three parameters. "The first is, ensure a sovereign, independent, viable Ukraine," Sullivan told me. "Number two is, maintain NATO unity. And number three is, avoid World War III"—or, as Horne remembers it, "don't get sucked into a war. No U.S. ground troops." Having these parameters helped, Horne recalls, "because when you have infinite options, it actually can lead to decision paralysis. So when you have things that are explicitly walled off by the commander in chief…it does help you hone in on what your priorities are."

With diplomatic efforts to defuse the situation going nowhere, and skepticism rife that Putin would actually invade, President Biden ordered the intelligence pointing to a Russian attack to be declassified and shared, in hope of jolting Zelensky, our allies, and the media into realizing what was coming. The move would steal the element of surprise from Putin, while hampering his ability to create a pretext for an attack.

On December 7, Biden spoke with Putin via SVTS in the JFK conference room. He warned the Russian leader that there would be serious consequences, economic and otherwise, of invading Ukraine. Biden's plan was to lay everything out on the table, but although the leaders spoke for two hours, Putin kept his cards close to the vest. The situation began to resemble a slow-motion car crash: You could see the impact coming but couldn't do anything to stop it.

The Tiger Team ramped up its preparations, testing the playbook with a series of tabletops—essentially role-playing exercises, where participants gamed out responses to every possible scenario. "It's really very unusual in foreign affairs and national security to have such advance warning before something truly history-making happens," Emily Horne told me. "We did have the luxury of a lot of time to really think creatively." In January 2022, the team delivered its playbook to the principals, then to President Biden, who signed off on it.

The stage was set. U.S. intel suggested that the Russians might move at any time, but with the winter Olympic games scheduled for February 4–20 in Beijing, most expected Putin to hold off. It seemed highly unlikely that he would launch an invasion while his neighbors to the east were hosting the games. After the frenzy of preparations, some in the White House dared to relax a bit.

But the respite would be short-lived.

————◄○►————

AT AROUND FIVE p.m. on February 10, "we got a piece of intelligence," national security official Matt Miller recalls. "Not getting into too many details, it made clear that Russia might attack before the end of the Olympics." Ten minutes later, Miller received another email, calling for an emergency meeting of the principals in the Sit Room at six p.m.

Because of the quick turnaround, many of the principals joined by SVTS. President Biden wasn't in the Sit Room when it began, but he and Vice President Kamala Harris walked in shortly after the meeting started. This was all-hands-on-deck—the moment the administration had been preparing for since early October.

"I'm sitting in the chair, running the meeting, like 'All right, this may happen as soon as...hours to days from now,'" Jake Sullivan recalls. As soon as the president walked in, Sullivan slid out of the chair at the head of the table, and President Biden settled into it and took charge.

He ordered two points of action. "One was to immediately downgrade some of the intelligence so we could share it with allies—NATO allies, Ukraine, obviously—and make them aware that this could happen in very short order," recalls Miller. This was an intensification of the intel-sharing strategy started in December. "And two was to work both inside the U.S. government, and with the allies we were planning these steps with, to make sure all of our response mechanisms were ready—the sanctions, the export controls, all the things that we were planning to go in a couple weeks."

For Emily Horne, whose fortieth birthday happened to fall on February 10, the day was full of strange contradictions. "My team brought me the saddest little cupcake in all the land," she recalls. "And I was so touched, because they'd been working their hearts out for months." Everyone was ready, Horne says—but the event they'd been planning for was one they dreaded. "You're waiting, sort of coiled and ready for action," she said. "But you're also really, really hoping that it never happens."

President Biden's decision to declassify and share intelligence was an unusual and highly strategic move. It set up a win-win scenario for the White House: If going public managed to cow Putin into calling off the invasion, catastrophe in Ukraine would be averted. U.S. intelligence might wind up with egg on its face, but that was a price worth paying. If, on the other hand, Putin forged ahead, U.S. intelligence efforts would be validated, and the White House would have a head start in organizing an allied response.

"The object of [releasing the intel] was less to stop them from invading, and more to shape the invasion in a way that was maximally to our advantage rather than theirs," Jake Sullivan told me. It was an effort to win the information space—something the United States had failed to do in the Afghanistan debacle.

"First, deny them the element of surprise, which they had in [the 2014 invasion of] Crimea and worked massively to their advantage because they created a fait accompli before the world had scrambled to do anything about it," Sullivan went on. "And the second was to deny them a pretext where they could say to the world, 'We had no choice, the Ukrainians are bombing us. The Ukrainians just killed a hundred ethnic Russians.'"

Seven years earlier, the Russians had tested the waters by invading Crimea and the Donbass. "Both times, they were able to achieve the element of surprise, and also the element of fuzziness: *What's happening exactly, and why is it happening?*" Sullivan told me. "And any time there's fuzziness in international politics, it allows everyone to kind of default to, 'Well, we're not really sure what's happening, so we shouldn't really do anything about it.'

"Clarity is not Russia's friend," he concludes. "And creating clarity about what was going to happen, and why it was happening, enabled the galvanizing of the coalition" that would oppose the invasion.

On Thursday, February 17, Secretary of State Blinken addressed the United Nations Security Council. He went into extraordinary detail about Russia's preparation for the invasion, the pretexts Putin was manufacturing to justify the attack, and the expected targets of Russian forces. "We've been warning the Ukrainian government of all that is coming," Blinken told the group. "And here today, we are laying it out in great detail, with the hope that by sharing what we know with the world, we can influence Russia to abandon the path of war and choose a different path while there's still time."

Blinken also acknowledged the specter of the 2003 Iraq WMD debacle. "I am mindful that some have called into question our information, recalling previous instances where intelligence ultimately did not bear out," he said. "But let me be clear: I am here today not to start a war, but to prevent one. The information I've presented here is validated by what we've seen unfolding in plain sight before our eyes for months."

This was the win-win strategy in action. "The goal of him going out was this last-ditch effort, let's see if we can prevent this from happening," Lissner told me. "So in some sense, success would have been getting it 'wrong.' But in the end, Putin went forward, and everything that we laid out ended up being validated by events that followed."

◄○►

In the early morning hours of Thursday, February 24, Russian troops stormed into Ukraine. Missiles rained from the sky, wreaking fiery havoc on cities such as Kharkiv and Dnipro and the capital city of Kyiv. In a lengthy speech, President Putin announced that this was a "special military operation" intended to "protect people who, for eight years now, have been facing humiliation and genocide perpetrated by the Kyiv regime." President Zelensky quickly declared martial law and cut off all diplomatic ties with Moscow. "Russia has embarked on a path of evil," he tweeted. "But Ukraine is defending itself."

Shortly after dawn broke in Washington, D.C., President Biden met with the NSC in the Situation Room. Vice President Harris, cabinet secretaries Antony Blinken, Lloyd Austin and Janet Yellen, CIA director William Burns, General Mark Milley and others— all wearing masks, per Covid protocol—crowded around the JFK conference room table, which was covered with coffee cups and paperwork. "People across the government closely consulted the Tiger Team playbook," Alex Bick notes with pride. "Which I've got to say as a planner is a pretty satisfying thing, since most of these break-glass playbooks are still collecting dust on some shelf of the defense department. This one had a life."

Since the Tiger Team had laid out clear steps, President Biden wasted no time in solidifying an allied response. "What we had planned was, as soon as this goes down, we're going to do...a G7 summit," recalls Jake Sullivan. "And we're going to show that there is unity. And we almost pre-negotiated, basically, joint statements that would come out of those things." Then they did something that would have been simply inconceivable in the original Situation Room: Modern video technology allowed them to create an instantaneous virtual summit of world leaders, who all popped up on the video screens in the JFK conference room. Imagine if, at the height of World War II, Roosevelt, Churchill and Stalin had been able to have daily video meetings, looking each other in the eye, while Hitler marched through Europe.

"It's like a Hollywood Squares–looking, kind of like a Zoom call," deputy national security adviser Jon Finer told me, with the leaders of Germany, Italy, Japan, the United Kingdom, France, and Canada all in little boxes on screen. "Think about how hard it would have been to get that group of leaders face-to-face."

The comfort with this technology was one of the few benefits of the ongoing pandemic. "It was this weird thing where you're using the technology of the Situation Room, but also the adaptation forced by Covid," says Miller. "People suddenly are used to doing video conference meetings—even heads of state."

President Biden rallied his G7 counterparts to line up behind Ukraine. "The fundamental message [was] that unity was going to be, in some ways, our most important strategic asset," Finer recalls. "And that preserving it would be challenging, but was just essential to supporting Ukraine in what was going to be a very long, difficult period ahead."

Suddenly, the president rose from his seat and walked out of the conference room. He ducked into a small secure telephone booth, sliding its glass door shut. In that tiny, anachronistic booth, he connected with Zelensky, who was hunkered down in the presidential compound in Kyiv. As the two men talked on the phone, "Zelensky was telling him an update from the ground about what was happening…basically describing a bunch of things they needed in terms of security assistance," Finer recalls. Biden would then poke his head out of the booth and tell Jake Sullivan, Secretary Austin and Secretary Blinken what Zelensky needed, and the information would be conveyed to the G7 leaders.

President Biden in the phone booth where he spoke with Zelensky. | *Official White House Photo by Adam Schultz*

"That phone booth is an amusing aside," Blinken told me. "It looks like a relic of the past, but ... it has a couple of classified phones in it, so that you could have a secure conversation, and also a private conversation." It feels incongruous in this age when phone booths don't really exist anymore, he admits. "It seems like something out of *Get Smart*"— the 1960s TV sendup of spy movies.

Hearing this, I couldn't help but think back to the scene in April 1961: Tazewell Shepard sits outside the Cabinet Room during the Bay of Pigs, waiting for Admiral Burke to pass along orders from President Kennedy, which Shepard then relays by phone to the Joint Chiefs of Staff. Six decades later, the technology is obviously superior, with secure phone lines and crisp real-time video bringing the world's leaders together at the push of a button. But the basics of person-to-person communication are, in many ways, unchanged. The core of any successful collaborative endeavor, from a summit of the most powerful people on earth to a tabletop exercise to a simple staff meeting, is the ability of humans to connect.

Yet with all the benefits, "there's something lost in the fact that we're not physically in the same room together," Wendy Sherman says. "What's lost is that bonding from that tiny room, and the business on the margins that you can do before the meeting starts and when the meeting ends, and the notes that you can't pass to the person sitting next to you, or the jokes you can't make about whatever somebody else is saying by passing a note to the person across the table."

So much has changed in the sixty-plus years since the Situation Room was established. And yet, the Cold War conditions that led to its creation have come full circle. Once again, the United States and Russia are adversaries. We're again engaged in a tense and dangerous conflict over another people's land. History is, in some ways, repeating itself. The difference is, we now live in a world where information flow is instantaneous, technology is ubiquitous and timelines are compressed.

"The world's a much more complicated place," says Wendy Sherman, "because it's not like there are just two powers, the Soviet Union and the United States. And there aren't two major nuclear powers. There's Chinese nuclear power, there's Pakistan, there's India, and of course the original nuclear powers of France and Great Britain... It's a multipolar world. It's not a bipolar world."

There are "lessons to be learned from the Cuban Missile Crisis," she told me, "but you don't want to overlearn it. It's a very different situation...Communication is so fast. So fast, that you don't have time to deliberate in the way that Kennedy did," she says, concluding that "the pressure to move faster is unfortunate." And this is why the Situation Room was, and remains, a crucial and irreplaceable part of any administration. Never again will a president have the luxury of taking extra time to deliberate a response: Between satellites, cell phones, social media, streaming video and the insatiable global appetite for information, the world learns almost instantly whenever a crisis arises.

"Time and the world do not stand still," President Kennedy remarked during a speech in Frankfurt in 1963. "Change is the law of life. And those who look only to the past or the present are certain to miss the future." No matter how much changes outside its walls in the years to come, the Sit Room will change along with it. Because it must.

Epilogue

WHSR

——◆——

WOW. IT FINALLY *looks like it does in the movies.*

That was my first thought when I entered the Situation Room for the first time in twenty-seven years. It was August 2023, a month before the renovation would be revealed to the world. As Sit Room director Marc Gustafson walked me through, I could hardly believe the difference from my days in the Clinton White House. The cramped, low-ceilinged, semi-analog series of rooms I remembered had been transformed into a digitally advanced, ergonomically designed, smartly configured complex.

The main JFK conference room is now wider, its flat ceiling replaced by floating cloud-style tiles with a backdrop of cool blue light, adjustable to other colors. Three walls are lined with screens and digital displays indicating the meeting's classification level, whether microphones are on, and the time zones in hot spots around the world. On the fourth wall, behind the chair at the head of the table, hangs a large presidential seal. In a nice design touch, this can be popped off and replaced with other seals, such as the vice president's or the executive office of the president, when someone other than POTUS is chairing a meeting.

The small conference room where President Obama and his team watched the bin Laden raid is gone, replaced by two breakout areas. But the room wasn't demolished: all the components were carefully saved and reassembled for display at the Obama presidential library in Chicago. Similarly, the phone booth where President Biden called Zelensky has been removed; it's now in storage for display at the Biden presidential library. This trend was started by the Reagan presidential library, which reassembled and displayed the former main conference room following the 2006 renovation.

In the newly updated watch center, duty officers monitor a multitude of screens from two rows of adjustable standing desks. A couple of glass-walled offices, for the director and deputy director, have switches to make their walls instantly opaque for privacy. And on the watch floor, there's a "sanitize" button that instantly clears all visible screens of secret material whenever someone without proper clearance enters the space.

In a nod to history, the mahogany is back. Most of the complex's walls are made of the deep, rich wood, ethically sourced in collaboration with the Rainforest Alliance. A presidential seal, carved from granite sourced from local quarries, is mounted on the wall outside the JFK conference room. Marie Harnly, the director of White House Situation Room Special Projects, served as the lead on the renovation, and she sought input from duty officers on everything from lighting to desks to chairs (everyone always has an opinion about chairs).

The demolition phase, undertaken mostly by robots, once again uncovered the old sunken courtyard columns dug up in 2006. But because the complex was renovated to have modular components, any future upgrades will happen piece by piece—nothing like the yearlong, total overhaul that shut the space down between August 2022 and August 2023. This decision was made to minimize future disruption of the Sit Room, keeping it as a centralized, efficient 24/7 nerve center for decades to come.

Funnily enough, it's not even called the "Sit Room" now. Sometime in the 2000s, people began calling it WHSR—pronounced "whizzer"—a term I'd never heard before researching this book. Emily Horne says she learned this just before her first meeting in the complex, during the Obama administration. "I was so excited, like, 'Oh my gosh, guys, we have a meeting in the Sit Room!' And someone sort of looked at me, like, 'We call it WHSR,'" she recalls with a laugh. "There was definitely a sense of, the cool kids call it WHSR." I suppose I'm not one of the cool kids, because I still can't bring myself to call it that.

WHILE TOURING THE renovated complex, I thought back to Doug Lute's observation that the Sit Room is made up of three Ps: place, process and people. The place is clearly in the best possible shape. What about the process and the people?

Over the course of the twelve administrations that have used the Situation Room, clear lessons have emerged about how it functions best. First, you need extraordinary trust: The kind the Obama team built up over years of working together before planning the bin Laden raid. The kind that decades of officials, both Republican and Democrat, had in Brent Scowcroft to be an honest broker. The kind that a group of unknown duty officers had in each other on 9/11, when they unanimously insisted on staying in the Sit Room despite the very real possibility that they would die there that day.

Trust is the foundation of teamwork. It enables people to express dissent—another vital component of an effective Situation Room. No president is served well by sycophants and groupthink; a healthy debate is critical to finding the best path forward. One need only look at the example of Vladimir Putin, who undoubtedly received little pushback when he decided to invade Ukraine. "The Achilles heel of any autocracy is that you don't have people who are willing or able to speak truth to power," Tony Blinken told me. "That's incredibly dangerous." The Sit Room's strength—more broadly, our strength as a democracy—depends upon having that give-and-take. The best decisions are made when all possible scenarios are considered and discussed, even if they are uncomfortable for the commander in chief. Perhaps especially so.

The decisions presidents make in the Situation Room are by definition the hardest ones to make, because anything easy will have already been solved by someone at a lower level. You want to make sure the president has the best possible information, which sometimes means going over it repeatedly in the most minute detail. The Sit Room experience, Bob Gates told me, is like flying a plane. It's "either hours and hours of excruciatingly boring debate over the same issues over and over and over again—or terrifying decisions that have to be made." Just as a pilot must be ready for any possibility, those in the Sit Room must be, too. In both cases, it can be a matter of life and death.

Finally, it's crucial to have a sense of history. Remembering the mistakes of the 1980 Desert One debacle was vital in planning the 2011 bin Laden raid. Understanding how the rogue operator Oliver North coopted the Sit Room for his own purposes helps prevent such abuses happening again. Acknowledging how Madeleine Albright maneuvered to give voice to women encourages greater diversity at the table. The ghosts of history—from LBJ's micromanaging to Nixon's absence, to the mad scrambling after Reagan was shot to the chaos of the Trump administration—hover over the Situation Room. The people who serve in it must master a balancing act: absorb the lessons of those moments without being paralyzed by them.

As the stories in this book have made clear, when we speak of the people in the Situation Room, we're talking about two distinct groups. There are the presidents, vice presidents, cabinet secretaries and NSC members—the principals—and their deputies and staff members. And then there are the duty officers, analysts, communicators and directors who make up the 24/7 Sit Room staff.

JFK's goal of centralizing decision-making in the White House with the NSC principals has only solidified in subsequent decades. That will likely continue. Presidents can't off-load crisis management. But what about the 24/7 staff? In the Sit Room's seventh decade of existence, will it continue to be made up of people like Gary Sick, who read thousands of pages a day to funnel information to the president? Or Mike Stiegler, who spoke of how "incredibly difficult" it is to boil a fifteen-page classified document down to three lines?

Eric Schmidt doesn't think so. The former CEO and chairman of Google and its parent company Alphabet, Schmidt expresses amazement at what people are still asked to do in environments such as the Situation Room. Intelligence analysts, he says, are "typically analyzing text and pictures. Why in the world would you have humans analyzing texts and pictures today? Makes no sense...that poor person is sitting there with pages and pages and pages and trying to look for correlates. That's exactly what computers do."

Schmidt believes that the national security apparatus should be relying more on artificial intelligence (AI). "We have all sorts of satellite information, which we get all the time, and humans are watching that stuff. That should all be automated," he told me. If Google oversaw national intelligence, he went on, "you'd build a bunch of AI algorithms to look for interesting things. It's easy to find them; that technology is well mature. You would surface them and some Google person would say, *Oh, that's interesting. Let me either run a new task or let me ask it to go analyze another question, or I'll ask the computer to analyze what I'm seeing and give me probabilities.* None of that, as best I can tell, occurs."

I remarked that the work of the AI algorithms sounds exactly like what the duty officers have been doing for all these decades: taking in reams of information and identifying what looks new or different.

"None of that makes any sense now," Schmidt said. "What you want is, you want humans to do reasoning that computers can't identify . . . I would never have humans look for patterns, because computers are so much better at it."

As I write this, AI has begun upending the workforce. It's sending shock waves through the worlds of technology, journalism, law, entertainment, publishing and many others. It is poised to alter the way humans write, edit, analyze and create. Schmidt is of course correct that the Situation Room will have to adapt to these changes: As technology evolves, so must the nerve center of the White House. And it's inevitable that, as this new era unfolds, the jobs people hold in the Sit Room will look less and less like they did for the first sixty years.

But there are things technology cannot replace. The Situation Room will always need, presidents will always need, America will always need the character these duty officers have brought to the White House basement every day. The ingenuity of Gary Bresnahan. The sensitivity of Sally Botsai. The creative vision of Jake Stewart. The sheer courage of Ed Padinske and Rob Hargis. The steady hand of Elliott Powell. The grace under pressure of Deb Loewer. The dedication to public service of Mike Stiegler. The quiet patriotism of those who serve in silence.

There's one more special part of the newly renovated Sit Room. It's a pillar in the watch center—the single structural element, besides the walls, that holds up the ceiling. Made of concrete, the pillar is covered with dark fabric to dampen sound. It's unremarkable, nothing you'd notice if you were in the room. But hidden underneath that fabric is something that made my throat catch: signatures. Dozens of signatures of officers who were serving in the complex as the renovation happened. Sarah May. Jared Fleming. Kim Lang. Brittney Hensley. Marc Gustafson.

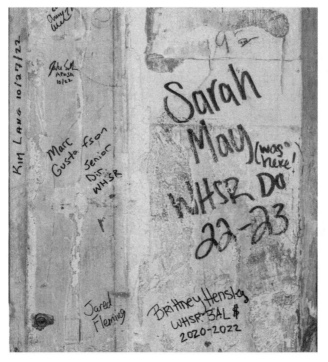

The concrete pillar, with signatures. | *Courtesy of WHSR Archives*

These are, like all those who have served since 1961, the unsung heroes of the Situation Room. Like the others, their names are preserved for posterity, but have been hidden from view.

Until now.

ACKNOWLEDGMENTS

This book was a true team effort. Lisa Dickey is the Platonic ideal of a co-writer. Curious, diligent, always upbeat. She has a quick pen, a clear mind and an open heart. I couldn't—and wouldn't—have written this book without her. Our researchers Emily Michel and Cameron Peters tracked down interviews, scoured the libraries and synthesized reams of information. Their work was impeccable. Any mistakes or oversights are on me. My indefatigable ABC producer Chris Donovan also provided invaluable fact-checking and research assistance. The original idea for this book came from the Javelin team—Matt Latimer and Keith Urbahn—who expertly shepherded us through the publication process.

Hachette Book Group gave us unwavering support. Our editors were superb. Sean Desmond guided us with enthusiasm, sound judgment and a strong sense of history. Colin Dickerman brought the project home with gusto. Thanks also to Zoe Karimy, Carolyn Kurek,

Andrew Goldberg, Rebecca Holland, Jim Datz, Ana Maria Allessi, Kim Sayle, Megan Perritt-Jacobsen and Lindsay Ricketts.

More than one hundred veterans of presidential administrations and the Situation Room agreed to be interviewed for this project. I'm grateful for their insights and time.

America's presidential libraries are a national treasure. We received invaluable assistance from Stacy Chandler at the John F. Kennedy Presidential Library; Jennifer Cuddeback, Lara Hall, Carrie Tallichet Smith and Chris Banks from the LBJ Presidential Library; Mark Updegrove and Hannah Green from the LBJ Foundation; Ryan Pettigrew from the Richard Nixon Presidential Library and Museum; Jim Byron and Jason Schwarts from the Richard Nixon Foundation; Brooke Clement, Geir Gunderson and Elizabeth Druga from the Gerald R. Ford Presidential Library and Museum; Brittany Parris, Ceri McCarron and Billy Glasco from the Jimmy Carter Library and Museum; Cate Sewell and Steve Branch from the Ronald Reagan Presidential Library and Museum; Chris Pembleton, Elizabeth Staats, Zachary Roberts and Mary Finch from the George H. W. Bush Presidential Library and Museum; Jay Barth, Dana Simmons and John Keller from the William J. Clinton Presidential Library and Museum; Sarah Haldeman and Sarah Barca from the George W. Bush Presidential Library; and Thomas Hayes from the Barack Obama Presidential Library.

President Biden's White House staff were generous with their time and guidance, especially Marc Gustafson, Adrienne Watson, Sean Savett, Marie Harnly, Adam Hodge and Kianna Castillo.

Thank you to my ABC colleagues for their support and teamwork, especially Simone Swink, Jonathan Greenberger, Nicole Katchis, Jen Pereira, Jen Joseph, John Santucci, Jon Cohen, Kerry Smith and Van Scott.

Leslie Sloan and Jami Kandel at Vision PR are the best in the business.

My good friend MJ Rosenberg read the manuscript with care and made it better, as did my longtime CAA agent Alan Berger and Alyssa Mastromonaco, who runs the production company Bedby8 that I started with my wife, Ali Wentworth.

Ali, Elliott and Harper deserve the most thanks. They are my joy.

NOTES

PROLOGUE: CENTER OF THE STORM

Publications: *White House Years* by Henry Kissinger; *Our Man: Richard Holbrooke and the End of the American Century* by George Packer

Interviews: Tom Donilon, Doug Lute, Mike Stiegler

CHAPTER I: AT THE CREATION

Publications and oral histories: "Organizational History of the National Security Council during the Kennedy and Johnson Administrations" by Bromley K. Smith; *Nerve Center: Inside the White House Situation Room* by Michael K. Bohn; *A Concept for Cold War Operations Report*—1961, John F. Kennedy Library; *Thirteen Days* by Robert F. Kennedy; *A Thousand Days: John F. Kennedy in the White House* by Arthur M. Schlesinger Jr.; Oral

History Interview with Godfrey T. McHugh—May 19, 1978, John F. Kennedy Library; Oral History Interview with Gerry M. McCabe—June 24, 1976, John F. Kennedy Library; *Under This Roof: The White House and the Presidency* by Paul Brandus; Presidential Recordings Digital Edition—University of Virginia Press; "The Information Needs of Presidents" by James W. Lucas for the Center for Information Policy Research at Harvard University—December 1991; Oral History Interview with Tazewell Shepard Jr.—April 3, 1964, John F. Kennedy Library; Lucius D. Battle, Oral History Interview—October 31, 1968, John F. Kennedy Library

Interviews: Deborah Birx, Valerie Jarrett, Condoleezza Rice, Jim Steinberg

CHAPTER 2: ALL THROUGH THE NIGHT

Publications and oral histories: The Miller Center's Presidential Recordings Program; *The Vantage Point: Perspectives of the Presidency, 1963–1969* by Lyndon B. Johnson; George Reedy's Oral History with the LBJ Library; The National Security Council Project—Oral History Roundtables, "The Role of the National Security Adviser," October 25, 1999, for the Center for International and Security Studies at Maryland—School of Public Affairs, University of Maryland and the Brookings Institution; *Reaching for Glory* by Michael Beschloss; Robert S. McNamara Oral History Interview by Walt Rostow for the LBJ Library—January 8, 1975; *Nerve Center* by Michael K. Bohn

Interviews: Luci Baines Johnson, Tom Johnson, Mark Updegrove

CHAPTER 3: "ALL HELL HAS BROKEN LOOSE"

Publications: *Years of Upheaval* by Henry Kissinger; *RN: The Memoirs of Richard Nixon* by Richard Nixon; *Master of the Game* by Martin Indyk; *One Man Against the World: The Tragedy of Richard Nixon* by Tim Weiner; "On Watch in the White House Basement for Armageddon," by James M. Naughton, *The New York Times*, May 10, 1977; "Stumbling Toward Armageddon," by Sergey Radchenko, *The New York Times*, October 9, 2018; Charles Stuart Kennedy and William Lloyd Stearman, Interview with William Lloyd Stearman. 1992. Manuscript/Mixed Material

Interviews: Sally Botsai, Garrett M. Graff, Henry Kissinger, Tim Weiner

CHAPTER 4: S.O.S.

Publications: *Nerve Center* by Michael K. Bohn; *A Time to Heal* by Gerald R. Ford; *Years of Renewal* by Henry Kissinger; *The Mayaguez Incident: Testing America's Resolve in the Post-Vietnam Era* by Robert J. Mahoney; "Reagan Told of Battle Six Hours Afterward," by Lee Lescaze, *The Washington Post*, August 20, 1981

Interviews: John Bolton, Sally Botsai, Kevin Dunay, Marc Gustafson, David Hume Kennerly, Robert Kimmitt, Jim Reed, Gayle Smith, Richard Norton Smith

CHAPTER 5: CLOSE ENCOUNTERS

Publications: *All Fall Down: America's Tragic Encounter with Iran* by Gary Sick; *Crisis: The True Story of an Unforgettable Year in the White House* by Hamilton Jordan; "Confessions of a Star Psychic," by Keith Harary, *Psychology Today*, November 1, 2004; *White House Diaries* by Jimmy Carter; *Power and Principle: Memoirs of the National Security Adviser, 1977–1981* by Zbigniew Brzezinski; *The Stargate Chronicles: Memoirs of a Psychic Spy* by Joseph McMoneagle; *Phenomena* by Annie Jacobsen; *Hard Choices: Critical Years in America's Foreign Policy* by Cyrus Vance; *Keeping Faith: Memoirs of a President* by Jimmy Carter

Interviews: Gary Bresnahan, Richard Clarke, Robert Gates, Anthony Lake, Joseph McMoneagle, Gary Sick, Jake Stewart

CHAPTER 6: THE HELM IS RIGHT HERE

Publications: *Nerve Center* by Michael K. Bohn; *All the Best, George Bush: My Life in Letters and Other Writings* by George Bush; *The Peacemaker: Ronald Reagan, the Cold War, and the World on the Brink* by William Inboden; *The Tower Commission Report*; Transcripts of March 30, 1981, audio tapes from Richard Allen's papers at the Ronald Reagan Presidential Library; *How Ronald Reagan Changed My Life* by Peter Robinson; President Ronald Reagan's White House Diaries, available at the Ronald Reagan Presidential Foundation and Institute; "Command and Control: Tested Under Fire," by Alan Peppard, *Dallas Morning News*, May 13, 2015;

"The Day Reagan Was Shot," by Richard V. Allen, *The Atlantic*, April 2001; "Intelligence Inside the White House: The Influence of Executive Style and Technology," by David A. Radi, Center for Information Policy Research at Harvard University, March 1997

Interviews: Gary Bresnahan, Tom Griscom, Will Inboden, Robert Kimmitt, William Martin, Peter Robinson, David Sedney

CHAPTER 7: RIGHT SIDE OF HISTORY

Publications: *The Politics of Diplomacy: Revolution, War and Peace, 1989–1992* by James Baker; *A World Transformed* by George Bush and Brent Scowcroft; *Nerve Center* by Michael K. Bohn; *All the Best, George Bush: My Life in Letters and Other Writings* by George Bush; *Destiny and Power* by Jon Meacham; *Transforming Our World: President George H. W. Bush and American Foreign Policy*, edited by Andrew S. Natsios and Andrew H. Card Jr.

Interviews: John Bolton, Gary Bresnahan, Richard Clarke, Robert Gates, Richard Haass, Robert Kimmitt, Jane Lute, David Radi, Condoleezza Rice, David Sedney

CHAPTER 8: PLEASE HOLD FOR THE PRESIDENT

Publications: *Nerve Center* by Michael K. Bohn; *Getting to Dayton: The Making of America's Bosnia Policy* by Ivo H. Daalder; *To End a War* by Richard Holbrooke; *6 Nightmares: Real Threats in a Dangerous World and How America Can Meet Them* by Anthony Lake; *My American Journey* by Colin Powell, with Joseph E. Persico; "The

Guy Behind the Guy: Samuel Nelson Drew and Peace-Building in the Balkans," by John Gans, *War on the Rocks*, July 18, 2019

Interviews: Gary Bresnahan, Tony Campanella, Richard Clarke, Ivo Daalder, Paula Dobriansky, Bonnie Glick, Rob Hargis, Anthony Lake, Jane Lute, Larry Pfeiffer, Elliott Powell, David Radi, Jim Reed, Drew Roberts, David Scheffer, Wendy Sherman, Gayle Smith, Jim Steinberg, Sandy Vershbow

CHAPTER 9: "THIS IS WHERE WE FIGHT FROM"

Publications: *Decision Points* by George W. Bush; *Spoken from the Heart* by Laura Bush; *No Higher Honor* by Condoleezza Rice; *The Only Plane in the Sky* by Garrett M. Graff

Interviews: Josh Bolten, John Bolton, Thomas Bossert, Gary Bresnahan, Richard Clarke, Kevin Dunay, Rahm Emanuel, Steve Hadley, Joe Hagin, Robert Hargis, Deborah Loewer, Doug Lute, Ed Padinske, Condoleezza Rice, Drew Roberts

CHAPTER 10: THE PACER

Publications: *The Finish: The Killing of Osama Bin Laden* by Mark Bowden; *Duty: Memoirs of a Secretary at War* by Robert M. Gates; *A Promised Land* by Barack Obama; *The World as It Is: A Memoir of the Obama White House* by Ben Rhodes; "Secret 'Kill List' Proves a Test of Obama's Principles and Will," by Jo Becker and Scott Shane, *The New York Times*, May 29, 2012; "'I'd Never Been Involved in Anything as Secret as This,'" by Garrett M. Graff,

Politico Magazine, April 30, 2021; "Getting Bin Laden," by Nicholas Schmidle, *The New Yorker*, August 1, 2011

Interviews: Gary Bresnahan, Richard Clarke, Kyle Cozad, Tom Donilon, Michèle Flournoy, Robert M. Gates, Mike Leiter, William H. McRaven, Ed Padinske, Leon Panetta, Larry Pfeiffer, Nick Rasmussen, Ben Rhodes, Drew Roberts, Gary Sick, Pete Souza

CHAPTER 11: POSTCARDS FROM THE EDGE

Publications: *The Divider: Trump in the White House, 2017–2021* by Peter Baker and Susan Glasser; *The Room Where It Happened: A White House Memoir* by John Bolton; *Unhinged: An Insider's Account of the Trump White House* by Omarosa Manigault Newman; "James Mattis Denounces President Trump, Describes Him as a Threat to the Constitution," by Jeffrey Goldberg, *The Atlantic*, June 3, 2020; "We in the 'Shallow State' Thought We Could Help. Instead, We Obscured the Reality of a Trump Presidency," by Sarah Isgur, *The Washington Post*, December 23, 2020

Interviews: Deborah Birx, John Bolton, Thomas Bossert, Anthony Fauci, Geoff Fowler, Omarosa Manigault Newman, Elizabeth Neumann, Larry Pfeiffer, Nick Rasmussen, Mike Stiegler, Alexander Vindman

CHAPTER 12: TIGER TEAM

Publications: "'Something Was Badly Wrong': When Washington Realized Russia Was Actually Invading Ukraine," by Garrett M. Graff, Erin Banco, Lara Seligman, Nahal Toosi and Alexander

Ward, *Politico Magazine*, February 24, 2023; "Inside the Successes, Missteps and Failures of Biden's Early Presidency," by Ashley Parker, Tyler Pager and Michael Scherer, *The Washington Post*, October 22, 2022; "Inside the White House Preparations for a Russian Invasion," by Ellen Nakashima and Ashley Parker, *The Washington Post*, February 14, 2022

Interviews: Alex Bick, Tony Blinken, Jon Finer, Emily Horne, Henry Kissinger, Ron Klain, Rebecca Lissner, Matt Miller, Wendy Sherman, Mike Stiegler, Jake Sullivan

EPILOGUE: WHSR

Interviews: Tony Blinken, Robert Gates, Marc Gustafson, Emily Horne, Eric Schmidt

Index

Note: *Italic page numbers* indicate photographs

Abbey Gate at Kabul International Airport, 299–300, 302–3, 305
Abbottabad, Pakistan, raid. *See* bin Laden raid
Able Archer 83, 132
Achille Lauro hijacking, 137
Adenauer, Konrad, 22
Afghanistan, 225, 245
　bin Laden raid, 249–50, 252, 260
　Soviet invasion of, 149
　U.S. withdrawal from, 299–302, 304–5, 307
Agnew, Spiro, 51–52, 57, 82

Air Force Academy, U.S., 165
Air Force One, 9, *94*, 146, 228, 231
　Bush and September 11 attacks, 206, 207, 214–19, *217*, 220–21
Air Force's Long Range Objectives, 9
Albright, Madeleine
　Bosnia War, 176–80, 183, 184
　women and diversity, 185–86, 188, 322
Alexander, Keith, 187–88
Allen, Richard, 117–21, 123–24
All Fall Down (Sick), 94

338

Alligator, the (shredder), 140
All Too Human
    (Stephanopoulos), 175
al-Qaeda, 190, 201, 215, 222–25,
    237–38. *See also* bin Laden,
    Osama; September 11 attacks
American Airlines Flight 77, 204
American President, The
    (movie), 192
Anderson, Patrick, 17
Andrews Air Force Base, 27, 68,
    114, 125
    bin Laden raid, 260–61
    September 11 attacks and,
        220–21
    Tiananmen Square massacre,
        154–55
Andropov, Yuri, 132, 141
anthrax, 224, 226, 282–83
Apollo 13, 307
Apprentice, The (TV series),
    271, 272
Aquino, Corazon, 157
Arlington National Cemetery,
    184
armored personnel carriers
    (APCs), 182–83
Arthur, Chester, 14
artificial intelligence (AI), 323–24
Asia-Pacific Economic
    Cooperation, 226
Athar, Sohaib, 267
attack on Pearl Harbor, 14, 221

Austin, Lloyd, 314, 316
Axelrod, David, 233

Baird, Zoë, 175
Baker, James
    Iraqi invasion of Kuwait, 159,
        161, 166
    Malta Summit, 157–58
    Reagan assassination attempt,
        117–18
    Tiananmen Square massacre,
        152, 153
Baker, James, Jr., 153
Baker, Peter, 292
Barksdale Air Force, 218
Barnes, Ben, 114
Battle, Lucius, 12
Battle of Khe Sanh, 37–38
Bay of Pigs, 10–12, 16, 316–17
Beal, Richard S., 21
Beck, Glenn, 200
Beckwith, Charlie, 100–101, 103,
    105–6, 247
Bedke, Curtis, 218
Beijing Olympic Games (2022),
    310, 311
Beirut Marine barracks
    bombing, 132
Berger, Sandy, 71, 187
    Bosnia War, 180–81, 184
    Clinton and Whitewater
        investigation, 197–99
Berlin Wall, 143–47, 149–51, 154

Berners-Lee, Tim, 134–35
Beschloss, Michael, 35
Bick, Alex, 307–9, 314
Biden, Hunter, 286
Biden, Joe, 73–74
    Afghanistan withdrawal,
        299–302, 304–5
    bin Laden raid, 252, 253,
        263–64, 303–4
    election of 2020, 1–2, 286,
        297–98
    Russian invasion of Ukraine,
        305–16, 316
    in the Situation Room,
        302–6
Biegun, Steve, 205–6
bin Laden, Osama
    manhunt for, 237–46
    September 11 attacks, 222,
        223
bin Laden raid, 250–70, 322
    Desert One comparisons,
        247, 248–51, 253, 254, 256,
        264, 322
    Iran hostage crisis
        comparison, 113
    planning and preparation,
        107–8, 243–49, 303–4
    telephone calls, 190
Birx, Deborah, 21, 282, 283–85
Black, E. F., 12
Black Hawk Down, 108–9,
    178, 258

Black Lives Matter, 2, 296
Blair, Tony, 189–90, 192–93
Blinken, Antony, 302–4, 306–7,
    313, 314, 316, 322
Bohn, Michael K., 22, 41, 83, 134,
    135, 140
Bolton, John, 230, 278–80
    Iraqi invasion of Kuwait, 159,
        166, 167
    Trump and, 72–73, 278–80,
        285–86
Bork, Robert, 59
Bosnia War, 109, 176–85
Bossert, Tom, 231–32, 275, 276,
    277–78
Botsai, Sarah "Sally," 53–55,
    83, 324
    Mayaguez incident, 85, 87
    Nixon's resignation, 67–68
    women and diversity, 186
    Yom Kippur War, 58–59
Bradlee, Ben, 11–12
Brady, James, 118, 123–24,
    127
Brady, Sarah, 127
Brandenburg Gate speech of
    Reagan, 142–46, 150
Brandus, Paul, 23–24
Brennan, John
    bin Laden manhunt, 240–41,
        243, 245
    bin Laden raid, 252–53, 255,
        258, 262

Bresnahan, Gary, 236, 324
  bin Laden raid, 199, 248,
    263–67
  Clinton and Whitewater
    investigation, 197–99
  communications technology,
    103, 136–37, 171, 195–96,
    214–15, 217, 229, 263–67
  email system, 136–37
  head-of-state calls, 195–96
  Iran hostage crisis, 103
  Reagan assassination
    attempt, 118
  September 11 attacks, 199,
    214–15, 217, 221
  Tiananmen Square massacre,
    153–56
  Y2K bug, 200–201
Brezhnev, Leonid, 46, 59–60,
  62–66, 132, 140–41
Brown, Harold, 99, 100, 105
Bryan, Bill, 283–85
Brzezinski, Zbigniew, 73, 89
  Iran hostage crisis, 92, 94–98,
    100, 102, 105–6, 111, 112
Budget Summit Agreement of
  1990, 171–72
Bulgaria, 149
Bundy, McGeorge, 12–13, 17–18,
  23–24, 40, 129
Burke, Arleigh, 11, 316–17
Burns, William, 314
Bush, Barbara, 169–70

Bush, George H. W., 148–56
  election of 1992, 172–73, 192
  fall of Berlin Wall, 149–51
  Gorbachev and Soviet Union,
    141–42, 148–51
  head-of-state calls, 195–96
  Iraqi invasion of Kuwait, 158,
    159–71, *163*
  "no new taxes" pledge, 171–72
  Reagan assassination attempt,
    116–17, 119, 124–25, 127–28
  in the Situation Room, 134,
    148–49, 303
  Tiananmen Square massacre,
    151–56
  video teleconferencing in
    Situation Room, 134
  waking up for late-night
    events, 73
Bush, George W., 278, 290
  presidential transition of
    Obama, 232–34
  September 11 attacks, 208–11,
    214–23, *217*, 224–26, 238
Bush, Laura, 213, 233
Butterfield, Alexander, 51–52

Campanella, Tony, 195, 196–97
Camp David, 16, 30, 162, 170,
  224, 227
Capitol attacks, 1–4, 294, *294*–98
Card, Andrew, 209, 210–11,
  218, 226

Carlucci, Frank, 100

Carl Vinson, U.S.S., 269

Carter, Jimmy, 88–115
  election of 1980, 130
  Iran hostage crisis, 92–109, *94*,
    112–15
  Operation Grill Flame, 89–90,
    91–93, 109–12
  waking up for late-night
    events, 73

Carter, Rosalynn, 89–92, 109,
  111–12, 113, 115

Castro, Fidel, 10–11

Ceausescu, Nicolae, 148, 149

Centers for Disease Control, 226

Central Command, U.S.
  (Centcom), 302

Charles III of England, 191–92

Cheney, Dick, 206, 217, 224,
  225, 226
  Iraqi invasion of Kuwait, 161,
    166, 168
  September 11 attacks, 214,
    217–18

Cheney, Lynne, 213

Chernenko, Konstantin, 141

Chertoff, Michael, 233

Chief of Naval Operations
  Intelligence Plot
  (CNO-IP), 270

China, Tiananmen Square
  massacre, 151–56, 199

Chirac, Jacques, 180

Christian, George, 39

Christopher, Warren, 105–6
  Bosnia War, 178, 180–81,
    181, 184

Churchill, Winston, 8, 15,
  171, 315

CIA (Central Intelligence Agency),
  18, 20, 22, 70
  Bay of Pigs, 10–12
  bin Laden manhunt and raid,
    238–40, 242, 251–52,
    256, 263
  Foreign Broadcast Information
    Service (FBIS), 24, 95–96
  Operation Grill Flame, 89–90,
    91–93, 109–12

Civil War, 13–14

Clapper, James, 252, 265

Clark, Wesley, 182–83, 184

Clarke, Richard, 157–58, 236
  Clinton and Whitewater
    investigation, 198
  Iran hostage crisis, 103
  Philippine coup attempt,
    157–58
  September 11 attacks, 212, 221,
    223–24
  United States embassy
    bombings, 71
  Y2K bug, 200–201

Cleveland Clinic, 192

Clifford, Clark, 39

Clinton, Bill, 174–99
  Bosnia War, 176–85, *181*
  election of 1992, 172–73, 192

head-of-state calls, 189–90, 192–93

inauguration of, 174–75

Lewinsky affair, 198, 200

Whitewater investigation, 198–99

Clinton, Hillary, 246, 247, 252–53

CNN, 153–54, 175, 209–10, 266, 269, 270

"code word" clearance, 127–28

Cohen, Michael, 273–74

Colby, William, 63–64

Cold War, 130–33, 140–51

Cuban Missile Crisis, 23–24, 44

Reagan and Brandenburg Gate speech, 142–46, 150

Reagan and Ivy League exercise, 129–30

Cole bombing, 238

Columbine High School, 200

Commodore 64, 134

Communism, 9, 130–31

Connally, John, 25–26, 27, 114

conspiracy theories, 176, 200, 286

continuity-of-government (COG), 3, 203–4

Contras, 138

Coolidge, Calvin, 14

Coral Sea, U.S.S., 84

Cosgriff, Kevin, 189, 196–97

Covid-19 pandemic, 2, 280–85

Cox, Archibald, 57, 59–60

Cozad, Kyle, 240–43, 248–49, 261

Crimea, 305, 312–13

Crisis (Jordan), 99, 100–101

Crisis Management Center (CMC), 135–36, 138, 140

Critical Intelligence Communications System (CRITICOMM), 70

Crutchfield, June, 45

Cuba

Bay of Pigs, 10–12

Mariel boatlift, 102–3

Cuban Missile Crisis, 23–24, 44, 317–18

Cuba Study Group, 12

Curveball (informant), 256

Cutler, Lloyd, 89, 102, 111–12

Czechoslovakia, 148, 149

Daalder, Ivo, 184–85

Daley, Bill, 259–60, 267

"dancing baby," 196

D'Andrea, Mike, 238–39

Darman, Richard, 117

Day After, The (movie), 132–33

Dean, John, 51–52

Deaver, Michael, 141

DEFCON (Defense Readiness Condition), 65

DEFCON 1, 65

DEFCON 2, 65

DEFCON 3, 65–66

DEFCON 4, 65, 127

DEFCON 5, 127

Defense Intelligence Agency, 20,
    58, 70, 89
Defense Intelligence College,
    15
de Gaulle, Charles, 22
Deng Xiaoping, 154
den Uyl, Johannes, 84–85
Desert One, 92–93, 97–109
    bin Laden raid comparisons,
    247, 248–51, 253, 254, 256,
    264, 322
Digital Equipment, 136
"dirty hands," 291
Divider, The (Baker and
    Glasser), 292
Dnipro missile strikes,
    314
Dobriansky, Paula, 188
Dobrynin, Anatoly, 43, 52
Dr. Strangelove (movie), 5, 5
Dolan, Tony, 143–44
Donaldson, Sam, 147
Donbass, 312–13
Donilon, Tom, 6
    bin Laden manhunt and raid,
    238, 243, 245, 246, 257–60,
    263, 273
    Obama presidential
    transition, 233
"Doomsday Clock," 133
Drew, Nelson, 183–84
Dulles, Allen, 20
Dunay, Kevin, 74, 233–34

Dunford, Joseph, 279
Duty (Gates), 253–54, 268

Eagleburger, Larry, 63, 154–55,
    159, 167
EEOB, 236–37
Egypt
    Six-Day War, 42–44, 45–49
    Yom Kippur War, 52–53
EgyptAir Flight 990, 200
Eisenhower, Dwight, 3, 15, 70,
    129
Eisenhower Executive Office
    Building (EEOB), 13–14,
    57–58, 214, 236, 237
    Crisis Management Center
    (CMC), 135–36, 138, 140
election of 1980, 130
election of 1992, 192
election of 2016, 287, 305
election of 2020 and Capitol
    attacks, 1–4, 294–98
Elsey, George, 15
el-Zayyat, Mohammed, 52
email system, 136–37
Emanuel, Rahm, 232–33,
    238–39
Emma E. Booker Elementary
    School, 208–9, 210–11
Enright, Charles D. "Chuck,"
    19–20, 21
Erdogan, Recep Tayyip, 193,
    194

Esper, Mark, 285–86
"Evil Empire" speech of Reagan, 131–32
Executive Committee of the National Security Council (EXCOMM), 23–24

Fauci, Anthony, 282–85
Fielding, Fred, 117
Finer, Jon, 315–16
Fitzwater, Marlin, 174
Flournoy, Michèle, 249, 257–58, 265
Foley, Tom, 171–72
Ford, Betty, 82–83
Ford, Gerald, 70–87
  daily schedule of, 84–85
  Mayaguez incident, 74–87, 86
  Nixon and Watergate scandal, 57, 68
Foreign Broadcast Information Service (FBIS), 24, 95–96
Fort Meade, 89
Fowler, Geoff, 272, 273
Frasure, Robert, 183

Gaddafi, Muammar, 71–72
Gallivan, James, 286–87
Gang of Eight, 161–62, 164
Gantt, Florence, 154–55
Gast, Philip, 100–101

Gates, Robert, 322
  bin Laden raid, 107–8, 247, 248, 249, 253–54, 257–58, 263, 264, 268
  Iraqi invasion of Kuwait, 159–60, 161, 166, 168, 169
  Operation Grill Flame, 89
  Philippine coup attempt, 157–58
  Tiananmen Square massacre, 150–51, 152
Geller, Uri, 91
General Services Administration (GSA), 201
Geneva Summit (1985), 142
Geochron, 135
George Washington University Hospital, 116, 120
Gephardt, Richard, 171–72
Gerard, Connie, 40
Gergen, David, 117–20, 124
Ginsburg, Robert, 38
glasnost, 141, 143
Glasser, Susan, 292
Glick, Bonnie, 186–87
Glover, Robert, 2
Goodpaster, Andrew, 15
Goodwin, Richard, 36
Google, 323–24
Gorbachev, Mikhail, 48–49, 141–47, 148, 150–51
Gorkin, Jess, 43–44
Graff, Garrett, 56, 58, 261, 265

Gray, Danielle, 237
Greenland, 292
Grenada, 132, 137
Griscom, Tom, 144, 145–46
Grumman F-14 Tomcats, 72
Gulf of Sidra incident, 71–72
Gulf War, 161, 167–69, 172,
    177, 189
Gustafson, Marc, 73–74, 319

Haass, Richard, 159–64, *163*,
    165, 169
Hadley, Steve, 195–96, 212–13,
    226, 233
Hagin, Joe, 227–32
Haig, Al, 52, 59–60, 62–64,
    117–24, 127
Haile Selassie, 9
Haitian coup d'état, 175
Hall, Fawn, 140
Hallett, Oliver, 24–28
Harary, Keith, 110–11
Hard Choices (Vance), 101
Hargis, Rob, 190, 191,
    194–95, 324
    September 11 attacks,
    203–14, 219
Harnly, Marie, 320
Harris, Kamala, 297, 311, 314
Hartmann, Robert, 78
Havel, Vaclav, 148, 149
Helsinki Summit (2018), 287
Hezbollah, 132, 138
Hill, Fiona, 287

Hinckley, John W., 25, 116–17,
    125, 129
Holbrooke, Richard, 6,
    182–83, 184
Holloway, James L., III, 79
Homeland Security, Department
    of (DHS), 283, 292, 293
Horne, Emily, 303, 309, 310,
    311–12, 321
hotlines, 43–49
House Judiciary Committee, 61
Howe, Jonathan, 63–64
Huckabee, Sarah, 272
Hughes, Karen, 206, 213
Hughes, Sarah T., 28
Hurricane Maria, 292
Hussein, Saddam, 225
    Iraqi invasion of Kuwait,
    159–71

Inboden, Will, 130, 137
Indiana University, 268
Internet, 134–35
Iran-Contra affair, 137–40, 142,
    165, 172
Iran hostage crisis, 92–109
    Desert One, 92–93, 97–109
    Operation Grill Flame, 109–12
Iranian shoot-down of American
    drone, 279
Iraq
    Gulf War, 161, 167–69, 172,
    177, 189
    head-of-state calls, 195–96

Iraqi invasion of Kuwait, 158,
159–71
Iraq War, 225, 244, 245
WMDs, 225, 256, 306–7, 313
Isgur, Sarah, 293
Israel
Six-Day War, 42–44, 45–49
Yom Kippur War, 52–53,
56–66
Ivy League exercise, 129–30

Jacobsen, Annie, 109–10
Jarrett, Valerie, 21, 235–37
jelly beans, 134
Jeremiah, Dave, 161
Johnson, A. E. H., 14
Johnson, Andrew, 200
Johnson, Lady Bird, 34, 46–47
Johnson, Luci Baines, 33–34
Johnson, Lyndon, 30–48
Great Society programs, 34
Kennedy assassination, 28,
30–31
management style and Situation
Room, 32, 37–41, 55, 78–79,
133–34
Pueblo incident, 75
Six-Day War, 42–44, 45–49
transcripts of tapes, 25, 31–37
Vietnam War, 30–41, 38, 78–79
Johnson, Tom, 32, 37–41, 49
Joint Chiefs of Staff (JCS), 20, 70,
97, 268
Jones, Alex, 200

Jones, David, 75–76, 100, 103–7
Jordan, 47
Jordan, Hamilton, 89, 98–102,
105–6

Kay, Gilda, 169
Kayani, Ashfaq Parvez, 267
Kelly, John, 271–72, 274, 291,
292, 293
Kennedy, Jacqueline, 8, 26,
28–29
Kennedy, John F., 318, 323
assassination of, 25–29, 30–31
Bay of Pigs, 10–12, 16, 316–17
creation of Situation Room,
8–9, 10, 12–13, 16–19,
20, 323
Cuban Missile Crisis, 23–24,
44
Kennedy, John F., Jr., 29
Kennedy, Patrick, 9
Kennedy, Robert F., 12
Kennerly, David Hume, 80–83,
84, *86*, 86–87
Kerr, Dick, 161
Kharkiv missile strikes, 314
Khe Sanh model, 37–38
Khmer Rouge and *Mayaguez*
incident, 69–70, 74–87, *86*
Khomeini, Ruhollah, 93, 95–96
Khrushchev, Nikita, 24,
43–44, 129
Kilduff, Malcolm, 27
Kim Jong Un, 279, 292

Kimmitt, Bob, 133, 136, 158
  Gulf of Sidrai incident, 71–72
  Iran-Contra affair, 137
  Iraqi invasion of Kuwait,
    160–61, 164–65
Kissinger, Henry, 6, 166
  Mayaguez incident, 69–70, 74,
    78–82, 85–86, 86
  Putin and Russian invasion of
    Ukraine, 305
  "shuttle diplomacy" of, 59–60
  "Situation Room syndrome"
    theory of, 55–56
  Yom Kippur War, 52–53,
    56–57, 56–67
Klain, Ron, 303
Koh Tang Island, 75–77, 87
Kompong Som, 77, 79
Korean Air Lines Flight 007,
  132
Kosygin, Alexei, 42–43, 45–49
Kruzel, Joseph, 183
Kushner, Jared, 285
Kyiv, 309, 314, 315

Lake, Anthony, 197, 236
  Black Hawk Down, 108–9, 178
  Bosnia War, 178–84, *181*
Lauder, Ronald, 292
Lavrov, Sergey, 305*n*
LBJ Ranch, 30, 40
LDX (Long Distance Xerography),
  41, 54, 83
Lebanon, 15, 138

Leiter, Mike, 238–39, 247–48,
  251–52, 256–57, 260, 264
Lewinsky, Monica, 198, 200
Libya and Gulf of Sidra incident,
  71–72
"lightning messages," 14
Lincoln, Abraham, 13–14
Lincoln Sitting Room, 14
Lissner, Rebecca, 307–8, 313
Little, George, 262
Lockheed C-130 Hercules, 102,
  103–4, 250
Lockheed C-141 Starlifters,
  154–55
Loewer, Deborah, 208–11,
  215–18, *217*, 220–24, 324
Long, Letitia, 261–62
Los Angeles International
  Airport, 201
Love Field, 28
Lucas, James W., 15–16
Lute, Doug, 6, 166, 229–30, 321
Lute, Jane, 166, 172, 177–78,
  187–88

Macmillan, Harold, 22
McCabe, Gerry, 12–13, 16–17
McCafferty, Art, 36–37, 41
McConnell, John Paul, 39
McDonough, Denis, 243, 258, 262
McFarland, K. T., 276–77
McFarlane, Robert, 86, 199
McHugh, Godfrey, 8–10, 12–13,
  16–19, 29

McKenzie, Kenneth F., Jr., 302
McKinley, William, 14
McMoneagle, Joseph, 89, 110
McNamara, Robert, 35, 42, 43, 45–46
McRaven, William, 243–45, 247, 249–51, 252, 256, 260, 262–67
Major, John, 192–93
Malta Summit (1989), 157–58
Mao Zedong, 151
Map Room, 14–15, 37, 198–99
Marcos, Ferdinand, 157–58
Mariel boatlift, 102–3
Martin, William, 136
Masirah Island, 102
Mattis, James, 274, 275, 285–86
Mayaguez incident, 69–70, 74–87, 86
Meese, Ed, 72, 118
Meir, Golda, 57
memorandum of conversation (memcon), 194–95
"M-hop," 155–56
Military Academy, U.S. (West Point), 165
Miller, Frank, 207
Miller, Katie, 282
Miller, Matt, 311, 315
Milley, Mark, 166, 314
Milosevic, Slobodan, 182–83
Mitchell, George, 171–72
Modern Family (TV show), 259
MOLINK (Moscow Link), 43–44
Mondale, Walter, 98, 102, 104–6

Moorer, Thomas, 63, 64, 65–66
Morell, Michael, 208, 260
Moscow Olympic Games (1980), 131
Moscow Summit (1991), 141, 146–47
Moscow-Washington Direct Communications Link, 44–49
Mossad, 91
Mount Igman, 182–83
Moyers, Bill, 36
Mullen, Mike, 252–53, 263–64, 267
Muskie, Edmund, 139
Muslim travel ban, 293

Napolitano, Janet, 233
National Association of Evangelicals, 131
National Geospatial Intelligence Agency, 262
National Institute of Allergy and Infectious Diseases, 282
National Military Command Center (NMCC), 22, 76–77, 85
National Security Agency (NSA), 20, 70, 113, 187
National Security Council (NSC), 20, 23–24, 133–34, 166, 224, 288
Defense Coordination, 88
National Security Planning Group (NSPG), 133–34

Nayef bin Abdulaziz, 192
Neal, John, 70
Nerve Center (Bohn), 22, 41, 83, 134, 135, 140
Neumann, Elizabeth, 290–93
Newman, Omarosa Manigault, 271–74
New York Times, 45, 54, 196
New York Yankees, 166
Nicaragua, 138
Nielsen, Kirstjen, 292
Nimitz, U.S.S., 102
9-11 attacks (2001), 3, 203–27, 321
Nivens, Lois, 46
Nixon, Richard, 51–68, 134
    avoidance of Situation Room, 54–56, 167
    resignation of, 67–68
    Saturday Night Massacre, 59–60
    Watergate scandal, 51–52, 57, 59, 61, 67
    Yom Kippur War, 52–53, 56–66
North, Oliver, 137–40, 165, 172, 322
North Korea, 73, 75, 175, 292
    Pueblo incident, 75
nuclear "football," 118–19

Obama, Barack, 235–70
    bin Laden manhunt, 237–38
    bin Laden raid, 199, 250–57, 259, 260–61, 263–67, 268, 303–4, 320, 321
    head-of-state calls, 190–91, 192
    inauguration of, 233–34
    presidential transition of, 232–34
Obama, Michelle, 235
O'Connell, Kevin, 169
Odom, Bill, 73
O'Donnell, Kenneth, 18, 28
Office of War Information, 44
Offutt Air Force Base, 218, 220
Oklahoma City bombing, 176
O'Leary, Dennis, 124
One Man Against the World (Weiner), 57
Operation Desert Shield, 161
Operation Desert Storm, 161, 177
Operation Eagle Claw, 92–93. *See also* Desert One
Operation Grill Flame, 89–90, 91–93, 109–12
Operation Rolling Thunder, 35
Oval Office, 14

Padinske, Ed, 324
    bin Laden raid, 269–70
    September 11 attacks, 203–8, 218–19, 222–23
Pakistan and bin Laden raid, 244–45, 249–50, 262, 267
Panetta, Leon, 184, 238–40, 243–45, 252–55, 263–64

Parade (magazine), 43–44
parapsychology and Operation
    Grill Flame, 89–90, 91–93,
    109–12
Parkland Hospital, 26
Parr, Jerry, 116–17
Peacemaker, The (Inboden),
    130, 137
Pence, Mike, 2–4, 282, 283
perestroika, 141, 143
Perry, William, 180–81, *181*, 184
Pershing II Weapon System, 132
personal computers (PCs), 134–35
Pfeiffer, Larry, 189, 191, 235,
    236–37, 272–73
Phenomena (Jacobsen), 109–10
Philippine coup attempt, 157–58
"piss-swisher," 63–64
Poindexter, John, 135–37, 138–39
Poland, 149
Pompeo, Mike, 279, 285
Porada, Irene, 272
Powell, Colin, 161
    Bosnia War, 176–77, 178
    Reagan's Brandenburg Gate
        speech, 144, 145–46
    September 11 attacks, 211, 226
Powell, Elliott, 189–90, 197, 201,
    202, 324
Powell, Jody, 98, 105–6
Powell Doctrine, 177
prank calls, 191–92
presidential briefings, 40

Presidential Emergency
    Operations Center (PEOC),
    206, 211–19
presidential head-of-state calls,
    189–97
Promised Land, A (Obama),
    252–53
Psychology Today (magazine),
    110–11
Pueblo incident, 75
Puerto Rico, 292
Pulitzer Prize, 81
Putin, Vladimir
    Biden's "killer" comment, 305–6
    Obama head-of-state call, 190–91
    Rice and September 11 attacks,
        219–20
    Russian invasion of Ukraine,
        160, 290, 305–6, 305*n*, 310,
        312, 313–14, 322
    Trump and, 278–79, 287,
        288, 290

Quayle, Dan, 161
Queen, Richard, 111

Radi, Dave, 148–49, 189
    communications technology,
        157, 159
    Iraqi invasion of Kuwait,
        161–62, 163, 166, 169, 170
    Tiananmen Square massacre,
        152–53

Radio Moscow, 24

Rainforest Alliance, 320

Rasmussen, Nick, 243, 245–47, 251–53, 255–56, 275–76

Reagan, Nancy, 145, 169

Reagan, Ronald
    assassination attempt, 25, 116–28, 131
    Brandenburg Gate speech, 142–46, 150
    election of 1980, 130
    "Evil Empire speech," 131–32
    Gulf of Sidra incident, 71–72
    Iran-Contra affair, 137–40, 142
    Iran hostage crisis, 93, 113–14
    Ivy League exercise, 129–30
    Situation Room, 133–37

Reed, Jim, 70–71, 192–93

Reed, Tom, 130

Reedy, George, 32

Regan, Don, 117, 123–24

"remote viewers," 89–90, 109–12

Ressam, Ahmed, 201

Reykjavik Summit (1986), 142

Rhodes, Ben, 237, 241–42, 254, 260–62

Rice, Condoleezza, 21, 148, 150–51
    Bush head-of-state call, 195–96
    Iraqi invasion of Kuwait, 163, 166
    September 11 attacks, 206–7, 211–14, 217–18, 219–20, 226–27, 305

Richardson, Elliot, 59–60

Roberts, Drew, 190–94, 213, 266–67

Robinson, Peter, 142–46, *145*

Rockefeller, Nelson, 75, 76

Rogers, William, 129

Romania, 148, 149

Roosevelt, Franklin D., 8, 14–15, 37, 315

Roosevelt, Theodore, 236

Rostow, Walt, 11
    Six-Day War, 42, 43, 45, 46
    Vietnam War, 31, 38, *38*, 39

Rove, Karl, 216

Ruff, Charles, 198–99

Rumsfeld, Donald, 211, 225
    Mayaguez incident, 85–86, *86*

Rusk, Dean, 25, 42, 43, 129

Russian interference in 2016 election, 287, 305

Russian invasion of Ukraine, 160, 290, 305–16, 322

Saigon, 32, 69, 300

Salinger, Pierre, 24–28

Sandinista National Liberation Front, 138

Saturday Night Massacre, 59–60

Saudi Arabia, 192

Schabowski, Günter, 149–50

Scheffer, David, 179–80, 182, 183

Schlesinger, James, 63–64, 77–78, 80, 85–86

Schmidt, Eric, 323–24

Schubert, Bob, 205

Schwarzkopf, Norman, 167–68

Scowcroft, Brent, 149, 177, 178, 279, 321

    Bush and election of 1992, 172–73

    Gulf War, 169

    Iraqi invasion of Kuwait, 160, 160*n*, 161, 162, 165–66, 167–68

    Mayaguez incident, 74, 77–79, 85–86, 87

    Philippine coup attempt, 157–58

    Reagan and Iran-Contra affair, 139

    Tiananmen Square massacre, 154–56

    waking up the president for late-night events, 73

    Yom Kippur War, 53, 56–57, 63, 68

Seabees (Naval Construction Battalions), 17

Secret Service, 2–3, 67, 116, 127, 205, 210, 215, 223, 241, 296–97

Secure Voice over Internet Protocol (VoIP), 231–32

Sedney, David, 138, 139–40, 152–53, 170, 191–92

September 11 attacks, 3, 203–27, 321

sexism, 185–89

Shalev, Mordechai, 52

Shalikashvili, John, 180–81, *181*, 184

Shanahan, Patrick, 279

Shepard, Tazewell, 11, 12–13, 16–17, 316–17

Sherman, John, 214

Sherman, Wendy, 188–89, 317–18

Shevardnadze, Eduard, 159

Short, Marc, 283

Shultz, George, 144, 146

Sick, Gary, 113, 323

    Iran hostage crisis, 93–97, *94*, 113, 114–15, 250–51

Sikorsky RH-53D Sea Stallions, 102

Sisco, Joseph, 52

Situation Room

    Afghanistan withdrawal, 301–2

    Bush and Iraqi invasion of Kuwait, 158, 159–71

    Bush and Tiananmen Square massacre, 151–56

    Capitol attacks, 1–4, 294–98

    Carter and Iran hostage crisis, 92–109, *94*

    Clinton and Bosnia War, 176–85

    communications technology, 22, 136–37, 222–32

    concrete pillar, 324–25, *325*

    Covid-19 pandemic, 280–85

    creation of, 4–5, 8–9, 10, 12–13, 16–19, 20

Situation Room (*cont.*)
  email system, 136–37
  Ford and *Mayaguez* incident,
    74–87, 86
  head-of-state calls, 189–97
  Hollywood's idea of, 5, 5
  hotlines, 43–49, 60
  Johnson and Six-Day War,
    42–44, 45–49
  Johnson and Vietnam War,
    30–41, 38
  Obama and bin Laden manhunt
    and raid, 238–40, 251–57,
    259–70
  Reagan and Iran-Contra affair,
    137–40, 142
  Reagan and Ivy League exercise,
    129–30
  Reagan assassination attempt,
    117–28
  renovations of, 227–32, 236–37,
    320–21, 324–25
  September 11 attacks, 203–8,
    218–27
  shredder (the Alligator), 140
  staffing, 20–22
  technology, 14, 22, 41, 54–55,
    134–37, 157–59, 196–97,
    227–32
  telephone calls, 189–93
  Trump and Omarosa incident,
    271–74
  use of term, 16–17

  women and sexism, 185–89
  Y2K bug, 200–202
"Situation Room syndrome"
  theory, 55–56
Six-Day War, 42–44, 45–49
6 Nightmares (Lake), 197
Smith, Bromley, 11, 18, 26, 39, 40
Smith, Gayle, 71, 185–86
Smith, Gerard, 44
Smith, Richard Norton, 82,
  83–84
Smith, Rosemary, 90
Smith, William French, 117,
  126–27
Sobray, Mary, 270
Sochi Olympic Games (2014), 305
Solidarity, 149
Somali Civil War, 108–9, 175,
  178, 258
Southern Governors
  Conference, 91
Souza, Pete, 237, 248, 261, 262,
  264–65
Soviet-Afghan War, 149
Spanish-American War, 14
Speakes, Larry, 72, 118, 120, 123
Special Coordination Committee
  (SCC), 94
Spence, Matt, 261
Spencer, Stuart, 130, 147
Srebrenica massacre, 180
Stalin, Joseph, 315
Stanford Research Institute, 89

Stapleton, Ruth Carter, 90–91
Starr, Kenneth, 198
State Department, 20, 22, 70, 136
Stearman, William Lloyd, 62
Steinberg, Jim, 21, 201–2
Stewart, Jake, 88–90, 92–93, 109, 111–12, 324
Stiegler, Mike, 280–81, 324
    Capitol attacks, 1–2, 3–4, 294–98
Stonestreet, Eric, 259
Strategic Air Command, 122
Strategic Defense Initiative (SDI), 132
Sukhoi Su-22s, 72
Sukhoi Su-57s, 132
Sullivan, Jake, 299, 301–2, 304–5, 307, 308–9, 311–16
Sununu, John, 161
Syria, 47–48, 52, 57, 61

"Tear down this wall!", 144–46
Tenet, George, 211
Thatcher, Margaret, 141, 150
This Is Spinal Tap (movie), 201
Thomas, Helen, 49
Thompson, Llewellyn, 43
Tiananmen Square massacre, 151–56, 199
Tiger Team, 307–15
Tillerson, Rex, 274, 275
Tillman, Mark, 216

Time to Heal, A (Ford), 75, 77, 79, 82
Tower, John, 139
Tower Commission, 139
Transforming Our World (Natsios and Card, ed.), 172
Troye, Olivia, 285
Truman, Harry S., 8, 15, 20
Trump, Donald, 271–98
    Afghanistan withdrawal, 299–300
    avoidance of Situation Room, 275–76, 278, 285–86
    Capitol attacks, 2–4, 294, 294–98
    Covid-19 pandemic, 280–85
    election of 2016, 287, 305
    Omarosa incident, 271–74
    Putin and, 278–79, 287, 288, 290
    waking up for late-night events, 72–73
    Zelensky phone call, 195, 286–87, 288–90
Trump Muslim travel ban, 293
Trump National Golf Club Bedminster, 292
TSA (Transportation Security Agency), 225
Tupolev Tu-22s, 90
Turner, Stan, 98, 107, 249

TWA Flight 800, 176
24 (TV series), 5

Ukraine
  Russian invasion of, 160, 290,
    305–16, 322
  Trump-Zelensky phone call,
    195, 286–87, 288–90
Under This Roof (Brandus),
    23–24
United Flight 93, 204
United Nations Security
    Council, 313
United States embassy bombings,
    71, 200, 238
Updegrove, Mark, 37, 38, 40, 41,
    47–49
USAID (United States
    Agency for International
    Development), 308

van Agt, Andreas, 128
Vance, Cyrus, 96–102, 108
Vantage Point, The (Johnson), 42,
    46, 48
Vaught, James, 100–101, 103,
    105–7
Velvet Revolution, 148,
    149
Vershbow, Sandy, 180–84
Vickers, Mike, 257, 258
video teleconferencing (VTC),
    134

Vietnam War, 30–41, 78–79, 300
Vindman, Alexander, 286–90

Walesa, Lech, 149
Washington, George, 13
Washington-Moscow Direct
    Communications Link, 44–49
Washington Post, 11–12, 72,
    196, 293
Washington Special Actions
    Group (WSAG), 53, 58
Watergate: A New History
    (Graff), 56
Watergate scandal, 51–52, 57, 59,
    61, 67
Watt, Murray, 112
WAYSIDE, 25–28
weapons of mass destruction
    (WMDs), 225, 256,
    306–7, 313
Webb, Brad, 248–49, 263, 264
Webster, William, 161
Weinberger, Caspar, 117,
    121–23, 125
Weiner, Tim, 57, 62
West Wing, The (TV series), 5
Wheeler, Earl "Bus," 39
White House, transcripts of tapes,
    24–28, 31–32–33, 35, 36–37,
    104–7, 117–24, 125–28
White House Communications
    Agency (WHCA), 20, 30, 46,
    136, 155, 227–28

White House Coronavirus Task
Force, 282–85
White House Correspondents'
Dinner (WHCD), 259–60
White House Daily Diary, 88–89
White House Diary (Carter), 114
White House Office of
Faith-Based and Community
Initiatives, 290
White House Situation Room. *See*
Situation Room
White House Situation Room
Special Projects, 320–21
White House Years, The
(Kissinger), 55
Whitewater investigation,
198–99
Williamsburg (yacht), 8
Wilson, U.S.S., 85–86
Wilson, Woodrow, 14
Wolfowitz, Paul, 161
women and diversity, 185–89, 322
World Trade Center bombing of
1993, 238

World Trade Center bombing
of 2001. *See* September 11
attacks
World Transformed, A (Bush and
Scowcroft), 160, 167
World War II, 171
World Wide Web, 134–35

Xi Jinping, 279

Y2K bug, 200–202
Yazdi, Ebrahim, 95–96
Years of Renewal (Kissinger), 74
Years of Upheaval (Kissinger), 60
Yellen, Janet, 314
Yom Kippur War, 52–53, 56–66

Zelensky, Volodymyr
Russian invasion of Ukraine,
306–7, 315–16
Trump phone call, 195, 286–87,
288–90
Zhivkov, Todor, 149
Zurhellen, Owen, 74–75

ABOUT THE AUTHOR

George Stephanopoulos is the host of *This Week* and the co-anchor of *Good Morning America*. Stephanopoulos joined ABC News in 1997 as an analyst for *This Week*. Prior to joining ABC News, he served in the Clinton administration as the senior adviser to the president for policy and strategy. He is the author of *All Too Human*, a *New York Times* bestseller.